Partners in Development

Partners in Development

An Analysis of AID-University Relations 1950-1966

by John M. Richardson Jr.

EAST LANSING

Michigan State University Press

1969

Standard Book Number: 87013–135–4

Library of Congress Catalog Card Number: 69–19769

TO
ROBERT T. HOLT

Manufactured in the United States of America

Foreword

THIS BOOK is the first to be produced from the research done in the Center for Comparative Studies in Technological Development and Social Change. An earlier version of this study was one portion of the final report of the CIC–Rural Development Research Project, Contract No. AID/csd–840. The direct costs of Dr. Richardson's analysis were just over ten thousand dollars, a small part of that large undertaking which involved expenditures of over one million dollars.

Foreign aid programs are a significant vehicle for introducing an advanced technology into the developing nations of the world. However, the experience of the foreign aid programs has clearly demonstrated that a bundle of tools and techniques cannot simply be packaged in the West and sent to a pre-industrial society with any hope of success. Social institutions must be built that can accommodate a new technology.

This is no new and startling discovery. Foreign aid officials have recognized the problem for a long time, but the question of how to aid in the building of successful institutions that can take root in a developing society is a difficult and complex problem for which there is no pat solution. The contract between the Agency for International Development (and its predecessors) and American universities is one attempt that has been made to support the building of institutions in developing areas. It has not been a uniformly successful program.

Dr. Richardson's book describes and analyzes the contract program from its inception in the early 1950's until 1966, concentrating attention on the Agency for International Development and its predecessors. As the history of the program unfolds and the same problems emerge in different periods and under different directors, it becomes apparent that the problems of supporting institution building do not derive solely from the situations found in the host countries. The organization of AID, the governmental and political setting in which it operates, the place of the university-contract program in the total operations of the Agency, the structure of American universities, and the professional and political context in which they operate all place severe restrictions on the policies and actions necessary for successful institution building.

Anyone who is interested in the problems of foreign aid will find this book valuable. But its relevance extends to a wider audience. Dr. Richardson's analysis is explicitly based on a theory of organizational behavior. This theoretical basis has enabled the author to cut through the web of complexities of day-to-day activities to identify the crucial problems. The book is thus a valuable contribution to the study of administrative behavior.

Robert T. Holt, Director
Center for Comparative Studies
in Technological Development
and Social Change
University of Minnesota

Contents

	Page
FOREWORD	v
PREFACE	xiii

PART ONE
FROM GENESIS TO HARMONY—A HISTORY OF STABILITY AND CHANGE IN AGENCY-UNIVERSITY RELATIONS — 1

CHAPTER I: *The Agency-University Relationship: An Overview* — 3
"I Bid You God's Speed" — 3
The Agency-University Relationship: Basic Concepts for Description and Analysis — 6
An Overview of Chronological Periods and Patterns of Participation in Agency-University Relations — 10

CHAPTER II: *The Period of Genesis (1949–1953)* — 13
"In the Beginning..." — 13
The Rationale for University Participation — 13
Patterns of Participation — 16
   The Utah State–Iran Project — 17
   The Oklahoma A and M–Ethiopia and Arkansas–Panama Projects — 19
   The Cornell–Los Baños Project — 22
Organizational Relationships — 24
   The Economic Cooperation Administration — 26
   The Technical Cooperation Administration — 27
Agency Policies Affecting University Participation — 32
Agency-University Relations During the Period of Genesis — 32

	Page
CHAPTER III: *The Period of Proliferation* (November 1953–June 1955)	34
Stassen's Philosophy and Objectives	34
Major Policy Changes Affecting University Participation	36
Organizational Changes	38
The Personnel Reduction Program	39
Stassen's Style of Administration	40
Patterns of Participation: The Proliferation of Contracts	43
Agency-University Relations at the Level of the Participating Universities	46
Agency-University Relations at the Level of the University Community	50
Conclusion: Aprez Moi . . .?	51
CHAPTER IV: *The Period of Retrenchment* (July 1955–September 1957)	53
John B. Hollister: A New Director and a New Approach	53
Organizational Changes	55
Major Policy Changes Affecting the University-Contract Program	56
Patterns of Participation	57
Agency-University Relations at the Level of the Participating Universities	58
Summary: The Causes of Deterioration	71
Agency-University Relations at the Level of the University Community	72
Activities of the National Association of State Universities and Land-Grant Colleges	73
Activities of the Committee on Institutional Projects Abroad of the American Council on Education	75
CHAPTER V: *The Period of Inertia* (September 1957–September 1961)	80
Introduction: A Leaderless Agency	80
Policy Changes Affecting the University-Contract Program	80
Organizational Changes and Administrative Practices	82
Patterns of Participation	84

Contents

	Page
Agency-University Relations at the Level of the University Community	85
Activities of the Committee on Institutional Projects Abroad of the American Council on Education	85
Activities of the NASULGC	92
Published Studies of the University-Contract Program and Their Impact	96
Agency-University Relations at the Level of the Participating Universities	101

CHAPTER VI: *The Interregnum (September 1961–December 1962)* ... 104
A Period of Transition ... 104
The Reorganization ... 104
Major Policy Changes Affecting Agency-University Relations ... 108
Patterns of Participation ... 109
Agency-University Relations ... 109

CHAPTER VII: *The Period of Harmony (1963–1966)* ... 112
David Bell ... 112
    Specific Initiatives and Policies ... 113
Policy Changes Affecting Agency-University Relations ... 116
Organizational Relationships and Issues ... 118
Patterns of Participation ... 121
    Inter-regional Differences in Patterns of Participation ... 121
    Diversification in Individual Patterns of Participation ... 122
Agency-University Relations at the Level of the University Community ... 126
    The Alliance Steering Committee on Rural Development ... 128
    The International Rural Development Office of the NASULGC ... 131
    The Conference on International Rural Development ... 133
Agency-University Relations at the Level of the Participating Universities ... 136

PART TWO
PERSISTENT ISSUES, ENVIRONMENTAL CONSTANTS AND BEHAVIORAL PATTERNS: AN ANALYSIS OF STABILITY AND CHANGE IN AGENCY-UNIVERSITY RELATIONS — 139

CHAPTER VIII: *Persisting and Unresolved Issues* — 141
Five Persisting and Unresolved Issues — 142
The Issue of "Equal Partnership" — 143
The Issue of University Autonomy Versus Agency Control — 145
The Issue of Contractual Form — 147
The Issue of Project Length — 151
Personnel Clearance: A Partially Resolved Persistent Issue — 155
Conclusion — 157

CHAPTER IX: *Historical Patterns and Individual Behavior: A Framework for Analysis* — 158
Historical Patterns — 158
Individual Behavior in Organizational Settings — 159
Attributes of Goals — 160
Behavioral Characteristics — 162
Conclusion — 165

CHAPTER X: *The Statics and Dynamics of Agency-University Relations* — 167
Program Goals and Procedures: Proximate Factors Contributing to Disharmony — 168
Environmental "Constants" — 180
    The "Settings" of University-Contract Projects — 181
    Congressional Influence — 182
    State Legislatures — 186
Institutional Variables: Persistent and Changing Patterns in the Agency and the Participating Universities — 187
    The Agency: Unchanging Behavior Amidst Organizational Instability — 187

Contents

	Page
The Universities: Liberal Ideals Amidst Institutional Conservatism	193
Summary	199
Summarizing the Analysis: A Matrix of Relationships	200
NOTES	209
APPENDIX I: *Documents Relating to the University-Contract Program*	232
APPENDIX II: *An Alternative to the Rationalistic Paradigm*	244
SELECTED BIBLIOGRAPHY	265

Preface

THIS STUDY was initiated under a sub-contract from the Agency for International Development and the Purdue Research Foundation to "prepare a report on the analysis of relevant literature and supplemental interview results giving particular emphasis to the principles which have guided AID-university cooperation in assisting the development of foreign agricultural education and research institutions." The report was to ". . . trace the evolution of relevant policies and practices and identity, insofar as is feasible, the reasons for significant changes over time and their implications to A.I.D., aid receiving countries and institutions, and the U.S. university community." As a component of the CIC–AID Rural Development Research Project, a major objective of the study was to provide background information for other members of the project team who were analysing specific aspects of the university-contract program in great detail.

When the study was initiated, more than three years ago, I was relatively unfamiliar with this area and began to research with few preconceptions of either a theoretical or substantive nature. The historical literature dealing with the contract program, as well as foreign assistance in general, was relatively sparse and it quickly became apparent that it would be necessary to devote a considerable portion of the report to synthesizing interviews, project records and documentary materials (mostly unpublished) in order to present a coherent picture of what had actually transpired during the life of the program. In the process of reconstructing this history, more than forty depth interviews were conducted by Professor Robert Holt and myself. In addition, I read through and abstracted the chronological files of eighteen university-contract projects and looked at twelve more in somewhat less detail.

In our interviews, particular attention was devoted to contacting individuals who had been associated with university contracting over a relatively long period of time or had a particularly significant impact on the program. Included in this group were former foreign assistance administrators such as Stanley Andrews, Harold Stassen and David Bell, high ranking officials in the Agency, such as D. A. Fitzgerald, E. N. Holmgreen and Edward Kunze and University Presidents such as John Hannah and John T. Caldwell. Later, many other individuals, both in the Agency and the university community were contacted to fill in missing details and discuss specific points where differing viewpoints had been uncovered.

It was primarily from interviews that the focus of the analysis became clear. To quote from Chapter I, ". . . this analysis of university contracting is essentially a story of two diverse types of organizations attempting to achieve a symbiosis in order to define and attain common goals." This concern led naturally to the literature on organization theory and in particular to the remarkably durable work of Herbert Simon, which inspired the "methodological individualistic" approach of the entire study and especially the framework presented in Chapter IX.

Hopefully, the study will be of interest to students of organization theory as well as those who are primarily concerned with problems of Agency-university relations and overseas technical assistance. Indeed, one message of this analysis of university contracting (perhaps the most important message) is that an explicit and well-founded theoretical framework is likely to make the policy alternatives relevant to a specific substantive problem clearer and more meaningful.

Obviously, the preparation of this study would have been inconceivable without the cooperation and encouragement of numerous individuals in the government and the university community who submitted to lengthy interviews (and in some cases re-interviews) and assisted me in digging out unpublished data relating to the program. It would be impossible in this brief introduction to acknowledge the assistance of each of them individually; however, to each goes my sincere thanks and deep gratitude.

A few individuals should receive special mention. During the early stages of the investigation, the historical perspective provided by Stanley Andrews, E. N. Holmgreen and D. A. Fitzgerald was invaluable. Later, each of these men read a preliminary draft of

Preface xv

the manuscript and added further comments from their rich store of experience in the foreign assistance and agricultural development fields. Other former Agency officials who took time from busy schedules to be interviewed included Harold Stassen, A. E. Moseman and David Bell. Messrs. Moseman and Bell also reviewed portions of the manuscript and made valuable comments.

I would also like to express my appreciation to President John Hannah and Dean Glen Taggart of Michigan State University, Chancellor John Caldwell and Dean Roy Luvvorn of North Carolina State University, Dean Jack Gray of Texas A and M University, Robert Jungenheimer of the University of Illinois and their respective staffs for the information and gracious hospitality which they provided. Former President O. Meredith Wilson of the University of Minnesota also took time from a busy schedule to offer some revealing insights regarding his long association with university contracting as did Russell Thackrey and Louis Howard of the NASULGC and Richard Humphrey of the American Council on Education. Later, Mr. Humphrey added his perceptive comments to a draft copy of the manuscript.

The preparation of the initial draft of the manuscript benefited greatly from unpublished data made available by Richard Duncan of the Syracuse Technical Assistance Research Project and Alan Michie of Education and World Affairs. The Illinois research group of the CIC–AID project, directed by William Thomson, provided hospitality, stimulating discussions and access to the project's central data archive superbly organized by Mrs. Kathleen Prop.

Throughout the research, writing and revision of the study I had the full cooperation and warm support of many officials in the Agency for International Development. As a result of my associations in the Agency, I gained new respect for the men who are charged with the difficult task of administering foreign assistance programs, often with little public recognition. Obviously, the men in the Agency whose candid and insightful comments provided the basis for a substantial portion of this work must remain anonymous. However, it does not seem inappropriate to gratefully acknowledge the backstopping which Robert MacMillan and Ernst Linde of the Agricultural Rural Development Service, Office of the War on Hunger and Curt Barker, the University Relations Officer, provided during my several trips to Washington.

The tactful assistance of Ira L. Baldwin and R. W. Jones,

CIC–Project Director and Associate Director respectively, was also most helpful. In addition to providing administrative support, both of these individuals drew from their experience in the contract program to provide substantive information and comment on successive drafts of the manuscript. I might add that—considering the differences in our backgrounds—both of these individuals were remarkably tolerant of some of my divergent opinions regarding the program. Professor Burton Sapin of the Political Science Department of the University of Minnesota also read two drafts of the manuscript and contributed critical but constructive comments.

My greatest debt of gratitude goes to the individual to whom this study is dedicated, Robert Holt. In addition to providing firm but flexible counsel during two major and innumerable minor revisions of this manuscript, Professor Holt has aided my professional and intellectual development in more ways than could be enumerated.

Of course, neither Professor Holt, nor any of the other individuals who have assisted me in so many ways are responsible for any errors or omissions or for the opinions contained herein. Indeed, many of them disagree strongly with some of the positions I have taken. But they are very much responsible for what ever characteristics of a positive nature the reader discerns.

John M. Richardson, Jr.
January, 1969

PART I

From Genesis to Harmony

A HISTORY OF STABILITY
  AND CHANGE IN AGENCY-
  UNIVERSITY RELATIONS

CHAPTER I

The Agency-University Relationship: An Overview

"I BID YOU GOD'S SPEED"

EARLY IN 1952, five faculty members from the Oklahoma Agricultural and Mechanical College arrived at Jimma, the capital of Kaffa province in Ethiopia. Their ultimate destination was a hillside in the rich, but undeveloped, agricultural land surrounding the capital where they were to establish and operate the Jimma Agricultural Secondary School. Of much greater importance, however, was the broader goal providing the rationale for this and similar enterprises. The five Oklahoma professors were charged with creating a setting in which the American Land-Grant idea could be transplanted to Ethiopian soil, to provide the motive force for agricultural and rural development.

What form and structure was envisioned for this new institution? The leader of the project group later remarked that the only preparation he received was a brief orientation by the director of the Technical Cooperation Administration program in Washington and a "Bid you God's speed." Naturally he and his colleagues had read as much as they could about Ethiopia in the hectic days before their departure. Furthermore, as faculty members of a Land-Grant institution they were well grounded in the tradition of putting knowledge to work for rural communities through teaching, research and extension. Beyond that, however, "all they knew was that they were to start a school, literally out of the bush and grass roots, to give Ethiopians the rudiments of a Land-Grant type agricultural education."[1]

The site of the prospective Jimma School had been designated by the Emperor after consultation with the Oklahoma group.[2] During the war it had served as barracks and industrial training center for the Italian Army. However, the buildings had been bombed and burned so that little but the outer shells remained. Eighty students, personally selected by the Emperor, were on hand for the opening of school in October 1952, and the first classes, without textbooks, were held under the trees.[3] At the same time, the students worked with their professors to convert some old stables into dormitories.

Much later, one foreign aid official characterized the Oklahoma team as "a group of crazy guys." "They didn't know there were things that just couldn't be done," he observed, "so they went ahead and did them. They had to cook over a campfire, but they trained their students in practical things."[4]

Oklahoma A and M was one of the five U.S. Land-Grant colleges and universities which first agreed to send staff members overseas, under government auspices, to participate in programs of institution building and rural development following the Land-Grant model. Other pilot projects were initiated about the same time in Iran, Iraq, Panama, Brazil and the Philippines.[5] The men who conceived these projects believed that making technical knowledge available to rural communities through service oriented institutions of higher education had contributed significantly to the development of the American agricultural system. They rightly regarded this system as one of the most productive and efficient in the world, but wondered if the essential components of this "miracle" of development could be introduced into other frontier settings, and lead to similar results. Hopefully the teams from Oklahoma A and M, Arizona, Arkansas, Cornell and Utah State would provide some of the answers.

More than fifteen years have elapsed since these beginnings. While few final answers regarding the transferability of the Land-Grant idea to non-western cultures are yet available, it is clear that the university-contract program—the use of American universities in overseas technical assistance projects—has become an established institution. As of December 1965, the Agency for International Development reported that contracts totaling more than one hundred and eighty-four million dollars were in force with one hundred and twenty-five colleges and universities.[6] In recent years, between thirty-five and forty-five million dollars has been expended annually by AID to support this program.

Several general observations can be made. First, the faith in the appropriateness of the Land-Grant idea (though not necessarily particular institutional forms) which provided the motive force for pilot projects during the early days seems undiminished. Second, the program which has emerged is very different from the one initially envisioned. On the positive side are the many solid accomplishments in the form of new or radically altered agricultural schools, colleges, and universities. Even more important are the new skills and changed attitudes which have made these institutions forces for development. Furthermore, the growth and present scope of the program can be interpreted, at least in part, as a success indicator.

Despite these accomplishments, however, published studies of the program and the interviews for this study reveal that many individuals associated with university contracts over the years have found this experience frustrating and even disillusioning. Some observers argue that the program has simply grown "like Topsy," without purpose or direction, and that in terms of attaining any coherent set of development or institution-building objectives, successes are significantly outweighed by failures.[7]

Weighing the evidence offered by advocates of university contracting against that provided by its detractors is not one of this study's purposes. However, there is an attempt to provide the historical perspective and an analytic framework which will make such assessments meaningful. The focus is not on the program as a whole but on a special aspect of it, the relationship between the aid-administering agency and the universities. In other words, this analysis of university contracting is essentially a story of two diverse types of organizations attempting to achieve a symbiosis in order to define and attain common goals. Thus, the phenomenon which is first described and then analyzed as a dependent variable is called the *Agency-university relationship*[8] (or sometimes, for reasons of style, *Agency-university relations*). The principal question which this study attempts to answer is, how has this relationship changed from 1950 to 1965 and why?

The Agency-university relationship is a complex phenomenon with no single history, no uniquely differentiable set of facts which "speak for themselves." It is documented in published studies describing and analyzing the university-contract program, in recommendations of Presidential working groups and commissions, in the Agency's "Congressional presentations" and in the published hearings of Congressional committees. It is found in the reports of university campus coordinators, chiefs of party and team members, and of mission directors, division chiefs, and other Agency personnel. An even more important source of this history is the perceptions and recollections of the individuals who have been associated with the program.

The term "history," however, should not be used in the singular. To university presidents, for example, the history of the Agency-university relationship is seen as a growth of consensus between themselves and ranking Agency officials regarding the objectives of university participation. To university business officers, it is the history of a gradual modification of contract and fiscal procedures to protect the universities in dealings with the Agency. To contract officers it is the history of a continuing struggle to bring the desires of university and mission personnel into congruity with the legal requirements of Federal contracting procedures. In fact, every individual who has participated in the Agency-university relationship has his own version of its history and of significant evolutionary patterns.

Documentary and personal sources of information about the university-contract program differ greatly in both "facts" and emphasis. Thus, even the descriptive part of this study is selective in choosing and depicting the events to which significance is attributed. The events themselves simply do not tell the story. For this reason, it seems useful to begin with a brief overview and some definitions of the concepts in terms of which the basic phenomena under investigation are presented.

The Agency-University Relationship: Basic Concepts for Description and Analysis

The "relationship" between two organizations is one of those slippery concepts often discussed in general terms as if it had a generally understood meaning. However, as one tries to define it, it becomes more and more complicated. In the case of "the universities" and "the Agency" we are dealing with extremely complex organizational entities which do not by any means speak with a single voice. Of course, "the universities" have no central organizational structure in common, although associations do exist in Washington which represent the university community in various ways. Furthermore, there are many possible dimensions of Agency-university relations and many relevant issues, some of which seem virtually impervious to generalization. Because of this complexity, a rather explicit conceptual scheme has been adopted in the hope of achieving a common frame of discourse with the reader.

First, Agency-university relations at the *level of the university community* and Agency-university relations *at the level of the participating universities* should be differentiated. The failure to make this distinction has limited the value of otherwise useful and interesting studies of the university-contract program. The failure to recognize that it exists has led to Agency and university policies based on false premises. The term "university community" is used to refer to organizations which represent and speak for all U.S. colleges and universities (such as the American Council on Education) or a major segment of them (such as the National Association of State Universities and Land-Grant Colleges [NASULGC]). By defining the university community in this way, it becomes possible to use a relatively small number of well-documented communications emanating from these organizations and from the Agency, as the primary referent for the concept, *degree of harmony of Agency-university relations at the level of the university community*. *Improving relations* (increasing harmony) and *deteriorating relations* (decreasing harmony) can then be discussed in relatively specific terms which will convey a fairly clear picture of the most significant issues related to improvement and deterioration at this level during different chronological periods.

It is fallacious to assume, however, as several previous studies have done, that the degree of harmony at the university community level can serve as the referent for the same phenomenon at the level of the participating universities. This level involves the interchanges resulting from the day-to-day activities of Agency personnel, usually low-level personnel, and representatives of particular participating universities. It is quite clear that major changes in relations can occur at the level of the university community without significantly affecting things at this level. We are dealing with two very different, and not directly related, phenomena.

The problem of coherent analysis at the level of the participating university is obviously more complex. There have been, during the history of the university-contract program, hundreds of thousands of interchanges between Agency and participating university personnel. Only a few of these are of consequence in themselves; but a number of them, in the aggregate, may be more important than anything that has occurred at the level of the university community. That there is no documented record of most of these interchanges does not make it any less important to think about Agency-participating university relations in this way. Such a record would be extremely difficult to establish in any case since the different parties to an interchange may have completely different perceptions of it. If no great importance is attached to any single incident, the lack of documentation should not be a major handicap. Among various participants and observers there is considerable agreement about series of interchanges of specific types (for example, those relating to audit disallowances) which, in the aggregate, have been of great consequence for relations between the Agency and the universities.

Despite agreement on this point, there may be little agreement as to what specific events comprised this aggregate. In fact, the aggregate probably has no concrete reality as it is viewed a little differently by each person who recognizes it as significant.

Given the caveats mentioned above, the concept, *degree of harmony in Agency-university relations at the level of the participating universities,* may be defined. The unit of analysis used for this purpose is called an *incident*. An incident is *any interchange between representatives of the Agency and representatives of a participating university related to the university-contract program.* A negative incident causes one or more of the parties to be irritated, angry or dissatisfied in some way. A positive (or neutral) incident leads to no irritation, anger or dissatisfaction.

Degree of harmony, then, is simply defined in terms of the ratio of negative incidents to total incidents. Thus, relations *improve* when the number of negative incidents decreases in relation to the total and they *deteriorate* when the number of negative incidents increases in relation to the total. This schema makes no distinction between incidents in terms of the setting in which they occur or other unique characteristics. Thus, incidents which occur at NASULGC conventions and incidents which occur in a contract officer's Washington office are both considered as of equal consequence.[9]

It would be possible to formulate a more elaborate model by developing weighted typologies in terms of which different types of incidents could be categorized. This could make the relationship between incidents and changes in degree of harmony more theoretically precise. However, such refinement would be of limited value since it was impossible, given the available resources, to count the incidents themselves. Thus, although a typological schema might be helpful in presenting historical data systematically, this study goes no further than the rather gross differentiations which can be derived from the dichotomy between negative incidents and positive incidents.

Although precise measurement is not possible, the concepts which have been presented do allow systematic linkages between data available on changes in policy, administrative procedures and attitudes within the Agency and data, primarily from interviews, suggestive of actual changes in the relationship. Rather specific statements can be made about changes in policy, organization, etc., that contributed to an increase or decrease in the number of negative incidents and *thus* to a change in Agency-university relations at the level of the participating universities.

The relationship between the staffing difficulties in the newly established Office of Contract Relations during 1956, and the concurrent deterioration in Agency-participating university relations provides an illustration of this approach. The great proliferation of contracts during 1954 and 1955 contributed to the great increase in incidents of all kinds. More universities were involved in more active contact with the Agency over more and different matters than had ever been the case before. The 1956 reorganization, which established the Office of Contract Relations, also established procedures which ensured that this Office would be a focal point for all contract actions. Thus, any question that a participating university had regarding contract matters had to be cleared through this office.

During 1956, the Agency was able to fill only about half of the staff positions authorized for the newly established Office. Very few of the new contract officers had had any previous experience with university contracts. With this inadequate, inexperienced staff, it was virtually impossible for the Office to meet the demands of the participating universities for quick decisions on contract actions, even when important activities in the field could not proceed until a decision had been made. Not only did the total number of incidents increase, but the staffing difficulties in the Office of Contract Relations contributed to a proportionately greater increase in negative incidents and, therefore, to the deterioration in relations between the Agency and the participating universities.

AN OVERVIEW OF CHRONOLOGICAL PERIODS AND PATTERNS OF PARTICIPATION IN AGENCY-UNIVERSITY RELATIONS

Changes in policy, personnel and organization within the Agency provide the basis for dividing this history into six chronological periods. Because of these changes, the Agency has had a significantly different orientation toward university contracting during each period, causing consequent changes in the degree of harmony of Agency-university relations at the university community or participating university level, or both. The periods are the following:

(1) *Genesis* (January 1949–Summer 1953). During this period, the university-contract program was conceived and the first projects initiated. A number of government agencies were associated with project administration: the Technical Cooperation Administration (TCA), Economic Cooperation Administration (ECA), Mutual Security Agency (MSA), Institute of Inter-American Affairs (IIAA), and the Office of Foreign Agricultural Relations (OFAR) of the Department of Agriculture (USDA). Projects were exclusively oriented toward agricultural and rural development. The program was experimental in nature and extremely limited in scope.

(2) *Proliferation* (Summer 1953–July 1955). The period of proliferation coincides with the tour of Harold E. Stassen as administrator of foreign assistance. During this period, responsibility for the administration of foreign assistance was consolidated under a single Agency, the Foreign Operations Administration (FOA). The university-contract program expanded rapidly, due largely to Stassen's policies.

(3) *Retrenchment* (July 1955–September 1957). The period of retrenchment gets its name from the philosophy and policies of

John B. Hollister, who served as director of the reorganized Agency, now called the International Cooperation Administration. Between July 1955 and September 1957 the expansion of university participation was halted as Director Hollister attempted to cut back the foreign assistance program and establish more uniform financial, legal and administrative procedures. There was a major deterioration in Agency-university relations.

(4) *Inertia* (September 1957–Summer 1961). During this period, there were four administrators but no major organizational or policy changes in the Agency. Numerous conferences were held between high ranking Agency and university officials concerning the university-contract program. However, there was little discernible improvement in Agency-university relations at the level of the participating universities.

(5) *Interregnum* (Summer 1961–December 1962). This might be called the period of confusion. The arrival of the "New Frontier" in Washington resulted in major organizational and personnel changes in the Agency. The short-term consequences of these changes for Agency-university relations were, to quote one observer, "chaotic."

(6) *Harmony* (December 1962–July 1966). The appointment of David Bell as administrator of AID marked the beginning of a period of harmony in Agency-university relations. During Bell's tenure, university participation was expanded and diversified. A major study and conference focusing on the university-contract program increased mutual understanding between Agency and university representatives. The most salient characteristic of this period, however, was Bell's administrative style. Since Bell's departure, further changes in policy and organization have occurred. However, it did not seem possible or appropriate to expand this study sufficiently to cover them in detail.

Patterns of Participation

In addition to changes in policy, organization and personnel and changes in Agency-university relations during each chronological period, there were also changes in aggregate and individual patterns of participation. Aggregate patterns of participation are defined by the number, general goals and geographic distribution of projects involving university participation. Individual patterns of participation are defined by significant characteristics of individual projects such as the nature of the relationship between the U.S. university and host government agencies, the degree of Agency regulation, the degree of home campus support for the team in the field, etc.

Changes in patterns of participation would be a legitimate topic for investigation in itself. However, this study is primarily concerned with these changes as possible intervening variables between policy, personnel and organizational changes in the Agency and changes in the degree of harmony of Agency-university relations.

In each of the chapters of Part I, similar topics are examined in roughly the same order. A narrative and discursive style has been used to permit a flexible approach to the data. Events which were emphasized in the literature or the interviews were not eliminated because they did not conform to some pre-determined conceptualization. Hopefully, enough basic information about the history and evolution of the university-contract program and administrative changes within the Agency has been included so that the study will be of value even to individuals who may have reservations about the conclusions and the approach used to present supporting evidence.

CHAPTER II

The Period of Genesis (1949–1953)

IN THE BEGINNING . . . .

SCHOLARS WHO describe, comment upon or analyze the history of the university-contract program like to speculate about the genesis of the program—to try to discover who first conceived of such a joint relationship and what his ideas were regarding its underlying philosophy and organization. It is impossible to say whether or not one man first envisioned a program involving the university as an instrument of technical assistance. It is clear, however, that the early projects reflected the ideas of a number of men who could be called "originators" of the program.

The first technical assistance projects involving university participation have been frequently characterized as "experimental"; "exploratory" might be a more appropriate term. At the time they were conceived, the "state of the art" of technical assistance was such that virtually every project, every policy, and every organizational arrangement was innovative and ground-breaking.

The Rationale for University Participation

The idea of institutional participation in technical assistance projects was neither the first, nor the only, method considered for tapping the resources of the Land-Grant universities. Although President Truman, in defining the objectives of "Point Four," stated that "our imponderable resources in technical knowledge are constantly growing and are inexhaustible,"[1] officials who had been involved in the relatively limited technical assistance programs administered by the Institute of Inter-American Affairs (IIAA) and the Office of Foreign Agricultural Relations (OFAR) of the Department of Agriculture recognized that mobilizing these resources for overseas programs under governmental sponsorship posed considerable problems. Even prior to the initiation of Point Four, a ranking OFAR official, Glen Taggart, had suggested the establishment of a pool of capable people, mostly from the universities, who would agree to participate in technical assistance projects and whose names and qualifications would be kept on file in Washington.[2] When a specific type of project was requested by a foreign government, the agency responsible for the project would then be able to find the person or persons who most closely met the qualifications that were desired. This idea of "loaning staff members to foreign projects" was presented to the university community by OFAR Technical Assistance Director, Ross Moore, in a speech before the Association of Land-Grant Colleges and Universities (NALGCU) in 1950.[3] However, a very different approach was to become the basis of university participation.

That institutional participation was forcefully volunteered by a few influential, internationally minded NALGCU officers was clearly a significant factor in the ultimate adoption of this approach. Shortly after Truman's address, the Association's executive committee empowered its officers to ". . . offer the facilities of this Association to the State Department and other Federal offices in furthering the . . . objectives [of the Point Four Program]."[4] Following this resolution, NALGCU President John Hannah formally offered the assistance of the universities to President Truman, on behalf of the Association. It should be emphasized that this initial offer of support reflected the "public service" orientation of a small group of representatives of the university community and a set of vaguely defined notions about the relevance of the "Land-Grant philosophy" and the "Land-Grant experience" to the problems of less developed nations. It did not reflect a consensus as to the most appropriate organizational relationships through which such support could be rendered or the exact form which it would take. As participation expanded in the 1950's, the university community developed and presented to the Agency a series of specific recommendations dealing with both philosophy and organization. These recommendations were, for

The Period of Genesis (1949–1953)

the most part, based on participating university experience during the program's early years. President Hannah later stated, "There was no specific decision at this point to enter into a long term program of international development, but Michigan State made it known to President Truman that it was flexible and willing to experiment. . . . [and was] interested in seeing whether the Land-Grant philosophy could be applied to educational ventures abroad."[5]

The first technical assistance projects involving university participation were described earlier as "exploratory." This description reflects the views of four of the government officials—Henry G. Bennett, E. N. Holmgreen, Stanley Andrews and D. A. Fitzgerald—who were most closely associated with the initial planning, implementation and administration of the program.[6] Each of these men was involved in the discussions and decisions which led to the first technical assistance projects involving universities and in determining formats for the first Agency-university contractual agreements. Although minor differences existed among them, they were in substantial agreement on all of the major questions regarding university participation. In particular, they believed in the relevance of the "Land-Grant idea" for promoting development. Furthermore, they took a realistic view of the existing level of knowledge and experience about the technical assistance process. Later, one of these originators summarized their basic philosophy:

> For the most part, we felt that these [developing] countries had never entered the twentieth century in education. What educational philosophy they had was based on 18th century Europe—educate a person so that he wouldn't have to work; give him knowledge so that he could sell it and only do it in a limited fashion. The idea of making knowledge actually work for *lots* of people was intuitively foreign to these thinkers. This is what our Land-Grant colleges had done, *wholesale*.
> The job, therefore, was to swing college education around by several degrees and begin a philosophy of taking knowledge to masses of people by way of a few educated ones who would give away their knowledge and not merely hold it for sale. This was the very basis of our Land-Grant college success.[7]

There was general agreement that some problems were unavoidable; that difficulties were going to arise during the early stages of the projects no matter what methods of implementation were chosen. Therefore, three basic decisions were reached concerning the scope and form of university participation:

First, the *types of projects* in which university participation would be enlisted should be limited to those fields in which the Land-Grant philosophy was particularly applicable, primarily agricultural and rural development.

Second, within these substantive areas, there should be experimentation with different patterns. *Project objectives* should be defined in such a way as to allow the university teams considerable flexibility in the field. Andrews and Holmgreen emphasized that it was the Land-Grant *idea* which they were hoping to "transplant," not the organizational forms of U.S. Land-Grant institutions.

Third, the *scope of participation* should be restricted to a limited number of projects so that participating universities could be carefully chosen and unforeseen problems could receive the personal attention of top administrative personnel in the respective agencies (TCA and MSA).

The notion of limited but flexible use of universities in overseas projects which guided the program during its early years merits special emphasis. None of the "originators" planned for or anticipated the massive expansion of the 1953–1956 period. During the early years, individual patterns of participation tended to reflect the characteristics of the different settings in which projects were located. Moreover, administrative procedures varied greatly from project to project.

Patterns of Participation

The most common type of project initiated during this period is generally referred to as a "sisterhood" relationship between an American university and an overseas educational institution. This arrangement had precedents that went back almost a century. As early as 1870, such a relationship had been formally established between Hokkaido University and the University of Massachusetts.[8] Less formal relationships existed between U.S. colleges and universities and institutions in the Philippines,[9] Iraq,[10] Panama,[11] and elsewhere. Although the fact of an earlier relationship contributed to the selection of a particular U.S. university for a particular project in several instances, the limited body of literature and personal experience in the area of overseas institutional involvement which existed as a result of these associations does not seem to have had any other significant impact on the new program.

Of course differences in overseas settings were contributing factors to differences in projects. However, equally important was the degree of involvement of each of the parties to the project and the degree of cooperation between them. New mechanisms of organization had to be worked out not only between the Agency and the university, but also between the home campus and its team in the field, the field team and the technical cooperation mission (TCM), the field team and the host institution (and host institution government) and between the TCM and its "parent" office in Washington. It is proper to speak of the patterns of participation which "emerged" from the initial contractual arrangements, because the salient characteristics of these patterns reflected the adaptation of the participating university and governmental personnel involved to significant differences in available resources, organizational relations and field situations. Such adaptation was, in part, a consequence of a conscious policy of defining project objectives vaguely and negotiating flexible contractual arrangements. The latitude granted to field and contract personnel was also, particularly in the case of TCA-administered projects, a result of an organizational fact of life during the early years of technical assistance programs. TCA simply did not have the resources and administrative machinery to exercise any significant degree of control over their programs, even if there had been a desire for such control.

A brief description of four of the projects initiated during this period will illustrate the three most common patterns of university participation and provide a basis for discussion of some of the problems which came to be associated with each pattern. Rather than give a complete resume of each project, the emphasis is on those characteristics resulting from significant differences in organizational arrangements during this formative period.

THE UTAH STATE–IRAN PROJECT

The pattern of participation in this project involved a *direct relationship between the field party of the participating U.S. insti-*

TABLE I

University-Contract Rural Development Projects Initiated and in Operation During the Period of Genesis

REGION	COUNTRY	U.S. INSTITUTION	HOST INSTITUTION	DATES
FAR EAST	Philippines	Cornell Univ.	University of the Philippines at Los Baños	1952–60
NESA	India	Univ. of Illinois	Allahabad Agricultural Institute	1952–Active*
NESA	Iran	Utah State Univ.	Government of Iran/Karaj College	1951–61
NESA	Iraq	Univ. of Arizona	Agricultural College at Aba-Ghraib	1951–61
LATIN AMERICA	Brazil	Purdue University	Rural University of the State of Minas Gerais	1951–Active
LATIN AMERICA	Colombia	Michigan State Univ.	2 National Universities	1951–59
LATIN AMERICA	Panama	Univ. of Arkansas	National Institute of Agriculture and Home Economics/Ministry of Agriculture	1951–57
AFRICA	Ethiopia	Oklahoma State U.	Government of Ethiopia	1952–Active

Summary Data: (1) Number of Contracts Initiated 8
 (2) Number of Active Contracts 8

Sources:
(a) *Interim Report* of the CIC-AID Rural Development Research Project, Appendix A
(b) ICA Statistical Reports on University Contracts
(c) "List of FOA financed technical cooperation contracts with universities—now in operation in cooperating countries and planned or in negotiation." Report submitted for the record by the Foreign Operations Administration to the Committee on Foreign Affairs, U.S. House of Representatives in connection with the testimony of Harold E. Stassen on the Mutual Security Act of 1954. *Hearings*, Eighty-Third Congress, Second Session, pp. 343–346.

*A second contract was negotiated with the University of Illinois in June 1955 to provide assistance to the government of the North Central Region of India. In 1958, the scope of the contract was reduced to focus on a "sisterhood" relationship with Kharagpur Institute and Uttar Pradesh University.

NOTE: Contracts listed as ACTIVE were active as of July 1, 1966.

tution and governmental institutions of the host country under the relatively close supervision of Technical Cooperation Mission "direct hire" officials. The project, backstopped by OFAR under the general supervision of TCA, was initiated by OFAR, under the authority of the Smith-Mundt Act,[12] prior to the establishment of TCA. The objectives and plan of work of the project provided for overall technical assistance in agriculture through cooperation with the Ministry of Agriculture, particularly the establishment of experiment stations and an extension service.[13]

The selection of Utah State University as the participating U.S. institution reflected a long history of association between Utah State and Iran. Of particular importance was the close personal relationship between Utah State President F. S. Harris and the Shah. Perhaps the most significant characteristic of this contract, from the standpoint of Agency-university relations, was the University's limited involvement in project operations. Basically, Utah State acted as a hiring agency for the Technical Cooperation Mission. The agricultural development program was developed by the mission director and agricultural division chief with a minimal amount of consultation with university personnel. The latter were closely integrated with the mission team and performed basically "direct hire" functions.

It will be noted later that projects in which university and direct hire personnel are performing similar functions have frequently been characterized by considerable hostility and noncooperation on the part of the direct hire personnel. That this situation did not exist in the Utah State contract may be, to a considerable degree, attributed to the fact that the chief of the TCM agriculture division was formerly on the staff of Utah State University and had originally come to Iran as a member of the university-contract team. In addition, President F. S. Harris became Mission Director after retiring from the University.

THE OKLAHOMA A AND M—ETHIOPIA AND ARKANSAS—PANAMA PROJECTS

The pattern of participation in these projects involved the *expansion of the "sisterhood" relationship with a higher educational institution in the host country into a direct relationship with host government agencies.* Since both of these projects are in themselves of considerable significance in the history of Agency-university relations, they will be considered separately.

The Oklahoma A and M–Ethiopia Project

The decision to initiate a project involving university participation in Ethiopia was to a considerable degree a consequence of the friendship of Emperor Haile Selassie and TCA Administrator Henry G. Bennett. The two men had discussed the possibility of establishing an agricultural college following the Land-Grant pattern in Ethiopia long before the Point Four Program had been proposed and had corresponded about the matter after Bennett became TCA Administrator. After Bennett's death in December 1951, the proposal for the establishment of a secondary school and an agricultural university was resubmitted to TCA by the Ethiopian government. Oklahoma A and M was the natural choice for the participating U.S. institution.

The contract (or "agreement") which, as in the case of the Utah State–Iran project, was administered and backstopped by OFAR, was designed to give the participating university wide flexibility. "In carrying out its obligations under this agreement," Oklahoma A and M was required to:

(1) Assist the government of Ethiopia in the establishment and operation of a college of agriculture.
(2) Assist the government of Ethiopia in the establishment and operation of a country-wide system of agricultural extension services to the people of rural areas.
(3) Assist the government of Ethiopia in the establishment and operation of agricultural research and experiment stations.
(4) Administer such other specific projects and operations and give such other assistance to the government of Ethiopia in related fields pertaining to the economic development of Ethiopia as the TCA may request and the college may accept.[14]

Although the Oklahoma team was primarily associated with developing the school at Jimma and the Imperial Ethiopian College of Agricultural and Mechanical Arts, team members became involved, at the request of the Ethiopian government, in diverse projects encompassing "everything under the sun." For example, soil surveys were undertaken by team members in areas remote from Kaffa province. A substantial portion of the work performed for the Ministry of Agriculture and other government ministries

The Period of Genesis (1949-1953)

was not even remotely associated with the agricultural college. Members of the Oklahoma team became, in fact, the Ethiopian government's principal advisors in agricultural development.

The chief factors contributing to the expansion of the Oklahoma team's original role illustrate several of the general observations about patterns of participation which were made above. These factors included:

(1) Ethiopia's great need for the additional functions which were performed,

(2) the Emperor's personal interest in agricultural development and in the activities of the Oklahoma team,

(3) the requests of the Ethiopian government ministries for additional assistance,

(4) the inability of the Technical Cooperation Mission's small staff to meet requests for assistance from the Ethiopian government,

(5) the cooperative attitude of the Technical Cooperation Mission, and

(6) the policy of the top administrators in OFAR and TCA, particularly Andrews, of encouraging university-contract teams, regardless of the terms in the contract, to meet host country needs as they arose in the field.

The University of Arkansas–Panama Project

This project was similar to the Oklahoma-Ethiopia project in the pattern of participation and the flexible nature of the stated project objectives in the contract. Although there was no previous relationship between Panama and Arkansas, the participating university was personally selected by Andrews after discussions with top university officials and officials of the Panamanian government. The contract was administered by OFAR under the general direction of the IIAA and TCA.[15] The project differed significantly from the one in Ethiopia, however, in the way that the functions of the Arkansas team expanded and in the nature of the relationship which evolved between the Technical Cooperation Mission, the university team and the Panamanian government. This aspect is worth considering because of the problems that arose after the abolition of TCA.

The National Institute of Agriculture and Home Economics of Panama, which the University of Arkansas had contracted to assist, was administered by the Ministry of Agriculture of the Panamanian government. The chief of the IIAA field party was directly associated with a *Servicio* whose functions were, to a considerable degree, parallel and competitive with those of the Ministry of Agriculture.[16] Because of these administrative arrangements, and because of a personal friendship which developed, the Minister of Agriculture developed the habit of going to the university chief of party rather than to the chief of the IIAA field party with his technical assistance problems. It was primarily for this reason that a pattern of participation similar to the Oklahoma A and M project developed. The Arkansas team also became involved in "everything under the sun" in the technical assistance field. The arrangement functioned with a minimum of friction during the period of permissive TCA administration but was to have serious consequences for relations between the Agency and the University of Arkansas after the governmental reorganization of August 1954.[17]

THE CORNELL–LOS BAÑOS PROJECT

This project is of particular interest because it became a model for many of the projects which were initiated from 1953 to 1960. The pattern of participation was a *contractually delimited "sisterhood" relationship* between Cornell University and the Agricultural College of the National University of the Philippines at Los Baños, oriented toward the development of the host country institution along lines suggested by the U.S. Land-Grant experience and philosophy. It was originally intended that the contract would be administered by OFAR, using Smith-Mundt and then Point Four funds, as a pilot agricultural program, but as a result of decisions embodied in the Mutual Security Act of 1951, the responsibility for technical assistance programs in the Philippines and other countries in the Far East which were determined to be of strategic significance was assigned to the newly established Mutual Security Agency.[18] Cornell University was selected as the participating institution at the request of the host country because of a long history of association between Cornell personnel and the National University of the Philippines.

The contractual agreement[19] defined the scope of services to be performed by the University in far greater detail than was characteristic of TCA/OFAR-administered contracts and clearly limited the activities of the university field party to those which were

The Period of Genesis (1949–1953)

relevant to the "sisterhood" relationship. The "scope of services to be performed" by Cornell University was detailed as follows:

(1) Prepare a report within 60 to 90 days of the effective date of this contract covering the present situation at Agricultural College. This report will include preliminary recommendations covering the current needs of the Agricultural College and identification of areas that need more detailed study.

(2) Assist the Agricultural College to formulate recommendations covering the requirements to develop into an institution that would render more adequate service to Philippine agriculture and the people.

(3) More specifically, to help carry out the recommendations formulated above, Cornell will provide specialists in various fields of agriculture as agreed upon by the Agricultural College and Cornell up to a maximum number of 12 specialists. Initially, the specialists will be limited to four.

(4) In addition to the teaching, demonstrations and research activities of the respective specialists outlined in Paragraph (3), each specialist may be required, with the assistance and advice of the College, to develop a list of, and recommend the kinds and quantities of supplies and equipment needed by the Agricultural College within the field of his specialty.

(5) The specialists will be expected to advise the Agricultural College as to the proper utilization of any materials, supplies or equipment furnished the Agricultural College by ECA or otherwise for the activity or activities represented by the respective specialist.

(6) Cornell will undertake to assist the College in selecting students and instructors for training in the United States. Cornell will also undertake to assist the Agricultural College in the necessary arrangements with appropriate United States or international agencies, organizations or institutes, public or private, for this training.[20]

The 1952 Cornell contract may be considered a direct ancestor of the present "standard" university contract. Under the contract, Cornell was authorized and required to perform the three basic functions which have characteristically been emphasized in university-contract projects, namely:

(1) the advising of the host institution staff by a field party from the participating U.S. institution,

(2) the supervision of the procurement and use of equipment provided under the provisions of the contract, and

(3) the supervision of a program of "participant training" at the U.S. institution.

It should be noted, however, that the predominance of this pattern of participation, which has, in general, been favored by the university community, is not clearly apparent until about 1956.

The administration of the Cornell contract was also similar in form to many of the subsequent university contracts. Administrative responsibility was exercised directly by MSA through its agricultural technical bureau (called the Food and Agriculture Division during this period).[21] Supervision of contract operations in the field was the responsibility of the Chief of the Food and Agriculture Division of the Mission, who reported both to the Mission Director and to the division (bureau) chief in Washington.[22]

The factors contributing to the relatively limited role of the Cornell team in the Philippine technical assistance program illustrate some of the differences between TCA and MSA administration. The four listed below are particularly significant.

(1) The resources of the MSA mission in the Philippines greatly exceeded those of the university-contract group. Thus there were advantages for officials of the host government in going to the mission director, rather than the university chief of party, with technical assistance problems.

(2) The functions of the university team were delimited by the contractual agreement. Additionally, the legal form of the contract was an agreement between Cornell and the Agricultural College of the National University of the Philippines at Los Baños.

(3) The contract was directly and relatively closely administered by MSA. Administration was not delegated to a participating government agency.

(4) The policy of the top MSA administrators clearly discouraged deviation from the specified objectives of the contract on the part of contractor personnel in the field. The meeting of host country needs as they arose was the specific responsibility of the mission director, his program officers and technical division chiefs.[23]

Organizational Relationships

The four technical assistance projects discussed above involved three different organizational relationships with agencies of the

U.S. government. The Cornell contract was administered by the Food and Agriculture Division of the Mutual Security Administration (MSA), an organization similar in both personnel and administrative structure to its predecessor, the ECA. The Oklahoma and Utah State contracts were under the general administrative direction of the Near East and African Development Service of the TCA, a subsidiary organization of the Department of State, but direct responsibility for contract administration and backstopping was delegated to OFAR. The Arkansas contract was under the general administrative direction of IIAA, an organization which performed the same function in TCA as the Near East and African Development Service, but retained its pre-TCA status as a "semi-autonomous government corporation" under its own directorship. As was true of the other TCA contracts, direct responsibility for administration and backstopping of the contracts was delegated to OFAR.

In many respects, for reasons which will be discussed below, the TCA- and MSA-administered contracts differed much less than might be imagined. However, the two major foreign assistance agencies, TCA and ECA/MSA, were guided by fundamentally different philosophies and reflected different organizational approaches to the problems associated with implementing programs of technical cooperation in "underdeveloped areas." These differences were a consequence of differences in personnel backgrounds, the settings in which the organizations had conducted most of their operations and the types of programs in which they had customarily engaged. The merits of the competing approaches were debated vigorously and with some hostility by ranking officials in the two agencies. Although the debate persists to this day, it ceased to be of importance within the government after the implementation of Presidential Reorganization Plan No. 7 of August 1, 1953. This plan established the Foreign Operations Administration (FOA) and signaled the triumph of the ECA approach. The reorganization, and perhaps more important, the personnel changes which accompanied it, contributed significantly to the establishment of patterns of administration and decision-making which affected the university-contract program for the next seven years. Thus the differences between the competing agencies, and the issues upon which their respective proponents disagreed, merit detailed consideration.

THE ECONOMIC COOPERATION ADMINISTRATION

The creation and evolution of the ECA have been analyzed and described in detail by Herbert Simon.[24] Simon emphasizes that "this organization grew and assumed a reasonably coherent form without ever apparently having been planned." The structure which emerged resulted from adaptation, over time, to the social, political and economic requirements of the post-war European situation, and the program which was designed to meet them. The Marshall Plan was a program of *capital development,* not technical assistance. There was relatively little emphasis on manpower training and education; the major objective was to rebuild the war-torn industrial plant of Europe. This point has, of course, been made many times before; but it assumes additional importance when examined from the perspective of Simon's analysis. The organization "adapted" to an environment and a set of program requirements which differed to *a very substantial degree* from the environment and program requirements of technical assistance programs. A second well-known characteristic of the European Recovery Program also merits special emphasis. The program was brilliantly, even startlingly, successful. A review of ECA's quarterly financial reports shows a high positive correlation between capital expended and improvements in the general financial health of the countries assisted as measured by many indicators. This success reinforced the views of those officials who argued that the ECA philosophy, the philosophy of capital development, was generally applicable.

From the perspective of this very brief discussion of the origins and philosophy of ECA, the significant characteristics of the organization may now be summarized.

(1) The organization was directly involved in the implementation of major U.S. foreign policy objectives in the Cold War.

(2) The top officials of the organization came, for the most part, from the U.S. business and financial community.

(3) The primary focus of the program administered by the organization was commodity support and capital development.

(4) The administrative structure which evolved to meet the requirements of this program was oriented to the control and maintenance of accountability for very large amounts of money.

Because of this, considerable emphasis was placed on *compliance control*[25] (enforcement of regulations) in the administrative procedures of the organization.

(5) Project objectives were integrated into country programs which were developed through joint negotiations between host country and U.S. personnel and defined according to rigorous economic criteria.

(6) The rebuilding requirements of the European Recovery Program required that the Agency be organized to engage in substantial contracting operations with private commercial contractors.

(7) Contract operations were carefully supervised by mission personnel who had substantial compliance control responsibilities.

(8) With rare exceptions, the programs of foreign assistance under the European Recovery Program were highly successful. Project objectives were not only achieved on schedule, they were achieved *ahead of schedule* and the entire program was phased out a year earlier than had been originally intended.

THE TECHNICAL COOPERATION ADMINISTRATION

Although "new" organizations frequently are created in government (especially in the foreign assistance field), they are often quite similar to predecessor organizations which performed similar functions. The Technical Cooperation Administration provides a case in point. The TCA drew many of its personnel and much of its philosophy from two organizations which were already administering technical assistance programs on a small scale. An examination of these two predecessors, the Institute of Inter-American Affairs (IIAA) and the Office of Foreign Agricultural Relations of the Department of Agriculture, provides useful insights into the basic differences between the ECA and TCA styles of administering technical assistance.

The Institute for Inter-American Affairs was the ancestor of the Alliance for Progress. Its scope of operations reflected the relatively low level of concern for Latin America which characterized American policy in the 1940's. In fact, the first technical assistance projects were initiated primarily to support American troops who were stationed in certain Latin American countries during the war.[26] After the war, IIAA projects reflected more general objectives in the areas of agricultural development, public health and education. The *Servicio* became the principal mechanism of technical assistance in Latin America. *Servicios* were jointly administered organizations in the recipient nations, which operated outside of normal governmental channels.

IIAA, which was chartered as a "semi-autonomous government corporation,"[27] has been criticized as a "holding company operation."[28] This criticism suggests the limited and highly decentralized pattern of administrative control which was characteristic of this agency. In comparison with its successors, the IIAA organization in Washington was minute. Moreover, while small missions were maintained in some countries, the mission chiefs did not, in most instances, have direct control over projects. "Country programming," in the ECA sense, was nonexistent.

It can be seen that the IIAA operation contrasted sharply with that of ECA. Its significant characteristics may be summarized:

(1) The organization was relatively free from association with major short-term U.S. foreign policy objectives.

(2) The program's primary focus was on technical assistance in the fields of agricultural development, public health and education.

(3) The resources available to the organization were relatively limited. Centralized administration was de-emphasized both in Washington and in the field.

(4) Large-scale contracting with private commercial organizations was minimal.

(5) The activities of the organization were "project oriented" rather than program oriented; project objectives were flexibly, even vaguely, defined; quantitative economic criteria were not emphasized.

(6) The officials of the organization were committed to the concept of the *Servicio* as the most effective organizational vehicle for the administration of technical assistance programs in the field.

The overall success of the IIAA program is difficult to evaluate, given its project oriented, fragmented character. However, by 1950 the *Servicios* had clearly made a discernible contribution to agriculture and rural development in many, although by no means all, of the areas in which projects had been undertaken and they were popular with the officials of Latin American governments.

A detailed discussion of TCA's other predecessor, OFAR, will be omitted. However, the following characteristics of this organization and its program should be emphasized.

(1) OFAR resources were extremely limited in comparison to those of ECA and even IIAA.

(2) Projects tended to be experimental[29] and research oriented.[30]

(3) Many OFAR officials had been closely associated with the agricultural extension and experiment station programs of Land-Grant colleges and universities.

Prior to the passage of the Act for International Development[31] (the authorizing legislation for the Point Four Program) in 1950, OFAR had engaged in some university contracting and was planning more under the authority of the Smith-Mundt Act.[32] However, these plans were altered by the establishment of the Technical Cooperation Administration.

Organizing to Administer Point Four: The Establishment of TCA and the Struggle Between the "Do-Gooders" and the "Big-Money Boys"

TCA became the organizational manifestation of Point Four. It was often called the "Point Four Agency." However, at the time of Truman's 1949 inaugural, the form of the agency, the nature and scope of its programs and its official relationships with other agencies engaged in overseas operations were by no means clear. The process of defining programs, areas of responsibility and organizational relationships by the newly appointed TCA officials precipitated a round of discussions in Washington which has been characterized by one of the active participants as "the struggle for survival [of TCA]," or "the fight between the 'do-gooders' and the 'big-money boys.'" The "do-gooders" were the administrators of TCA and OFAR, and their staffs, and some other State Department officials. The "big-money boys" were high ranking officials in the Economic Cooperation Administration and in the Office of the Director for International Security Affairs in the State Department.[33]

To fully understand this struggle, it should be remembered that by the end of 1951, ECA was successfully working itself out of business in Western Europe. A drastic contraction of personnel and appropriations appeared inevitable unless new responsibilities in other areas could be undertaken. Thus the intensity of the debate over control of the Point Four Program—which had, eventually, to be resolved by President Truman himself—can be explained, at least in part, by the fact that for *both agencies* the fundamental issue was survival.

The major substantive matters on which the debate focused were the following:

(1) The degree of relationship between project objectives and short-term U.S. foreign policy objectives.

(2) The degree of emphasis on capital development in technical assistance programs.

(3) The degree of delegation of responsibilities for program implementation to contractors and other government agencies.

(4) Matters of general orientation to programming and project selection, specifically, the degree to which projects should be integrated into "country programs" and the relevance of quantitative economic criteria for the definition of objectives and evaluation of technical assistance projects and programs.

(5) The degree of control to be exercised by a central "headquarters agency" over field personnel.

(6) The degree of control to be exercised by Agency missions in the field over contractors.

In more general terms, the issue under discussion was simply the relevance of the IIAA experience in Latin America as opposed to the ECA experience in Europe for the patterning of technical assistance programs under the new program.

The struggle was temporarily resolved with the passage of the Mutual Security Act of 1951 which changed the name of ECA to MSA and assigned this agency responsibility for coordinated programs of technical and military assistance in "underdeveloped areas" having *strategic significance*.[34] The responsibility for administering technical assistance programs in the rest of the "underdeveloped" world was assigned to the TCA, which was formally established by Executive Order 10159 of September 8, 1950, and Departmental Announcement 212 of October 27, 1950.

The Mutual Security Act was a compromise which, like a modern-day Treaty of Tordesillas, divided the world into spheres of influence, TCA countries and MSA countries.[35] It resolved the issues of contention between the two agencies geographically, but not substantively, and did little to reduce the intensity of feeling between the competing groups.

Significant Characteristics of TCA Programs

The basic characteristics of the two agencies from which TCA drew many of its personnel and much of its philosophy have been reviewed. Major segments of the TCA programs (including the university-contract projects) were, as noted above, directly administered by these two agencies under the TCA umbrella. The significant characteristics of technical assistance programs administered by TCA may, therefore, be summarized briefly.

(1) The policy of TCA was consciously to divorce itself from any association with immediate U.S. foreign policy objectives. Even the painting of U.S. insignia on equipment and other materials distributed under the program was specifically prohibited. "Point Four had simple goals," emphasized Administrator Andrews.[36] "There were no objectives except long term stability and no political strings attached to the granting of aid. The basis of projects was simply a joint agreement to work toward the achievement of mutually acceptable goals which were established by the host country."

(2) The organization was "field oriented." The responsibility for decisions concerning the initiation and administration of projects was decentralized. The Washington organization was oriented toward advisory and "backstopping" functions rather than supervisory, compliance control functions.

(3) Projects were farmed out to other government agencies, particularly the Department of the Interior and the Department of Agriculture, whenever possible and these organizations were granted considerable autonomy in their administration.

(4) Flexibility was emphasized in project agreements, and modification of projects to meet changing situations in the field was encouraged.

In general terms, the objective of TCA-administered technical assistance was viewed as "building people" rather than "building things." Education, particularly in the fields of agriculture and public health, was emphasized. The use of capital development projects to achieve the goals of Point Four was not encouraged. Obviously the initiation of university-contract projects and the individual patterns of participation which emerged reflected this orientation.

Agency Policies Affecting University Participation

The similarities between the policies of the two agencies with regard to university contracts reflected the common rationale of the officials who were most concerned with the program during its initial stages and the fact that these decision-makers were in a position to define the administrative procedures by which this rationale was implemented. Because of this, the struggle between the agencies was less consequential for the university-contract program than it might otherwise have been. It will be recalled from the earlier discussion that in both agencies:

(1) Participating universities were carefully selected by persons who had full knowledge of the programs which were to be undertaken and of the capabilities of the universities.

(2) Participation was limited to the fields of agricultural and rural development, fields in which the "Land-Grant philosophy" seemed relevant and the universities were believed to have special competence.

(3) The number of projects was deliberately limited. Because of the experimental nature of the program, projects were only initiated in field settings where they had been specifically requested by the host government and where university participation was deemed to be the most appropriate means of meeting project objectives. The limited scope of contract operations permitted the ranking officials concerned with the success of the program to devote considerable attention to its operational aspects.

The differences between the policies of the two agencies reflected the differences in organizational mechanisms through which the essentially common rationale was implemented. Thus, TCA projects placed greater emphasis on contractor autonomy, flexibility in the field, and the use of participating government agencies to perform backstopping functions. The autonomy of ECA (MSA) contract teams was more limited.

Agency-University Relations During the Period of Genesis

During this early period, the meetings of the Association of Land-Grant Colleges and Universities were used as a forum by

Agency officials to state general ideas regarding Agency-university participation in technical assistance programs, but it is not really appropriate to speak of the existence of a relationship at this level. The university-contract program had not, as yet, become an activity involving substantial numbers of American universities and for this reason it was given scant attention, in comparison to later periods, by the university community.

At the level of the participating universities there was a relatively high degree of harmony in the relationship but, because of the small size of the program, it was of relatively little significance in comparison to other programs of the different agencies. The most significant factor contributing to the relatively infrequent occurrence of negative incidents was the high level of consensus and communication which existed between cognizant government and university officials. Because of the limited scope of the program, a small group of high officials in the agencies (ECA, TCA, OFAR, MSA, IIAA) and the participating universities were involved in most of the incidents which occurred. These men shared the belief that the Land-Grant experience and philosophy were relevant to the objectives of the Point Four Program and were willing to experiment. The level of agreement was such that, during this brief period, which, in terms of actual contract operations was less than two years, it is really inappropriate to speak of the "Agency side" and the "university side," though this distinction is often used when discussing Agency-university relations in later periods.

This is not to suggest that the early projects were freer from operating problems than their successors. However, it is to suggest that the high degree of consensus among the participants about the underlying rationale of the program and the "command attention" and administrative flexibility which were possible due to its limited scope permitted these problems to be resolved more rapidly and efficiently than in later periods. This will become clearer during the examination of the problems the Agency faced as it attempted to cope with the vastly increased numbers of contracts which were initiated during the period of proliferation.

CHAPTER III

The Period of Proliferation (November 1953–June 1955)

THE STATUS of the university-contract program has never been (and, in all likelihood, will never be) a major consideration in the selection of foreign aid administrators. Nor has this program been a usual focal point of Agency activity.[1] It is doubtful if anyone envisioned the consequences for university participation in technical assistance which would follow the appointment of a former governor, presidential candidate and university president, Harold Stassen, to the Directorship of the Foreign Operations Administration (FOA). It seems likely that the university-contract program would have moved in a very different direction had Stassen not served at the head of FOA from January 1953 through June 1955.[2]

Stassen's Philosophy and Objectives

In the Fall of 1953, Stassen asked for the opportunity[3] to address NASULGC's Sixty-Seventh Annual Convention in order to make a special plea for increased university participation in the foreign assistance program. His speech must be regarded as a landmark in the history of Agency-university relations. "We have reached a conclusion," Stassen stated, "that we should present to you a very direct plea for assistance in a new and expanded way—a way which we feel will translate to the world scene to a very major extent, the kind of an association and development that occurred within the United States." He continued:

> This is our proposal and our suggestion: We are prepared to enter into new, broad, long term contracts with the Land-Grant colleges

The Period of Proliferation (November 1953–June 1955)

in the United States in relationship to specific underdeveloped countries and the educational institutions within those countries. We are prepared on the basis of three year contracts to set agreed upon objectives of accomplishments, and broad outlines of the method of program and to leave to a very major extent the decentralized implementation of research and education and extension work to the institutions within the United States which have the relevant particular kind of training and experience. . . . We contemplate activity in those areas in which the institution has demonstrated competence within the United States.[4]

Stassen outlined his proposed program for the university presidents in some detail. FOA would negotiate broad-range contracts with their institutions, which might include, in addition to agriculture, areas such as home economics, engineering, public administration and resource development. His hope was that expanded Land-Grant university participation would promote the development of a "two way flow between the individual country and the college with great progress and benefit to both."[5]

The proposed program reflected a coherent rationale[6] regarding university participation in technical assistance projects which was similar in many respects to the philosophy guiding the initiators of the program.[7] First, Stassen wanted to open up channels for growth and development that would be flexible and responsive to the needs of individual countries. By using universities, he hoped that the "bottlenecks" of the Washington bureaucracy could be circumvented and that the channels could become institutionalized. "I believed that education was the essence of development," he emphasized, "that we had to teach teachers or teach the teachers who would teach the teachers; that this would be the keystone to development."[8]

A second reason for expanding university participation was political. Stassen hoped that an increased emphasis on contracts would foster Congressional support for long-term commitments in the foreign assistance program at a time when conservative elements in Congress were challenging the basic idea of aid.

Finally, he hoped that expanded university participation would be a way of improving the quality of personnel in the foreign assistance program. University professors had been reluctant to participate in direct governmental service because of the loss of long-term institutional ties with their universities which this entailed. The new program would, through the mechanism of institutional participation, remove this impediment.

Stassen brought the perspective of a university president as well as that of a high ranking administrator and politician to the program. This greatly enhanced his ability to communicate with NASULGC members both as a group and individually. He emphasized that the university-governmental relationship was intended to be mutually beneficial; that contracts were not intended to be a drain on university resources; that universities could gain a needed international dimension through participation in overseas projects.

There is general agreement that the objectives envisioned by Stassen were not achieved by the policies formulated to implement them. Some of the reasons for this will be discussed below. These objectives have been described in some detail, however, because they are one of the least understood aspects of the remarkable proliferation of university contracts during Stassen's eventful, but brief period in office. For the patterns of university participation which evolved and the issues which arose between the Agency and the universities reflected organizational changes, personnel policies, specific policy directives and a style of administration which eventually impeded the attainment of the program's fundamental goals. Because of this, the period of proliferation is remembered by Agency and university personnel alike as a time of growing disillusionment and misunderstanding.

Major Policy Changes Affecting University Participation

Major policy changes originating outside of the Agency significantly affected the university-contract program during the period of proliferation. These changes originated in both the executive branch of the government and in the Congress.

The policy changes originating in the executive branch reflected basic philosophical differences between the newly elected Republican Administration of President Eisenhower and its predecessor regarding foreign assistance. First, there was increased emphasis on the use of foreign assistance programs to achieve major (Cold War) foreign policy objectives. A central agency was established to integrate and administer both technical assistance and mutual security programs. To a considerable degree the non-political philosophy of the Point Four Program was rejected.[9] Second, there was an increased emphasis on the use of non-governmental, contract personnel instead of government direct hire personnel in foreign assistance programs, a reflection of Republican opposition to "big government."

The attitude of the Congress toward foreign aid was more hostile and skeptical than it had been during the previous Administration. Both the Marshall Plan and the Point Four Program had enjoyed wide Congressional support, but charges of waste and corruption were leveled against them—as well as against many other Truman Administration programs—during the 1952 election campaign. The election results, of course, shifted control of Congress to the Republicans. Following the election, the foreign assistance program was investigated by several Congressional committees.[10] As a result of these investigations, the mutual security legislation passed in 1953 included a provision added by the Congress, but not opposed by the Administration, requiring the Director of Foreign Operations to reduce Agency personnel by not less than twenty-five percent prior to January 1, 1954.[11]

A second consequence of growing Congressional skepticism was the establishment of more detailed regulations and compliance control procedures in the area of personnel security. This change in policy, which was to have distinctly adverse consequences for Agency-university relations, was particularly related to the activities of Senator Joseph McCarthy and his permanent Investigations Subcommittee of the Senate Committee on Government Operations.[12]

There were also several important policy changes originating within the Agency. Some of these were primarily reactions to executive and Congressional directives. Others were the result of Stassen's personal initiatives.

From the standpoint of the university-contract program, the most important change was Stassen's directive to bureau and mission chiefs to "get university contracts."[13] A minimum goal of one contract per mission was established. A second change was the increased emphasis, at the Washington headquarters level of the Agency, on the integration of all foreign assistance operations in each country into an overall country plan. "One of the first things we did," Stassen noted, "was to set up a research unit. Extensive analyses of the different countries were undertaken. We had charts and other devices to stay on top of things."[14] Following the pattern established in ECA, mission directors were directed to assume full supervisory authority over project operations. Particular emphasis was placed on "getting control"[15] of those projects which had been administered by TCA. Finally, there was an attempt, only partially successful, to establish uniform fiscal and legal procedures throughout the Agency.

These new policies reflected a major shift in direction for the Agency, and particularly, the triumph of the ECA approach to foreign aid. This becomes even clearer when the concurrent organizational and personnel changes are examined.

Organizational Changes

In August 1953, the new Administration consolidated all foreign assistance operations under a single agency, the Foreign Operations Administration.[16] Although the agency was given a new name, it differed little in either organization or personnel from MSA. From the standpoint of technical assistance programs, the projects which had been administered by TCA were simply absorbed by a newly labeled Mutual Security Agency.

The reorganization transferred administrative responsibility for the rapidly expanding university-contract program to a much larger organization with a greater variety of concerns than had characterized TCA and OFAR. Moreover, FOA differed fundamentally in organizational structure from these two predecessor agencies. The expansion of contracting meant that responsibility for decisions affecting the day-to-day operations of university projects was relegated to much lower level personnel in the Agency than responsibility for major policy decisions. Thus, at a time when the problems with individual projects tended to increase because of the proliferation of contracts, the involvement of new personnel, and new administrative procedures, the amount of time that policy-makers within the Agency could devote to matters concerning individual projects was reduced sharply. A manifestation of this change was the creation of the office of

The Period of Proliferation (November 1953–June 1955)

University Contracts Coordinator. The sole function of this essentially powerless position[17] was to "expedite" decision-making related to the university-contract program.

THE PERSONNEL REDUCTION PROGRAM

The organizational changes in the Agency cannot be considered apart from the substantial changes in personnel which accompanied them. The degree to which factors influencing these changes combined to ensure that persons who would be most competent to administer an expanded university-contract program, and more important, who could work congenially and harmoniously with universities, were eliminated from the Agency, is truly remarkable.

First, personnel were eliminated because of the change in national administrations and the prevailing Republican attitudes toward the Point Four Program. None of the personnel who had served in policy-making positions in TCA were appointed to the new Agency.

Second, personnel were eliminated by the implementation of a personnel selection and evaluation program. Stassen, it will be recalled, was directed by the Congress to reduce Agency personnel by twenty-five percent. The procedures used to implement the reduction were (1) an examination administered to all Agency personnel, (2) a rating system by which superiors evaluated and rated their subordinates, and (3) the personal decision of the director himself.[18] Many "old hands" in the Agency—persons who had been associated over a long period of time with IIAA and persons who had been recruited through the influence of Dr. Bennett—found these procedures to be intolerable and simply resigned rather than submitting to evaluation and examination. Some individuals, particularly former TCA officials, argue that the evaluative system was biased for political reasons, but no convincing evidence that this was so has been uncovered. The evaluative system apparently was an attempt to meet the requirements imposed by Congress in a rational manner. However, along with some beneficial effects, the system did have the unfortunate side effect of contributing to the resignation or retirement of some of the more competent and experienced people associated with predecessor agencies, particularly TCA.

A third source of personnel attrition was the reorganization itself. Personnel were simply "reorganized" out of their jobs. The centralization of responsibility for all foreign assistance programs within the MSA organizational structure meant that many jobs in TCA no longer existed. Though new positions were found for a few of the former incumbents of these jobs, many simply left the Agency.

It is difficult to make an objective judgment regarding the relative competence of the persons who remained with the Agency (primarily MSA employees) in comparison with those who did not (primarily TCA employees). One cannot escape the impression, however, that many who left the Agency during this period did so for reasons that had little to do with their relative competence in comparison with those who remained. Among this group were a number of men whose background, philosophy, and experience would have enabled them to make a substantial contribution to the expanded university-contract program.

STASSEN'S STYLE OF ADMINISTRATION

Adding to the general picture of change was Stassen's forceful style of administration. It is frequently said that the Agency has been "leaderless" throughout much of its existence. However, this generalization is certainly not applicable to the period of proliferation. Agency officials who served during this period often speak of "Stassenation" when describing what occurred. Some use this term nostalgically; others, grimly.

Investigation of the FOA organization does not fully reveal the character of the changes introduced by Stassen to ensure that he would be able to exercise personal supervisory control over all aspects of Agency decision-making and that important problems would be quickly brought to him for resolution. "Given the scope of foreign aid—programs in operation in over eighty countries and territories—we were faced with an extremely difficult administrative problem," he later observed. "There had been a lot of sloppy administration and there had to be an administrative clamp down. I tried to set up an organization that would bring key problems to the attention of the director. There was a system of secretarial follow-up to ensure that policies were carried out. There was also a weekly staff meeting to check on these things."[19]

The Period of Proliferation (November 1953–June 1955)

The mechanism established to serve this objective, "to bring key problems to the attention of the director," was a sort of check and balance system within the Agency. The power of several of the technical service bureaus was increased to counterbalance the power of the geographic area bureaus. With a vaguely defined structure of authority, differences among the bureaus had to be resolved by the director. Unfortunately this arrangement conflicted with Stassen's objective of increasing autonomy in the field. The co-equal power of mission directors (under geographic bureaus) and "functional" division chiefs (under technical service bureaus) meant that, even at this level, disagreements often had to be referred to Washington. One critic later observed that "this system stalled everything in the field for eighteen months."[20] It is true that, following the ECA pattern, the power of the mission director over projects was increased in the former "TCA countries"; but, in the area of university contracting at least, the nature of the increased power was such that it was used primarily as a compliance control instrument to enforce conformity to Washington-originated directives.

A second facet of Stassen's style of administration which was of particular consequence for Agency-university relations was his habit of issuing major policy directives without prior consultation and discussion among his subordinates. Agency personnel called such directives "SSS" (Stassen says so) policies. One of these policies was the expansion of university contracts to the minimum level of one contract per mission. The practice of issuing directives without prior consultation was by no means unique to Stassen among Agency administrators. What was unique was that Stassen's personal energy, the reorganized administrative structure, and the sweeping authority granted him by the Congress to remove personnel ensured that all policies with which the director was personally concerned would be implemented throughout the Agency. These factors did not ensure that such policies would be enthusiastically supported, however. In fact, the proliferation of contracts created a legacy of hostility in the Agency toward university participation and led to a substantial increase in negative incidents following Stassen's departure.

This hostility seems to have been particularly prevalent among personnel involved in the mechanics of program administration, the day-to-day decision-making through which coordination and cooperation were supposed to be achieved. A number of factors contributed to this unfortunate situation.

First of all, many of the Agency's personnel at this level were strong proponents of the ECA–MSA capital development philosophy. They were firmly committed to the maintenance of supervisory control over contractor operations, the use of quantitative indicators to measure performance, and the integration of project objectives and political objectives. University contracts, on the other hand, seemed reminiscent of the old TCA approach emphasizing apolitical objectives, flexibility and contractor autonomy in the field. Many officials, especially those with no background in agriculture or the Land-Grant system, contemptuously viewed this approach as administratively lax and politically naive.

A second factor was Stassen's personal unpopularity among many, though by no means all, of the middle level personnel in the Agency. The "SSS" policies, the vigorous exercise of control "from above" and the unpopular personnel evaluation system all contributed to this. This unpopularity tended, in some instances, to focus on university contracting because it was one of the programs with which Stassen was most closely identified. Furthermore, officials who lagged in the implementation of the directive to "get contracts" for whatever reason—and there were certainly legitimate reasons for not having a university contract in some missions—found themselves faced with the prospect of making lengthy explanations to the director or with the loss of their position.

Personnel in the field, especially in Latin America, tended to have particularly negative views toward universities. University personnel, especially those whose projects involved the performance of essentially direct hire functions, were viewed as threats to job security. These feelings were intensified by the fact that the proliferation of contracts and drastic personnel cutbacks in the Agency coincided. In addition, contract personnel made demands on mission resources in the field which the missions had not been adequately prepared to meet. When their demands were not granted, they often complained to Washington that the Agency was not living up to its side of the contract. Finally, it must be recognized that many of the university personnel who were sent overseas during this period were ill prepared and poorly backstopped. A few were simply incompetent. They could hardly have been expected to impress mission personnel already predisposed to judge them unfavorably.[21]

Patterns of Participation: The Proliferation of Contracts

The rapid growth in contracts for rural and agricultural development is presented in Table II. However, this does not by any means portray the total picture of expansion during this period, with its consequent load on the administrative and decision-making processes of the Agency. Agency contract operations expanded from eight projects in rural and agricultural development involving seven Land-Grant institutions to eighty-one projects in everything from medicine to political science, involving more than sixty institutions including Land-Grant colleges and universities, private colleges and universities, trade and business schools.

One official closely associated with the pre-Stassen university-contract program offered a graphic picture of the situation resulting from Stassen's forceful and far-reaching initiatives.

> The thing turned out in a way which we never had intended. Suddenly we had globs of contracts . . . all over the world. There was a race to get contracts. Mission people who knew somebody in a college or university would simply contact them to start a contract. . . . But the idea was not yet well developed. The people overseas didn't understand what was being talked about when we talked about college contracts . . . many of the colleges and host institutions didn't want contracts or if they did, weren't ready for them. So a mat of contracts spread out over the world in the next two or three years in a highly disorganized manner. Sometimes three or four institutions would be in the same country doing different things. In the haste to get contracts, there was no time to bring order out of chaos . . . out of this glob of college contracts.[22]

Only one really new pattern of individual participation emerged during this period. It was characterized by a low level of involvement and commitment both by the university and by the Agency. The only reason for the existence of projects following this pattern was Stassen's drive to "get contracts." Generally they involved a direct relationship between the university "team"[23] and a host government agency or ministry under direct mission supervision.

TABLE II

University-Contract Rural Development Projects Initiated During the Period of Proliferation

REGION	COUNTRY	U.S. INSTITUTION	HOST INSTITUTION	DATES
FAR EAST	Thailand	Oregon State Univ.	Kasetsart University	1954–60
	Korea	U. of Minnesota	Seoul National University	1954–62
NESA	Afganistan	Univ. of Wyoming	Kabul University	1954–Active
	India	Univ. of Illinois	Ministry of Food and Agriculture, North Central Region	1955–Active*
	India	Kansas State Univ.	Ministry of Food and Agriculture, Central Region	1956–Active**
	India	Ohio State Univ.	Government, Ministry of Food and Agriculture, Northwest Region	1955–Active
	India	Univ. of Tennessee	Government, Ministry of Food and Agriculture, Northeast Region	1956–Active**
	India	Univ. of Missouri	Government, Ministry of Food and Agriculture, Northeast Region	1957–Active**
	Pakistan	Washington State U.	Punjab University, Ministry of Agriculture	1954–Active
	Turkey	Univ. of Nebraska	Ataturk University	1954–Active
	Israel	State Univ. of N.Y.	Government (direct hire functions under mission direction)	1954–58
	Jordan	Montana State Univ.	Government, Ministry of Agriculture (2 contracts; direct hire functions under mission direction)	1954–57

LATIN AMERICA			
	Chile	U. of California	University of Concepción; Agricultural Research and Extension (2 contracts)	1954–57
	Costa Rica	Univ. of Florida	Servicio and Ministry of Agriculture	1954–60
	Ecuador	Univ. of Idaho	Universities of Quito and Guayaquil	1954–57
	Mexico	Texas A & M	Escuela Superior de Agricultura	1954–56
	Mexico	U. of Pennsylvania	Ministry of Agriculture/USOM; Research and Training	1954–58
	Peru	North Carolina State University	National School of Agriculture, Government, Ministry of Agriculture	1954–Active
AFRICA	None			

Summary Data: (1) Number of contracts initiated   20
(2) Number of contracts terminated none
(3) Number of active contracts   28

Sources: See TABLE I, p. 18.

*The second Illinois contract in India differed substantially from the first and was the result of an entirely different set of negotiations. It was not simply an extension and reorientation of the first contract.

**Negotiations for these contracts were initiated during the period of proliferation. With the exception of the Missouri contract, funds were also available.

NOTE: Contracts listed as ACTIVE were active as of July 1, 1966.

In addition, the pattern which had characterized the Oklahoma State and Arkansas projects began to be altered as newly appointed mission directors tried to extend their control over contracts which had been administered by TCA. The expanded responsibilities which the university field teams had assumed were gradually reduced.

Agency-University Relations at the Level of the Participating Universities

Many of the participants in the university-contract program, as well as those who have studied it in some detail, point to the period of the Stassen administration from 1953 to mid-1955 as one in which a serious deterioration in Agency-participating university relations occurred. However, the public record as well as detailed interviews with knowledgeable people does not support this evaluation. The nadir of Agency-university relations came in 1956–57. Although many of the difficulties that existed at this time can be traced to policies and practices initiated by Stassen, during his tenure in office, the deterioration in relations was relatively insignificant. This view is supported by the absence of serious manifestations of dissatisfaction at the level of the university community.

The lack of any significant evidence of deterioration during this period (especially in comparison with the period which followed) can be explained by the following factors.

(1) Most of the projects initiated during the period of proliferation did not actually begin operation until late in 1954 or 1955. Thus, the increase in the *total number of incidents* over the preceding period was relatively small.[24]

(2) Because of the relatively short operational period of most of the projects, there was little opportunity for incidents involving fiscal and financial matters to occur. For a number of reasons which will be explored below, these types of incidents were the most likely to be negative.

(3) Stassen's interest in university contracts and administrative ability limited the occurrence of negative incidents by giving university-contract matters a high priority within the Agency and ensuring that major problems were brought to his attention.

The Period of Proliferation (November 1953–June 1955)   47

(4) High ranking officials of the participating universities were not personally involved in many of the projects during this period. Thus it was less likely that incidents involving them would occur.

(5) Incidents which did involve high ranking university officials also tended to involve Stassen himself and, therefore, were frequently positive rather than negative.

This final factor merits particular emphasis since it suggests the degree of communication between the highest level of the Agency and the participating universities. In cases of serious misunderstanding, Stassen's policy was simply to call the president of the concerned university and try to work things out.[25] This channel provided a means of smoothing over many irritating problems before they became major exacerbating issues.

Although the period of proliferation was not marked by a serious deterioration in relations, problems—and negative incidents—began to occur with increasing frequency during the closing months of Stassen's regime. Some of these were directly related to organizational changes, the proliferation of contracts and Stassen's administrative style. This suggests that a considerable deterioration in relations might have occurred during succeeding years, even if a man who was more sympathetic to university contracting had been appointed as Stassen's successor.

Three problem areas merit particular attention because of the long-term nature of the issues which were raised. These can be categorized under the headings of (1) bureaucratic red tape, (2) mutual lack of commitment and (3) adjustment.

"Red Tape" Problems

"Red tape" is a term frequently used to denote certain kinds of problems which arise in large organizations, especially government bureaucracies. However, it is rarely defined explicitly. In annual reports of participating universities, criticisms of bureaucratic red tape in the Agency appeared with increasing frequency after 1953.[26] After Stassen's departure the phrase *rigidity and interference* began to be used by universities and in official statements from the university community. The difference in terminology suggests an important distinction between types of problems in the Agency-university relationship.

Problems of bureaucratic red tape arose where Agency and university personnel at the operating level were unable to work out a satisfactory solution, given existing organizational and administrative mechanisms, to problems associated with the achievement of goals to which *both were committed.* Appendix I reproduces the record of a series of incidents involving equipment procurement, taken from the files of one of the larger university-contract projects, which illustrates this problem. The source of the difficulty in this case was the difference between the procurement regulations of the Agency and those of the university, plus a lack of effective communication mechanisms between the two parties. Many comparable examples can be found in university and Agency files.

The difference between these types of problems and the problems of rigidity and interference which were more characteristic of the period of retrenchment (and subsequent periods) was that in the latter case, lack of commitment to common goals made some of the responsible decision-makers unwilling to work out the organizational impediments to effective cooperation. The high priority of the university-contract program during the period of proliferation minimized the occurrence of such problems.

Mutual Lack of Commitment Problems

Problems of *mutual lack of commitment* arose in several projects initiated as a result of the directive to "get contracts." In these projects, the mission and bureau complied with the directive, but little thought was devoted to project planning or the selection of the participating institution. Apparently, the feeling among the responsible officials was that once they could say they had a contract, that was sufficient. On the university side also, the *idea* of having a contract was an important motivation; however, home campus backstopping was minimal or non-existent for the persons who were recruited as "university personnel"[27] and little attention was given to the problems which almost invariably developed in the field. Often the duties of campus coordinator were assigned to a part-time graduate assistant.

The terminal reports of technicians who participated in projects characterized by mutual lack of commitment make rather poignant reading. In the introduction to his chronological summary, one participant reported:

Each day I expected that I would receive a definite assignment. I finally asked about a range resource development program and was

The Period of Proliferation (November 1953–June 1955) 49

informed that none had been developed and that when the [host] government wanted such a program they would ask for it.[28]

Later in the same report, he observed that "from about July 20th to August 15th, there was nothing for me to do . . . ." Another participant reported the following "hindrances" to his work:

1. There was no program prepared for me to follow or to build upon. I had to start from the beginning.
   a. Several months elapsed before I found out with whom I could work.
   b. I was told by [Chief of USOM Agricultural Division] that there was no government official responsible for or interested in range work.
2. I was told that contracts with government officials were to be made by the chief of the department and not by a technician.
3. When I asked how my ideas and proposals for range work development could be brought to the attention of the government here, [Chief of USOM Agricultural Division] stated "if the government wants them, they will ask for them."
4. The language barrier is serious, I had no counterpart.
5. When I wished to enroll in morning [language] classes to gain some knowledge of the language, I was told by [Chief of USOM Agricultural Division] "the director does not approve; technicians should be in the field." . . .[29]

Many of these projects were discontinued by the Agency when the initial contractual agreement expired, normally after two years. However, they left a residue of ill feeling on both sides and, in some cases hampered subsequent (and better organized) efforts to initiate university projects in the same settings.

Adjustment Problems

Several of the TCA-initiated projects, where the university team had expanded its operations and university personnel had established direct and congenial working relationships with important government officials, encountered problems of adjustment.

FOA mission officials who came in contact with this kind of project tended to feel that the informal relationships which had been established violated the concept of country programming under mission direction and the official chain of command. University representatives felt that the FOA officials were inexperienced, did not understand the field situation, and were interfering with their legitimate responsibilities. The degree to which these differences became exacerbated seems, in the three projects which were most plagued by these types of problems, to have depended primarily on the personalities involved. In two cases, the problems were worked out over a period of time and the direct hire functions which had been performed by the U.S. university field party were gradually assumed by mission personnel. In one instance, personal differences between the mission director and the chief of party lead to a hardening of attitudes on both sides and the problems eventually became so severe that they led to the termination of the contract by the U.S. university.[30]

Agency-University Relations at the Level of the University Community

The need for official expressions of dissatisfaction by the university community was kept relatively low during this period by the high level of communication which existed between the Agency and the individual participating universities. Consequently, Agency-university relations at this level remained relatively quiescent. A mild expression of dissatisfaction was placed in the record of the NASULGC convention in 1953, but this did not represent a serious attempt to pressure the Agency to modify its procedures. It is unlikely that it was even noted by the Agency.[31]

As both the Agency and university community representatives foresaw the possibilities of increased operational difficulties,[32] the NASULGC was asked to establish a "full time shop" to serve as liaison between the participating universities and the Agency.[33] Following discussions between representatives of NASULGC, FOA and the USDA, the American Council on Education was requested, in January 1954, "to establish a service to help facilitate effective relationships in technical cooperation between United States educational agencies and institutions and the Foreign Operations Administration and between institutions of cooperating countries."[34] Responding to this request, the Council, with financial assistance from the Ford Foundation, established the Committee on Institutional Projects Abroad (CIPA), with a Washington staff office, in the Summer of 1954.

Although the Committee did not begin to play a major role in Agency-university community relations until November of the following year, four months after the end of the period of proliferation, its establishment is properly viewed as a landmark for two reasons. First, the events leading up to the submission of the request for such a committee to the American Council on Education marked a fundamental change in the relationship between the Agency and the Association of Land-Grant Colleges and Universities. For the first time, Agency representatives went to the Association, not merely to express the notion that university participation would be a good thing, or to solicit such participation, but to request assistance in solving operational problems associated with the program. Second, the establishment of the Committee created a focal point for establishing communication between ranking Agency officials and leading representatives of the participating universities. Although relatively unimportant during the remaining months of Stassen's administration, such a focal point became extremely important in the years which followed.

Conclusion: Aprez Moi...?

Some analysts have viewed the development of the university-contract program as analogous to the growth of a maturing organism. While such an analogy is of limited usefulness, the term "adolescent" could be appropriately applied to the period just considered. Like an adolescent, the program grew rapidly in all directions; at times, the head seemed to have little control over the extremities. Both the Agency and the participating universities undertook activities which exceeded their resources and experience. In terms of the numbers of projects in operation the program had reached its full growth; however, its mature form was, as yet, undetermined.

The problem with the analogy appears during an examination of the years following Harold Stassen's departure from the Agency, for the program did not assume a more mature and developed form. Instead, its very existence often seemed doubtful. Thus, while the policies of proliferation provided the basis for future growth, they also altered the program in a way which made a deterioration in Agency-university relations probable, if not inevitable.

CHAPTER IV

The Period of Retrenchment (July 1955–September 1957)

John B. Hollister: A New Director and a New Approach

HAROLD STASSEN's association with the foreign assistance program terminated with the third reorganization of the Agency in as many years. His successor, John B. Hollister, who was named director of the newly created International Cooperation Administration, differed from Stassen in many respects. A former law partner of the late Senator Robert A. Taft, Hollister shared Taft's conservative philosophy regarding foreign and fiscal policy. He had become closely associated with the foreign assistance program in an investigatory capacity as Executive Director of the Hoover Commission and shared the views expressed in the Commission report; namely, that "mistakes and waste" had characterized the U.S. foreign aid program[1] and that "important savings" could be made through more efficient administration.[2]

Hollister's objective was to cut back the excesses which he believed characterized the Stassen regime. This approach was consistent with his personal views toward foreign assistance and with the drive for economy in government which was being pressed by Treasury Secretary Humphrey, as well as with prevalent Congressional attitudes. In the interests of economy, he tended to oppose the initiation of new projects, the continuation of old ones and anything else which cost money.[3] Agency personnel joked that he had a large cash register installed in his office and spent most of his time personally and reluctantly doling out the barest minimum of funds to operate the program. Some persons who served in ICA during this period have expressed the opinion that his intention was to "destroy" the program.[4] The period of retrenchment is referred to as "the Dark Ages" by old hands in the Agency.

Although some university personnel believe that Hollister specifically opposed university contracts, this view is not entirely accurate. Hollister was opposed to technical assistance projects in general because they were difficult to administer financially and because of their characteristic high ratio of personnel to funds expended; however, it is unlikely that university contracts were singled out for special attention. On the other hand, it is clear that he was not especially interested in the university-contract program, took few pains to inform himself about it and did not actively participate in decisions related to its administration. This allowed others who were not favorably disposed toward universities to have a much freer hand than they had under Stassen.

A policy directive issued to guide the Agency in reviewing fiscal year 1958 proposals is especially revealing of Hollister's administrative style and philosophy.[5] It emphasized that (a) project goals would be defined in quantitative terms (a particularly difficult task in the case of many university projects),[6] (b) project proposals would have to be supported by detailed documentation in order to even be considered and (c) all cognizant offices would review and comment on proposals in detail prior to consideration by the Director.[7] The directive specified to missions that all project plans at their inception would indicate a specific termination date and indicated that "any project which has continued for a number of years and does not indicate a definite and reasonable *early* termination date" would receive special attention in the review of the 1957 budget.

This policy greatly complicated and lengthened the clearance process for most projects. Matters were further complicated by the fact that Hollister was not particularly interested in maintaining the system which had enabled his predecessor to be aware of major problems and to exercise control over all aspects of Agency operations. Thus, during the period of retrenchment, the "check and balance system" began to break down and legal, contracting and fiscal management personnel assumed a preponderant influence in Agency decision-making processes. Agency personnel became increasingly skilled in determining which of the unpopular directives from above had to be implemented and which could be given lip service only. The Agency developed a

The Period of Retrenchment (July 1955–September 1957) 55

"life of its own,"[8] exclusive of decisions made at the top. Subordinate Agency officials lived with the policies and whims of the Director, but did not actively support them.

Organizational Changes

At the beginning of Hollister's tenure, the name of the foreign aid administering agency was changed from the Foreign Operations Administration to the International Cooperation Administration (ICA). The "new" organization became a "semi-autonomous agency" under the direct administrative control of the Department of State.[9] From the standpoint of the university-contract program, however, the change from FOA to ICA was little more than a change in name. The administrative structure was still basically similar to ECA and operating relationships remained essentially the same.

The establishment of a central contracting office in March 1956, had more important consequences. Previously, "some 12 divisions or offices had the authority to negotiate, enter into and administer contracts."[10] The reorganization transferred these responsibilities to the Office of Contract Relations, which was staffed by a newly recruited group of contract specialists under the direction of former MSA controller, Edward E. Kunze.

More will be said about contract specialists (or contract officers) below; however, the underlying rationale of a central contract office should be briefly discussed at this point. In general terms, the idea was that the legal and substantive aspects of contracted projects could be separated administratively and thus that those things which all contracting operations had in common were more important than those things which differentiated one project from another. Ideally, then, technical specialists in various areas would present the contract specialist with a statement of what needed to be done, and he would put this statement in the proper legal form to procure the required services. This system seems to have worked relatively well in the case of contractual arrangements with commercial companies for specific types of services. However, it was not so successful in the case of university contracts.

University personnel soon came to regard the new contract office as a bottleneck in the Agency. During the first year of operation at least, problems in personnel recruitment rather than new procedures were the major source of the numerous delays which exasperated team members, campus coordinators and university presidents. At the time of its establishment, in March 1956, the office was authorized to fill fifty-nine positions (contract officers and administrators). As of June 20, 1956, only twenty-nine of the positions had been filled. Not until November 1956 was the Agency successful in recruiting a substantial number of the persons with the capabilities required and not until January 1957 was staffing completed.[11]

A second factor also complicated the work of the new office (and irritated the universities). During the Summer of 1955, there was a substantial personnel turnover in the Office of the General Counsel of the Agency. Subsequently, a number of legal rulings were issued which altered procedures in the area of university contracting, particularly with regard to acceptable financial management procedures on the part of the universities.[12] These new rulings caused considerable embarrassment for Agency contract negotiators and major difficulties for a number of university business officers. The negotiators were forced to inform the universities that a number of procedures hitherto acceptable would no longer be permitted. Unfortunately, this involved more than simply adjusting to the new procedures on the part of the participating universities. Post-audits were performed by Agency auditors who drew no distinction between the period when the universities had been operating under the initial and under the revised interpretations. Consequently substantial disallowances were imposed on the universities,[13] and repayment to the government of previously expended funds was required.

Major Policy Changes Affecting the University-Contract Program

There were no changes in national policy directly affecting the university-contract program during the period of retrenchment. Treasury Secretary Humphrey's drive for economy in government began during this period, however, and Hollister's retrenchment program was, in part, a manifestation of this.

Within the Agency, four significant changes were initiated. Two of these, the emphasis on economy and the requirement of early termination of projects, have already been discussed. A third change was the introduction of standard contracting procedures for university contracts. The universities provided the impetus for this innovation, which is properly regarded as a landmark because it represents the first major change in Agency procedures strongly affected by pressure from the university community. These developments are discussed in greater detail below in the section on Agency-university community relations.

The fourth change dwarfs the others in its significance for Agency-university relations. This was the de-emphasis of university contracts. Hugh Mohrabacher, assistant university contracts coordinator, tells part of the story in this way:

> The new policy was first announced at a meeting of Latin American mission and *Servicio* directors in Rio. When I went before the group, I noticed that I was somewhat coolly received. Stassen's drive to get contracts had aroused considerable hostility and opposition and I am sure they looked at me as just another guy who was coming down from Washington to tell them to get more contracts.
>
> However this all changed when I introduced my presentation with the following statement: "Gentlemen, the message that I bring you is that university contracts are no longer a sacred cow." There was an audible sigh of relief, I could feel the air clear immediately. . . .[14]

The news of this de-emphasis—and it was considered good news, particularly by field personnel—spread quickly throughout the Agency. Some, but not all, of the contracts which were under negotiation and for which FY '56 funds had been appropriated were completed. However, the number of new contracts tapered off drastically in 1957. It was a predictable reaction to the "get contracts" policy and the dissatisfaction which it had generated. Perhaps even more important, the priority given to university-contract matters in Agency decision-making processes dropped substantially.

Patterns of Participation

The effects of de-emphasizing university contracts are partially revealed by Table III. Most of the new contracts which were initiated had been under negotiation during the Stassen Administration. Furthermore, the necessary funds had already been appropriated in many cases.

A number of contracts were discontinued. Several "low commitment" projects were quickly concluded because the Agency simply refused to extend them beyond the initial termination date specified. Three other contracts were discontinued because of participating university dissatisfaction with Agency policies and administrative procedures.

Individual patterns of participation show increasing uniformity after the period of retrenchment. Most of the contracts which survived were of the "sisterhood" relationship type. This uniformity persisted until 1962 when the Latin American Bureau of the Agency (The Alliance for Progress) again began initiating contracts involving a direct relationship between university field teams and host government agencies.

Agency-University Relations at the Level of the Participating Universities

It was suggested above that the deterioration in Agency-university relations was much greater during the period of retrenchment than during the preceding period of proliferation even though many of the decisions contributing to the deterioration were made during the earlier period. The differences between the two periods which support this contention are readily apparent. The rationale and administrative style of Director Hollister and the changes in organization, policy and personnel greatly increased the probability that negative incidents would occur. At the same time, the projects initiated during the period of proliferation reached a stage where the occurrence of incidents likely to be negative (especially those involving legal and fiscal matters) was unavoidable. Thus, nearly all of the factors which, during the period of proliferation, had limited the occurrence of negative incidents were altered. The result was a rapid and significant deterioration in Agency-participating university relations.

Appendix I provides examples, from university contract files, which illustrate typical kinds of incidents. The reader who wishes

TABLE III

University-Contract Rural Development Projects Initiated and Terminated During the Period of Retrenchment

REGION	COUNTRY	U.S. INSTITUTION	HOST INSTITUTION	DATES
Contracts Initiated:				
FAR EAST	Indonesia	Univ. of Kentucky	University of Indonesia at Bogor	1957–Active
	Japan	U. of Massachusetts	Hokkaido University	1957–61
NESA	None			
LATIN AMERICA	Guatemala	Univ. of Kentucky	University of San Carlos	1957–61
AFRICA	None			
Contracts Terminated:				
FAR EAST	None			
NESA	Jordan	Montana State Univ.	Ministry of Agriculture (2 contracts; direct hire functions under mission direction)	1954–56/57
LATIN AMERICA	Chile	Univ. of California	University of Concepción; Agricultural Research and Extension (2 contracts)	1954–57
	Ecuador	Univ. of Idaho	Universities of Quito and Guayaquil	1954–57
AFRICA	None			

Summary Data: (1) Number of contracts initiated   3
                (2) Number of contracts terminated   5
                (3) Number of active contracts   26

Sources: See TABLE I, p. 18.
NOTE: Contracts listed as ACTIVE were active as of July 1, 1966.

to understand some of the problems encountered, from the perspective of individual contractors, will find it helpful to look over some of these cases before proceeding further.

As the discussion above suggests, negative incidents were caused by a multiplicity of interrelated factors. However, it is possible to identify four major problem areas which seem particularly significant.

First, delays in reaching decisions relating to university-contract matters became endemic within the Agency. Many university personnel, in fact, seem to regard delays as the major cause of negative incidents during the period of retrenchment. The factors contributing most significantly to the delays were the increasing complexity of Agency decision-making procedures, chronic staffing problems, and the relatively low priority of the university-contract program in relation to other pressing concerns of Agency personnel. The problems which arose because of these factors are called *structural problems*.

Second, there were disagreements and misunderstandings over regulations and procedures which had been established for administering contract funds. Problems in this area are termed *financial management problems*.

Third, differences of viewpoint existed between the Agency and the participating universities regarding the most appropriate nature of the contract instrument, contract interpretations and matters related to the "boilerplate" provisions of the contract. These can be called *contractual problems*.

Fourth, the Agency and the universities frequently defined project goals differently, even when agreement was reached on a statement of project objectives in the contract. Furthermore, the parties disagreed about the degree to which the participating university should be allowed to determine the means by which project goals were to be achieved. Problems in this area are called *fundamental conceptual problems*.

Because of the long-term character of the issues involved, each of these problem areas will be examined in some detail.

Structural Problems

During the life of any university contract, numerous situations arise which require authoritative decisions and interpretations by Agency representatives in the field or in Washington. This is particularly true in the early stages of project operations (particularly with an inexperienced university) and also when the contract is coming up for extension or termination. Matters requiring interpretation of contract provisions require particular attention. So do matters involving the accounting for project funds.

During the period of retrenchment the Agency began to require "clearances" before participating universities could take final action on numerous routine matters. For example, clearance was required for appointments of overseas staff members and participant trainees, salaries of overseas staff members, and inspection trips by U.S. university officials. Of course, all matters involving deviation from regulations and requirements stipulated in the contract required clearance; because contracts were usually written and negotiated in Washington, deviations were invariably necessary.

The point which needs emphasis is not that clearances were good or bad in themselves, but that this system required regular and timely action by the Agency for contract operations to proceed at all. During this period such action often was not forthcoming. It is clear that Agency personnel were not deliberately impeding things in many instances. Most of the delays in action on more or less routine requests from the participating universities can be attributed to (1) the complexity of the procedures required for action, (2) staffing difficulties in ICA and (3) the low priority of the university-contract program in relation to other Agency activities.

1. The complexity of procedures required for action:

The increased emphasis within the Agency on uniformity and centralization ensured that all requests for approval and interpretation would be dealt with according to formalized procedures. Because of the "check and balance" system established by Stassen, most decisions, even fairly routine ones, had to be cleared through several offices. During the Stassen regime, this system kept delays at a minimum by quickly bringing problems to the Director's attention. However, Hollister apparently did not want to use the system in this way. Consequently, the processes of decision-making bogged down as the amount of work required in the review and clearance processes increased. Forwarding final, carefully documented *decisions* to the Director rather than *problems for decision* was emphasized.

An example of clearance procedures will illustrate the way in which the decision process worked. If a participating university requested a salary clearance for an overseas staff member, this request was reviewed by:

(a) technical personnel in the cognizant technical division of the U.S. Overseas Mission (USOM),

(b) program officers and controller personnel in the USOM,

(c) the cognizant country desk officer and program officer in the appropriate ICA/Washington regional office,

(d) technical field specialists and the project manager in the cognizant technical service office, and

(e) the contract officer (who might consult with legal specialists and financial analysts) in the Office of Contract Relations.[15]

If differences of viewpoint developed at any stage, consultations with superiors in the different offices and negotiations among the offices were required until an acceptable decision was reached. In the case of a routine salary clearance, consultation and negotiation would probably be minimal. However, even under the best conditions, the clearance process tended to be tortuous.

2. Staffing difficulties in ICA:

Furthermore, it should be emphasized that the complex procedures discussed above were designed for a fully staffed organization. ICA was seriously understaffed during the period of retrenchment.[16] Problems of understaffing did not, however, lead to any simplification of clearance, interpretation and approval procedures. In fact, as noted above, the trend was in the opposite direction.

The difficulties encountered by the newly created Office of Contract Relations provide a relevant example. This office was a particularly important link in the chain of decision relating to the university-contract program because the contract provided the legal basis for project operations and especially for expenditures of government funds. The proliferation of contracts in 1954 and 1955 led to a substantial increase in requests for contract actions[17] in 1956, the first year that the office was established. Because of staffing difficulties and the relatively low priority of the university-contract program, it was simply impossible for the office to meet the demands placed upon it by the participating universities. Decisions which were vital to operations in the field were often delayed for two or three months, sometimes longer.

3. The low priority of the university-contract program in relation to other Agency activities:

Complex procedures and staffing difficulties affected all Agency programs to some degree, although by no means equally. In some programs, delays and inattention to problems could not be tolerated. Thus it was necessary for overworked Agency personnel to establish an informal priority system to ensure that programs of major importance received primary attention. High priority matters were those which

(a) received Congressional attention—particularly the preparation of the annual "Congressional presentation,"
(b) were personal concerns of the director,
(c) required Presidential decision by law,
(d) involved the expenditure of large amounts of money,
(e) were related to major foreign policy interests of the U.S., or
(f) involved the employment of large numbers of Agency personnel.[18] According to these criteria, matters relating to the university-contract program received extremely low priority. Consequently, unless the Agency personnel involved were personally interested in some aspect of the program or somebody's demands became particularly strident, these matters tended to be pushed aside or dealt with in an offhand manner.

Financial Management Problems

Procedures relating to the payment of indirect costs were a major source of negative incidents. During the period of retrenchment, the first audits of overhead expenses based on provisional rates were completed for many of the contracts initiated during the first year of the period of proliferation. The results of these audits led, in many cases, to negative incidents involving ranking university officials. To discuss the causes of these incidents, it is necessary to outline Agency procedures for determining provisional overhead rates and the payment of indirect costs.[19]

All university contracts negotiated prior to 1962[20] specified, in accordance with Federal contracting regulations, the following procedures for overhead payments:

(1) The assignment of a provisional overhead rate in the contract, and the budgeting of funds for indirect costs according to this rate,

(2) An audit of operations under the contract to determine actual indirect costs, and

(3) Repayment by the contractor to the Agency of any differences between the two figures.[21]

These provisions led to numerous incidents in which participating universities were required to return funds to the Agency. Both the inexperience of university business offices with Federal contracting regulations and the lack of clear-cut criteria for determining what constituted a legitimate indirect cost for a university contributed to readjustments downward of overhead rates. The criteria for determining indirect costs were based on commercial contracting experience and the documentation requirements validating indirect costs were based on the procedures of commercial contractors. Consequently, during the early years of the university-contract program, the decision as to whether a given expenditure for indirect costs had been validly incurred had to be left to the judgment of Federal auditors. Almost invariably, the decisions of the auditors were unfavorable to the universities. The first round of audits of contracts initiated during the period of proliferation occurred during 1956 and 1957. In many instances, there were readjustments downward to overhead rates and consequent demands for repayment.

The post-audits conducted to determine whether expenditures of Federal funds by the contractors were justified by the provisions of the contract and in accordance with Federal regulations could also lead to demands for repayment. Usually, the auditors would "disallow" certain expenditures for one reason or another. The situation which developed during the period of retrenchment has been concisely summarized in the *Glick Report*.

> The contracts drafted in this period [of proliferation] showed extremely poor craftsmanship. Contract terms were so ambiguous that they paved the way for frequent disallowances by FOA and ICA auditors, with subsequent legitimate complaints from contractors that they had been led astray by the Agency's own negotiators.[22]

The *Glick Report* fails to mention, however, a major source of these difficulties; namely, the personnel changes in the Agency's legal staff and consequent reinterpretations of contract provisions and of allowable procedures. As in the case of overhead, disallowance problems were exacerbated by the inexperience of university business offices with Federal contracting and documentation requirements. A further complicating factor was the shortage of staff in the ICA auditing office, which meant that contracts often did not receive their first audit until two, even three, years after the start of operations. Because of this delay, universities could expend "unauthorized" funds for relatively long periods of time before the "errors" were uncovered. In these cases, disallowances frequently amounted to many thousands of dollars. After their first audit, university officials quickly became aware of the potential problems. In many cases business officers *requested* an audit during the early months of operation under a new contract. However, these requests were all too frequently denied because of the backlog of work in the auditing division and the low priority accorded to university-contract matters. This forced some universities to go to the cumbersome extreme of submitting every invoice justifying expenditures under the contract of the Agency for immediate audit. Even when these procedures were used, the Agency would only approve these expenditures provisionally, subject to final audit.[23]

Disallowances and re-evaluations of overhead rates created a special problem for participating universities which tended to involve top university administrators. In simple terms, the problem was: "Where is the money going to come from?" Although the overhead or other expenditures had been disallowed, *the money had already been spent.* There was certainly nothing "left over" for the university to return to the Agency. This meant that the repayment funds for disallowed expenditures or differences between the provisional and actual overhead rates had to be included in university budgets as a new item for the next fiscal year. This requirement led to unpleasant sessions between university presidents and the appropriations committees of the state legislatures. Needless to say, items in the university budget for substantial repayments to a Federal agency—on occasion involving as much as one hundred thousand dollars—were not kindly received by state legislators, who often opposed university involvement in international programs in the first place. Though there is no evidence that a state legislature ever actually disapproved a repayment item, university officials were caught in the middle of an unpleasant and extremely difficult situation which was unlikely to dispose them kindly toward Agency fiscal procedures.

Contractual Problems

The differences between USDA administration of the annual supporting funds which were made available to Land-Grant universities and ICA administration of contracts constituted a potential source of negative incidents which was particularly significant in Agency relations with these institutions. USDA funds were made available to Land-Grant colleges and universities on a grant basis through a simple letter of commitment. Of course, the universities were required to make reports of the expenditures of these funds, but they were not subjected to the complex requirements associated with Federal contracting procedures. As one university official reported:

> The arduous process of writing the contract and the length of the contract were surprising to many of the academic personnel with a background in agriculture. We had been working with the Department of Agriculture for years and had operated, for their research grants, under simple one page memoranda of agreement. We had sort of assumed that working with ICA would be similar.[24]

Throughout this period, particularly after the initial difficulties with the contracts arose, universities began requesting that funds be made available to them on a grant basis rather than a contractual basis. If that was not possible, they requested that the contract be made more flexible and less complex. The Agency was severely limited in this area by Federal contracting and General Accounting Office regulations. Furthermore, most Agency officials were not sympathetic to the grant idea. They felt that their programs required tighter controls than a grant arrangement would permit. In many cases, their experiences with universities during the period of proliferation had tended to confirm these views. Thus, the continued demands of university representatives for a more flexible instrument and the unwillingness, and in some cases inability, of Agency representatives to comply led to negative incidents.

Another problem was the lack of uniformity of contracts. Prior to 1956, as many as twelve different offices within the Agency could negotiate contracts. Prior to 1957, there was no standard university contract. Consequently there were substantial differences between contracts, even when two universities were performing the same function. Differences in benefits received depended to a considerable degree on the demands of the individual universities and on the skill of the negotiators for each side. Negative incidents occurred when officials of one contracting university discovered that another had received preferential treatment in some area covered by a similar contract and requested that the Agency amend their contract to conform to the more liberal provisions.[25] The university representatives felt that the Agency tended to act "quite capriciously" in these matters and that the notion that each university should go out and try to get the best deal for themselves was not in accordance with the philosophy of "equal partnership" between the Agency and the universities.[26] For the Agency, however, enacting such amendments was not a simple matter. In many cases it was impossible. Agency negotiators were limited by the GAO-enforced "value received provision" in Federal contracting regulations which stated that a contract could not be amended to the benefit of the contractor unless additional value received to the government could be clearly demonstrated. Such demonstration was difficult or impossible in the case of many of the amendments which the university representatives requested. However, the Agency's position was interpreted as "rigid" by the universities.

Fundamental Conceptual Problems

It is much more difficult to identify specific incidents in this area since fundamental conceptual differences tended to produce negative incidents revolving around procedural matters. However, the issues involved were viewed by both parties as significant. Additionally, these issues were a major topic of discussion between the Agency and the university community, particularly after 1957.

The two parties to a contract often disagreed about the most appropriate project goals. These differences would arise even after a set of project objectives had been formalized. Most frequently they arose between the overseas university team and the Agency field representatives. For example, in projects involving a "sisterhood" relationship, university representatives tended to emphasize the development of a research capability in the host institution faculty as an appropriate goal. Agency personnel, however, tended to emphasize more "practical" matters such as the capability of the host institution to graduate some specified number of students in a given field.[27]

Even when there was general agreement about project goals, there was no guarantee that attaining those goals would be given the same priority by university and Agency representatives. The necessity for deciding among several goals in a given setting could often lead to negative incidents. A mission director's decision, given limited resources, to fund a university-contract project below the level deemed necessary by university representatives in order to fund another project which he believed of equal or greater importance would be an example of this type of situation.

Differences could also arise regarding the relative weight to be assigned to goals and prescribed procedures in conducting project operations where the two seemed to conflict. This again was a matter of priority. Both parties might agree about goals and the appropriate means for attaining them, but one party might refuse to modify established procedures to reflect this agreement. For example, a mission director might decide not to allow a chief of party to "go over the head" of a mission division chief in matters related to some aspect of contract operations even though both he and the chief of party agreed that such a modification of procedures would contribute to the achievement of project goals. In many cases, ICA/Washington was the party unwilling to make modifications. However, the universities were by no means entirely free from fault in this respect.

Finally, the Agency and the universities often differed about who was more competent to make decisions about project operations. Differences in this area often became manifest (on the individual project level) in goals-versus-procedures negative incidents, but the universities tended to be more concerned about the basic problem than about any specific incident. A succinct statement of the view generally held by university officials on this issue was presented in a semi-annual report submitted to the Agency. The quoted passage is entitled "responsibility necessitates freedom."

> It is doubtful whether any plan could be evolved which would make easy the activities contemplated in the [host country] contract. However, from the educational point of view, a far more effective job could be done by the Contractor if he had greater freedom of action. The [U.S. institution] has the sole responsibility for the operations and her reputation rests upon the results secured.
> Most of the controversies between the [U.S. institution] and ICA and the inevitable delays which resulted, might have been avoided.

The Period of Retrenchment (July 1955–September 1957)

> How much better it would have been had the Contractor been permitted, within the broad objectives of the contract and the total funds provided, to have the final responsibility for all decisions involving the educational program without the necessity of securing approval from ICA/Washington. It appears that much of the "fine print" which is written into university contracts and limits the Contractor's freedom in educational matters has greater applicability to contracts with business or industry than to a responsible university.
>
> Would it be unreasonable to suggest, even at this late date that ICA/Washington eliminate the present close controls especially in the case of educational decisions and limit its efforts to the selection of reputable institutions to render desired educational services, and to the approval of a suitable contract governing the proposed operations. Where sufficient care has been given to the selection of the institution, should the university be hampered by Washington decisions concerning matters of an educational nature which the Contractor is in a much better position to decide than are ICA staff members.[28]

Before concluding the discussion of fundamental conceptual problems, the issues of security and publication clearance must be considered. Problems in these areas stemmed from the same types of general differences between the two parties as those discussed above, but were manifested in a somewhat different way.

In the area of security, difficulties were caused by the fact that a full field investigation (background investigation) was required for all direct hire personnel serving in overseas assignments, regardless of their position. This reflected the increased emphasis on security regulations following the McCarthy investigations. The Agency's official position with regard to clearances of university personnel in overseas assignments was that, since they were "performing the same or nearly identical duties [as direct hire personnel]," they should be subjected to the same full field investigation.[29] The policy for home campus personnel was to clear only the campus coordinator and other officials who might have direct and individual contact with participant trainees in an official capacity.

Probably any program of security investigations involving university professors and administrators would have led to some negative incidents because of the emphasis placed by the universities on individuality and academic freedom. The Agency reported[30] in 1957 that the average time for clearances was eleven to twelve days, that no complaints had been made except in the case of isolated incidents, and that a great majority of the universities had made no objection to the clearance procedures. Despite this favorable picture, differences involving security matters were of sufficient magnitude to cause negative incidents involving ranking university officials and expressions of dissatisfaction at the level of the university community. It is clear that criticism could be directed at both parties. On the university side, this was an area in which, particularly during this period of generally strained relations and hostility, administrative officials and individual team members tended to be particularly intransigent. On the Agency side, the policies implemented by individual security officers and investigators were occasionally narrow and inflexible. Long delays in processing compounded the problems.

The Agency's policy of publication clearance was based on the same principle as the policy of security clearance; namely, that "university-contract personnel stationed overseas have close official relations with United States government employees and, in the minds of the host country representatives with whom they come in contact, little or no distinction is made between them and Federal employees on regular rolls."[31] Therefore, university and direct hire technicians should be subject to essentially the same regulations. With regard to publications written in the field, Agency regulations provided for:

(1) Clearance by the mission
(2) Clearance by the office of public reports, ICA/Washington
(3) Submission by ICA/Washington after clearance to the university, institution or publisher recommended by the writer.

ICA/Washington reserved the right to return the article to the mission with "suggestions for further action" if major changes were recommended.[32] University personnel tended to take exception to the general principle upon which the clearance requirements were based, maintaining that their employees should only be subjected to such government regulations in the field as applied to U.S. citizens generally or were specifically stated in the contract. Agency censorship of publications was regarded as an abridgment of academic freedom.[33]

In many instances, it is difficult to determine whether the primary source of negative incidents occurring during this period was the specific substantive issues in terms of which disagreements

The Period of Retrenchment (July 1955–September 1957) 71

were manifested, or simply the uncooperative and unfriendly attitudes which developed between many university and Agency representatives. This "climate" in Agency-university relations has been noted by many commentators. For example, the *Glick Report* states:

> People newly transferred to Washington from field operations who have accompanied contractors to these sessions have expressed their amazement at the rigidity and unfriendliness that characterizes these (contract) negotiations.[34]

and the *Gelband Report* notes:

> At . . . times, the situation at the operating level was so strained that the Committee [on Institutional Projects Abroad] believed it wisest merely to provide a forum for the discussion of the areas of contention.[35]

The findings of these reports have been confirmed by the interviews conducted for this study. Typical statements describing this period were: "when Agency and university representatives were in the same room you could feel the hostility in the air" and "things were just awful during that period . . . just awful."

It has been noted that Stassen's policies contributed to uncooperative, even hostile, attitudes towards university contracts among many Agency officials. Hostility was increased by substantive disagreements, particularly in cases where Agency representatives believed the universities had failed to live up to the terms of their contract or requested "special treatment." Requests by university representatives which were classified as "special treatment" in the Agency were justified in terms of the concept of "equal partnership" by university officials. Moreover, complaints about the "purchase psychology" and "rigidity" of Agency officials were frequently expressed, both informally and in official reports. This climate provided a sort of "accelerator effect" for the occurrence of negative incidents revolving around substantive matters.

SUMMARY: THE CAUSES OF DETERIORATION

The factors contributing to the deterioration in Agency-participating university relations may be summarized as follows:

(1) The full impact of the contracts negotiated during the period of proliferation affected the Agency during this period. Thus, the total number of incidents increased substantially.

(2) A large number of these incidents involved financial management and procedural matters associated with contract interpretation, and were therefore incidents having a high probability of being negative.

(3) The added load on the Agency came when it was plagued by understaffing and inexperience, particularly in areas where large numbers of potentially negative incidents were likely to occur. Changes in organization and procedures compounded the problem by increasing the workload.

(4) The change in directors lowered the priority of the university-contract program. Additionally, it eliminated an important channel of communication between the highest level of the Agency and high ranking university officials.

(5) The change in directors also eliminated an important source of consensus with respect to basic program goals and objectives between the Agency and the participating universities.

(6) The increase in negative incidents in all areas tended to have an "accelerator effect" on the personal hostility already existing between some Agency and university representatives.

Agency-University Relations at the Level of the University Community

Beginning with the period of retrenchment, increasing attention must be devoted to relations between the Agency and the organizations which have "represented"[36] the university community in dealings with the Agency during much of the time that the program has been in operation, namely the American Council on Education's Committee on Institutional Projects Abroad (CIPA) and the Association of State Universities and Land-Grant Colleges. During this and subsequent periods the activities of these organizations affected the relationship between the Agency and the participating universities by: (1) providing a source of information for ranking Agency officials about negative incidents at the operating level and about the universities' attitude toward these incidents; (2) providing forums for discussion between ranking university and Agency officials about the causes of negative incidents and the most appropriate means for improving Agency-university relations (These "forums" were also sources of positive and negative incidents in their own right.); and (3) putting "pressure" on the Agency to make changes in areas where large numbers of negative incidents involving high ranking university officials were occurring. In this and the following chapters the activities of each of the major university community organizations will be examined in some detail.

ACTIVITIES OF THE NATIONAL ASSOCIATION OF STATE UNIVERSITIES AND LAND-GRANT COLLEGES

Prior to the period of retrenchment, the annual NASULGC conventions were used by Agency officials to discuss university participation in international technical assistance programs in general terms and, in the case of Stassen, to solicit university participation in such programs. The request submitted to the Association by Agency officials for assistance in solving operational problems constituted a major landmark in relations with the university community. In the period of retrenchment, the Association, through its Committee on Technical Cooperation, exercised general surveillance over developments in the program. Through correspondence, personal contact and the annual *Proceedings* of the convention, the Committee made ranking government officials both within and outside of the Agency aware of the increasing dissatisfaction of the participating universities with the program and submitted recommendations for improving the situation. Additionally, in the numerous informal discussions of the program which took place at the Association's annual conventions, high university officials became aware of negative incidents occurring in projects other than their own.

In the 1955 *Proceedings*, the Committee on Technical Cooperation reported:

> There has been a growing concern among participating institutions over difficulties encountered in administration of contracts and it is recommended that these problems be brought to the attention of the Committee on Institutional Projects Abroad of the American

Council on Education and the proper officials of the International Cooperation Administration.[37]

The tone of the Committee report in the 1956 *Proceedings* reflected the deterioration in Agency-university relations during 1956. The report recommended that the situation be brought to the attention of government officials *outside* of the International Cooperation Administration who had the power to initiate corrective action.

> The Committe has repeatedly called attention to the difficulties encountered in attempting to operate the university-contract program effectively. Last year, it issued a special note of warning and expressed a growing concern among participating institutions over difficulties incurred in the administration and operation of these contracts. In the interim, certain steps were taken by ICA to counter these difficulties, among them the establishment of a centralized contracting office. The Committee is obliged to note that, far from ameliorating the problems existing a year ago, the Agency's interim measures have appeared to increase them. The Committee is convinced that with present administrative organization and lack of major concern for and support of institutional contracts abroad at top ICA administrative levels, the program will continue to deteriorate and fall far short of its intended contribution to the fulfillment of the intent of Congress to improve the well being of free peoples through international cooperation and technical assistance. The Committee is constrained to agree that, unless the administrative problems are speedily resolved, the Agency must be prepared for withdrawal of many institutions from the program.
>
> The Committee recommends that the Association invite the attention of the President of the United States and the Congress to the inevitable breakdown which is imminent unless drastic action is taken by the government at a very early date. As a constructive first step, we urge consideration of the proposal to centralize responsibility for the university-contract program at the highest possible government level, either within or outside of ICA, and that this office be clothed with sufficient authority not only to resolve existing problems but also to plan and execute a positive and effective program in the future.[38]

This statement is the most sweeping indictment of the Agency policies ever issued officially by the university community. A very low degree of harmony in Agency-university community relations had been reached. In the months which followed, however, things began to improve gradually as a result of initiatives taken by CIPA.

ACTIVITIES OF THE COMMITTEE ON INSTITUTIONAL PROJECTS ABROAD OF THE AMERICAN COUNCIL ON EDUCATION

During the period of retrenchment the CIPA became an active and important force in Agency-university relations by sponsoring two "Conferences on University Contracts Abroad" for mutual discussion of problems associated with the operation of the program and by initiating a series of negotiations which led to the adoption of standard contracting procedures by the Agency.

The first Conference on University Contracts Abroad was convened in November 1955, at Michigan State University to "encourage discussion of . . . the contract program."[39] After two days of discussions involving both Agency and university representatives, the conference passed a resolution which ". . . affirmed the universities' belief in the fundamental objectives of university cooperation in foreign technical assistance and indicated the willingness of American higher education to continue to work with the government of the United States in the attainment of these objectives."[40] The Committee also emphasized the importance of clarifying the objectives of the program in the following resolution:

> A clear statement of public policy by the United States government is required in order to provide for effective long range planning and full integration of the program within contracting institutions . . . the principle governing the relationship between the government and the universities in this program must be one of cooperative partnership rather than that of employer and employee.[41]

The Committee's efforts to improve communications between the two parties were not always successful. In April 1956, it arranged a special State Department briefing for university presidents and other high officials. The briefing, conducted by Secretary of State Dulles and other senior officers of the Department, was supposed to emphasize the relationship between the contract program and U.S. foreign policy objectives.[42] A second purpose was to convince skeptical presidents that the program was viewed with favor at the highest levels of the State Department.[43] Instead of doing this, however, the presentation confirmed the suspicions of the skeptics. Participants considered it an insult and a disaster. To be more specific, Hollister impressed the presidents with his *dis*interest and *lack of* support for the program. Secretary Dulles was so poorly briefed that he gave the impression of hardly knowing what university contracts were all about.[44] CIPA turned to other approaches.

A second Annual Conference on University Contracts Abroad was sponsored by the Committee in 1956. The tone of the discussions provided another indication of the deterioration in Agency-university relations. In fact, a ranking Agency official cited this conference as marking the nadir of the relationship.[45] The conference was called to provide "a forum for expressing the sharply mounting dissatisfaction of university contractors with what they regarded as the obstructive operating methods of the ICA."[46] At the conclusion of the conference, the participants endorsed the NASULGC resolution "inveighing against ICA contract policies, program administration and lack of concern with program objectives"[47] which was based on the report of the Association's committee on overseas technical assistance.[48]

The Adoption of the Standard Contract

The CIPA's most concretely productive activity during this period was the development of recommendations and the initiation of negotiations between the Agency and university representatives which led to the adoption of the first standard university contract. This activity reflected the Committee's concern with attempting to solve the most pressing problems associated with the program on the operating level so that both parties could begin to concern themselves with broader, more substantive issues.[49]

The Committee began by carefully examining the illustrative contract then in use. On the basis of its findings and a reading of university opinion, it recommended in June 1956 that the Agency substitute a grant-in-aid technique. The recommendation argued that this arrangement would "liberalize the legal and financial relationship between the Agency and the institutions so as to leave the universities free to fulfill the academic functions for which they are engaged, in their terms as well as those of ICA."[50]

The Period of Retrenchment (July 1955–September 1957)   77

This proposal was not favorably received by Agency officials. In assessing this reaction, it must be recognized that university performance under many of the contracts negotiated during the period of proliferation was hardly such as to create a favorable climate for the liberalization of regulations (see above, p. 48). In addition, ranking officials felt that they would be abdicating too much control over their programs at a time when they were trying to increase integration and program control on the country level. Accordingly, the Agency responded with an alternative proposal offering policy revisions of seventeen troublesome areas in the existing contract.[51] The CIPA submitted the proposal to the participating universities, but the reaction was generally unfavorable. The consensus among the university representatives was that the changes did not go far enough.

Feeling that an impasse had been reached and recognizing that the grant-in-aid technique would not be accepted by the Agency, the Committee retained CIPA member and University of Nebraska Chancellor Clifford N. Hardin on a part-time basis. Chancellor Hardin, with the Committee's executive staff, began the formulation of a new set of recommended contract revisions. Although the working group was constrained in areas where Agency representatives stated that revision would be impossible because of Federal contracting requirements and GAO regulations, they developed a revised set of proposals which were presented to a special session of the entire Committee in 1957. In a letter to Deputy Director Fitzgerald concerning the new recommendations, President Adams (of the ACE) stated: "the new procedures promise materially to alleviate the operating problems experienced hitherto, [but, the Committee is] fully aware that completion of the implementing documentation will alone make concrete and meaningful the general principles . . . discussed."[52]

The Committee proposals formed the basis of discussion at a conference of ICA representatives and university business officers which was called to work out problems and put in final form the proposal to be submitted to the Agency. The committee of business officers was generally satisfied with the proposal that had been developed and reported to ICA that it was "a workable document that places responsibility for our programs precisely where it belongs, that is squarely on the contractors, and at the same time assures ICA of the necessary controls. Many of the problem areas which we believe have been resolved," the report continued, "have existed since the first contracts were negotiated back in the early days of the ECA."[53]

Subsequently, CIPA Chairman John Hannah, President of Michigan State University, reported to the presidents of the participating universities that "general adoption of the new contract procedures will provide a salutory legal and administrative basis for the challenging educational task to be performed under the university-contract program."[54]

The contract, though it fell far short of the hopes of many university representatives, did establish uniformity in the troublesome "boilerplate" areas. The negotiations can also be viewed as a landmark in that they represent the first instance of Agency and university representatives meeting together over a relatively long period to attempt to work out operating problems. Although the gradual adoption of the standard contract did not, perhaps, cause a significant reduction in the number of negative incidents between the Agency and the participating universities, it did mark the beginning of a new era in the relationship at the level of the university community.

The need for improving this relationship was impressed upon ranking ICA officials during the 1957 hearings of the Senate Foreign Relations Committee on the foreign aid program. The hearings represent the first documented evidence of Congressional concern with the threatened "breakdown in relations between the Agency and the participating universities." Most of the questioning on university-contract matters was conducted by Senator Wayne Morse, who had been visited by several "disgusted" university presidents,[55] and had familiarized himself with major criticisms of the program emanating from the CIPA, NASULGC and other sources.

During his appearance before the Committee, Hollister was questioned on specific instances of delays in answering correspondence and problems related to security clearances and post-audits of contracts. Morse quoted the allegations of university presidents that there was "an absence of real understanding and support for inter-university contract operations at the highest levels in ICA."[56] In connection with the Director's testimony, ICA was required to prepare and submit detailed reports to the Committee on several specific incidents raised by Morse and on

The Period of Retrenchment (July 1955–September 1957)

general policy regarding the use of university contracts.[57] Concluding his testimony, Hollister stated his belief that university contracts were "one of the finest things we do" and asserted that he was "continually checking" the program to iron out problems and make things work more smoothly.[58]

These hearings did not lead to any significant policy initiatives on the part of the Agency, but they did impress ranking Agency personnel with the need to placate the university presidents and improve relations at this level.

Thus, the analysis of this difficult period for Agency-university relations does not conclude on an entirely negative note. Though the program was faced with serious problems, Agency officials were becoming aware of some of the mechanisms through which greater harmony could be promoted. It is not surprising that improving relations at the level of the university community was one of the most significant patterns to emerge in the years following the period of retrenchment. Unfortunately, eliminating negative incidents at the level of the participating universities was a more complicated matter. Amelioration of the divisive issues which had developed at this level would take much longer.

CHAPTER V

The Period of Inertia (September 1957– September 1961)

Introduction: A Leaderless Agency

THE CHARACTER of the Agency during the periods of proliferation and retrenchment was strongly influenced by Stassen and Hollister respectively. The contrast with the period of inertia is striking. From 1957 through 1961, the Agency had four separate directors.[1] Only one of these appointees held his position for as long as twenty months (and he was seriously ill for much of that period). This rapid turnover contributed to the limited influence which the directors were able to exercise.

Many analysts of foreign assistance have noted the slight impact which these men had upon the Agency, an assessment confirmed by the interviews for this study. Few of the Agency and university officials who were questioned could remember anything significant about the individuals who served as Director during this period. In fact, most had difficulty even remembering the names of these men.[2] Although the office of Director was never unfilled officially, the Agency was, in the sense of having positive direction from the top, a leaderless organization.

Policy Changes Affecting the University-Contract Program

After Stassen, university contracting had moved far from the center of the stage of Agency operations. Thus, the modest

The Period of Inertia (September 1957–September 1961)

initiatives undertaken in foreign aid during the twilight years of the Eisenhower Administration[3] had little effect on project activities or Agency-university community relations. Nor were there any policy changes within the Agency of particular consequence, though a modification in an irritating publication clearance requirement was well received by university officials and team members.[4]

Congressional policy towards foreign aid, however, was another matter, though the effects were largely indirect. During this period, appropriations bills for the Agency were subject to increasing scrutiny, especially in the House of Representatives. Spearheaded by its Foreign Operations Subcommittee, under the direction of Representative Otto Passman, the House Appropriations Committee attempted to impose specific and "across the board" cuts in authorized budgets of about ten percent annually.[5] Despite the "appellate" function performed by the corresponding Senate Committee, the annual cuts averaged more than five percent.[6] More important than the specific cuts, were the undesirable spill-over effects of the increasingly tortuous authorizing and appropriating process. In order to consider these effects, it will be necessary to look a little more closely at this process as it operated during this period.

It should be remembered that in a very real sense, it is the Congress, not some group of developing nations, which constitutes the effective clientele of the Agency. Without Congressional approval in the form of annual appropriations, the Agency could not survive. Thus Agency personnel have always been extremely sensitive to Congressional attitudes.[7] Certainly this was true during the period of inertia.

Unfortunately, one of the most powerful members of the House Appropriations Committee, Representative Otto Passman,[8] tended to take a strongly negative attitude toward foreign assistance. In fact, when he was appointed to the chairmanship of the Foreign Operations Subcommittee, he observed that he had never voted for a foreign aid appropriations bill,[9] a pattern of opposition which did not change after he assumed a firm grip on the Agency's purse strings.

Beginning in this period, the authorizing and appropriating process began to assume a patterned, almost ritualistic, character which persisted through 1965.[10] The administration would propose the annual foreign aid legislation, usually with an incremental increase over the previous year. In early spring the relatively sympathetic House Foreign Affairs and Senate Foreign Relations Committee would go over the presentation books and listen to the pleas of Agency officials that the full amount requested be authorized. Limited cuts would be imposed and the authorizing legislation would usually be passed by mid-May.

This, however, was just the beginning. Next the presentation books would be moved to new committee rooms and Agency officials would repeat their testimony before the respective appropriations sub-committees of the House and Senate. Here the hearings tended to be more arduous, and the cuts more severe. Almost invariably the House Appropriations Committee would cut much more deeply than the Senate. Then the differences would have to be worked out in conference committee before a workable bill could be passed. Often it was October or November, sometimes even later, before Agency officials knew how much money they would have to operate on for the fiscal year.

The nature of this process injected an air of uncertainty into Agency operations. Officials could not make firm long-term commitments to universities or other contractors. Often the hiring of contract personnel and the extension of contracts in the field were adversely affected. Furthermore, Agency officials were continually harassed about their failure to "complete" any projects, particularly technical assistance projects, and about their inability to show demonstrable results from the input of foreign aid funds.[11] The attitudes and procedures which these kinds of pressures engendered were particularly harmful to Agency-university relations.

Organizational Changes and Administrative Practices

Organizational instability has been endemic in the Agency throughout its history. However, during the period of inertia, the administrative structure and patterns of decision-making affecting university contracts remained relatively stable. There were no formal organizational changes which significantly influenced Agency-university relations. A minor change with generally bene-

The Period of Inertia (September 1957–September 1961) 83

ficial effects was the division of responsibilities with regard to commercial and "cost" contracts which occurred in the Office of Contract Relations shortly after the end of Hollister's tenure. An Assistant Director of Contract Relations for Non-Profit Contracts was designated and assigned the concurrent responsibility of university-contracts coordinator. At the same time, a small number of contract officers were designated to deal exclusively with non-profit contracts.[12]

Although there were no formal changes of importance, the character of Agency operations did change during this period. Three characteristics stand out in particular, namely (1) the increasing resistance of Agency personnel to policy and procedural changes initiated by the director, (2) the coequal status of "line" (geographic area) and "staff" technical service bureaus in Agency decision-making processes and (3) the dominant position of D. A. Fitzgerald, the Deputy Director for Operations, in the Agency.

The capacity for passive resistance to and non-support of policies emanating from the Office of the Director, among Agency personnel, had begun to develop during Hollister's term in office. However, it appears that this pattern predominated to an unusually high degree during the period of inertia. The often repeated statement that the Agency had no direction "from the top" is based on the fact that policy initiatives of the Directors produced little or no discernible effect on Agency operations. Certainly this was true in the area of university contracting. Policy directives supporting the position of the university community and emphasizing the need for greater understanding of and cooperation with the participating universities were issued on several occasions, but there is no evidence that these ever filtered down to operating levels of the Agency.[13]

To the degree that effective leadership was exercised in the Agency, it was provided by D. A. Fitzgerald. The dominant position of "Dr. Fitz" during these years is often mentioned by both Agency and university personnel. The reasons for this dominance were partly personal and partly a consequence of ICA's organizational structure.

The reader will recall that after Stassen's reorganization, what amounted to two "chains of command" were established in the Agency. The technical service offices (staff) shared coequal status with the geographic area offices (line) in the decision-making process.[14] Consequently, no one of these offices could direct an action to be performed by any others. As the *Glick Report* later observed, "this was almost literally administration by unanimous consent."[15] If all of the heads of the various units agreed on a program, then action could go forward. However, if any one strongly disapproved, no action could be taken until the differences were compromised. Fitzgerald's unique position of authority in this system was outlined by the *Glick Report*:

> ... it is both startling and true that he was the only officer, other than the Administrator, who could make a decision and direct that action to go forward ... no officer below the Deputy Director for Operations could summon people to his office, announce that no further delay would be tolerated, listen to the opposing contentions and then make a binding decision.[16]

Fitzgerald's power derived from other factors as well, especially his personal characteristics as an administrator. He had the capacity to see both sides of the problems which were brought to his attention and to create consensus as well as directing compliance. The only adverse comment which is usually heard about him is that he was a "bottleneck" in the Agency during this period. There were so many important matters regarding ICA operations which had to be brought to his attention that "it sometimes took weeks to get to him."[17] From the standpoint of Agency-university relations, it is fortunate that Fitzgerald was both an originator and a supporter of the university-contract program. A ranking NASULGC official commented, "If things really got bad, I could always call Fitz and he would straighten it out; but Fitz was so busy that I hated to take his time."[18] Despite his ability, however, the Deputy Director for Operations was not in a position to initiate major policies. He could only attempt to see that the cumbersome administrative machinery functioned as best it could according to the established patterns.

Patterns of Participation

Nine contracts were initiated during the period of inertia and eight were discontinued. Additionally, two contracts were altered in form from a university–host government relationship to a university–host institution ("sisterhood") relationship.

Few generalizations can be made about these developments. In general, the policy established under Hollister, limiting contracts to a "sisterhood" relationship, continued to be followed. There was increasing pressure from Representative Passman's Committee in 1959 and 1960 to "finish" some projects and the decision to close out the Cornell project in the Philippines and the Oregon State project in Thailand reflected this pressure. The early termination of the Arizona–Iraq project was the result of political developments in the host country.

Agency-University Relations at the Level of the University Community

Relations at the level of the university community began to improve considerably after Hollister's departure and the negotiations which led to endorsement of the standard contract by the Committee on Institutional Projects Abroad. The most significant indicator of this improvement was the change in orientation and tone of CIPA conference discussions and the official statements and recommendations emanating from the CIPA and NASULGC. There were no more predictions of "breakdown" in the relationship. Both organizations tended to shift from a concern with immediate operational problems to a concern with more fundamental problem areas of the program. This shift in orientation in part reflected and in part contributed to a growing willingness on the part of ranking Agency officials to consult with the university community on programmatic and substantive as well as operational matters.

ACTIVITIES OF THE COMMITTEE ON INSTITUTIONAL PROJECTS ABROAD OF THE AMERICAN COUNCIL ON EDUCATION

By mid-1957, when the first supporting grant from the Ford Foundation expired, Committee members felt that substantial progress had been made toward solving the operational and management problems associated with the program.[19] However, they

TABLE IV

*University-Contract Rural Development Projects
Initiated and Terminated During the Period of Inertia*

REGION	COUNTRY	U.S. INSTITUTION	HOST INSTITUTION	DATES
Contracts Initiated:				
FAR EAST	Philippines	State Univ. of N.Y.	University of the Philippines, College of Forestry	1960–65*
	Cambodia	Univ. of Georgia	National College of Agriculture, Animal Husbandry and Forestry	1960–63
	China	Michigan State Univ.	National Taiwan University and Taiwan Provincial Chung Hsing University	1960–64
	Vietnam	Univ. of Georgia	National College of Agriculture, Animal Husbandry and Forestry	1960–62
	Pakistan	Colorado State Univ.	Peshawar University	1958–64
	Pakistan	Texas A & M	University of Dacca	1958–66

NOTE: The Utah State-Iran and State University of New York-Israel contracts changed to the "sisterhood relationship" pattern during this period.

LATIN AMERICA	Peru	Iowa State	Instituto de Reforma Agraria y Colonización	1961–Active
	Paraguay	Montana State Univ.	National University of Asuncion	1960–63
AFRICA	Nigeria	Michigan State Univ.	Government of Eastern Region of Nigeria, University of Nigeria	1960–66

Contracts Terminated:

FAR EAST	Philippines	Cornell Univ.	University of the Philippines at Los Baños, College of Forestry (2 contracts)	1952/57–60*
	Thailand	Oregon State Univ.	Kasetsart University	1954–60
	Japan	U. of Massachusetts	Hokkaido University	1957–61
NESA	Iraq	Univ. of Arizona	Agricultural College at Aba-Ghraib	1952–59
LATIN AMERICA	Colombia	Michigan State Univ.	2 National Universities	1951–59
	Costa Rica	Univ. of Florida	Servicio and Ministry of Agriculture	1954–60
	Mexico	Univ. of Pennsylvania	Ministry of Agriculture/USOM Research and Training	1954–58
AFRICA	None			

Summary Data: (1) Number of contracts initiated 9
(2) Number of contracts terminated 8
(3) Number of active contracts 27

Sources: See TABLE I, p. 18.

*The State University of New York contract in the Philippines was a continuation of the Cornell contract.

NOTE: Contracts listed as ACTIVE were active as of July 1, 1966.

believed there was a need to direct the attention of both the government and the universities to more substantive issues of policy and planning if the program was to achieve its potential. Consequently, a three-year extension of the Ford Foundation grant was requested by the Committee "to continue (its) work . . . reoriented in part to meet the need for educational policy determination."[20]

The major areas on which the Committee focused its attention during this period were long-term concerns, still subjects of discussion ten years later. These included:

(1) the effects of international involvement on the participating U.S. universities,

(2) the adequacy of university resources for effective participation in international programs, and ways of enhancing those resources,

(3) the most appropriate organizational and legislative arrangements for supporting such programs, and

(4) ways in which the planning and programming process could be improved to promote more effective university participation.

In conjunction with these concerns, the Committee submitted, through its parent organization, a number of specific recommendations to the government. These focused on the four major areas of planning, program administration, research and policy-making. By examining the recommendations, it is possible to identify the most significant problems of the era as they were perceived by the university community. Specifically, the Committee recommended the following:[21]

(1) *A "long range" viewpoint in project planning:* In response to an ICA request for an analysis of the contract process, the Executive Director of CIPA stated:

> The university-contract program does not escape attention in the continuing debate about the relative short- and long-range characteristics of specific public programs. It is essential to remember in this connection that important "political decisions" affecting foreign aid often reflect the short-, rather than the long-range view. In the light of this tendency, it is necessary to stress that most technical cooperation projects, and notably the university contracts, demonstrate their greatest utility over the very long pull indeed. They cannot produce the quick and tangible results so congenial to American habits of thinking. To expect them to flourish uninhibited by

the annual Congressional crossfire of short range challenges is to exhibit a certain naivete. . . . The technical cooperation aspects of foreign aid, in the large, then, and the university programs in particular, should be viewed as relatively long-term instruments of public policy. Their effect is penetrative and cumulative, and to do effective business through them is to require commitments of substantial duration.[22]

(2) *Centralization of authority for the program at a high level in the Agency:* In 1959, when ICA seemed to be contemplating reorganization, CIPA Executive Director Humphrey communicated the prevailing university sentiment on the organizational status problem:

Broadly, it is recommended that authority and responsibility for the ICA university-contract program be centralized, at as high an administrative echelon as is practicable. The principal reasons are three.

(1) concentration of administrative concern at a point of some influence within the Agency appears to be the only way in which to assure more than moderate impetus to program development,

(2) a single point of authority within ICA is badly needed by the contractors, not only for contract negotiations, but also for substantive program planning, and

(3) the internal diffusion of authority and responsibility between the political, functional, geographic and fiscal-legal shops has in practice, proved a heavy drag upon the program since its inception.[23]

(3) *The inclusion of a research component in university contracts:* In their studies of the program, Committee members found that the resources of many of the U.S. universities had been seriously strained or were simply inadequate to meet the commitments which they had undertaken. They concluded "that one way for the universities to move toward the desired capability would be to engage in extensive research activities and therefore attempted to convince the ICA of the necessity for including research funds in its contracts."[24] The Committee's view was transmitted to ICA in a letter from Richard Humphrey to the Director of the Office of Contract Relations:

. . . contract related research . . . would make more effective the university contribution to any project it is called upon to assist. It is recommended that the ICA establish as a matter of policy that it is appropriate and desirable to provide authorization and funds for research and staff development where attainment of the objectives of the contract program would be furthered thereby. . . . Although it may be assumed that the ICA will endeavor to contract with the university best qualified for the intended task, it will often happen that no university will be fully prepared for the assignment. . . . If these assumptions are valid, it follows that the objectives sought through many governmental projects abroad may not be fully attainable owing to deficiencies in knowledge and properly qualified manpower in the United States. Consequently it is desirable to enable institutions that have been asked to undertake difficult assignments abroad to strengthen their resources for the assignment where this appears to be necessary to the full success of the project.[25]

(4) *The involvement of the university community in the determination of policy and the individual universities in project planning:* A document issued by the Council's Commission on Educational Affairs reflected the concerns of the Committee in this area:

> . . . higher education has become more and more aware of the fact that, while government may often rely upon its counsel in devising means for attaining public objectives, it too seldom, perhaps, calls upon the academic community at the point where the objective is being framed, the policy determined. . . . The increasing reluctance of universities . . . to retain the role of mere agents of government policy, combined with the pressures of mounting enrollments which tend to render international commitments less and less competitive, suggest that some way must be found by government to take the universities into its policy confidence lest it substantially lose their cooperation in international programs in the period immediately ahead.[26]

The Committee's desire to place the Agency-university cooperative relationship in broader perspective was reflected in the discussions and presentations at the four annual conferences which were sponsored during 1957–60. The conferences made a valuable contribution to improved Agency-university community relations by serving as a forum in which Agency and university officials could let off steam and communicate on broad-range problems in a relatively neutral setting. Equally important were the opportunities for informal communications which these gatherings provided.

Two of the special conferences sponsored by the Committee

The Period of Inertia (September 1957–September 1961)   91

also merit brief attention. The Bloomington Conference on the Impact of University Contracts on the American University marked the first major attempt by the universities to evaluate themselves at the university community level.[27] The discussions increased the participants' awareness that all of the faults in the program did not lie with the Agency and marked the beginning of a greater emphasis on developing an international dimension in the universities. The effectiveness of participant training and home campus backstopping were also topics of formal and informal discussion. The Annapolis Conference on International Education, sponsored by the Committee in conjunction with the Bureau of International Cultural Relations of the Department of State,[28] and attended by ranking government officials and heads of major foundations as well as university presidents, is especially well remembered by participants. The focus of the conference was on the importance of long-range planning, particularly in the area of personnel needs in international educational programs. However, the contribution of the conference toward promoting mutual understanding between government and university representatives was far more important than the specific recommendations which emerged. One of the participating university presidents remarked that it was not until after this Conference that he felt that the government had any appreciation of "the need for predictability on the part of the participating universities."[29] ACE President Adams expressed his satisfaction with the Conference in his 1958–59 *Annual Report,* which stated, "Nowhere has the Committee's objective of promoting awareness of the long range commitments to human resource development been more strikingly advanced than through the Annapolis Conference discussions."[30]

The existence of the CIPA was terminated when its second Ford Foundation grant expired in December 1960. In evaluating its role during the six years of its existence, the Committee concluded:

By the end of the second CIPA grant period, . . . both the government and the academic community had come a long way in raising the level of their approach to the problems and potentialities of the contract program. While a direct causal relationship between the Committee's activities and the change in attitudes of the two other parties cannot be claimed with objectivity, . . .[31] we have shared in an important phase of the evolution of the inter-university program at a time when the Council could play a useful role. That role ... was primarily to raise the sights of the institutional-governmental relationship.[32]

In retrospect, this assessment must be qualified somewhat. The change in attitudes and "raising of sights" which occurred at the level of the university community is well documented. However, among lower level personnel in both the Agency and the universities, CIPA's activities went virtually unnoticed. Before discussing some of the reasons for this phenomenon, the concurrent activities of the National Association of State Universities and Land-Grant Colleges should be examined briefly.

ACTIVITIES OF THE NASULGC

It is clear that the major spokesman for the university community during this period was the CIPA. However, although little mention of Agency-university relations is found in the annual NASULGC *Proceedings* from 1957 through 1960, officials of the Land-Grant institutions played major roles in activities of the CIPA and the executive office of the Association, through Executive Secretary Russell Thackrey, maintained close liaison with the Committee staff and with the Agency.[33]

At the 1961 (Centennial) Convention, the Association again began to make its voice heard officially. The report of International Study Group I on "The Special Role of Land-Grant Colleges and State Universities in Meeting the Needs of Developing Nations" said little about Agency-university relations that had not been said at CIPA conventions in previous years. However, the tone of the report, which focused on specific operational problems as well as more general substantive ones, indicated that perhaps the CIPA had been somewhat optimistic in its assessment of the improvement in relations. "Responsibility for bookkeeping and fiscal management," the study group stated, "may seem like minor issues, but for those who operate the program in the host country, they often become the cloud that hides the sun. There have been elegant plans for more independence for universities involved in contract operations, but little real progress."[34] The need for Congressional initiative to change the direction of the program was emphasized by the study group.

The Period of Inertia (September 1957–September 1961) 93

This [lack of progress] stems in part from the failure of Congress to provide a charter, so to speak and perhaps even a formula for the granting of funds as it did in the case of agricultural research and agricultural extension work.

In the beginning, universities were brought into the program of ICA more for the purpose of helping [the Agency] with its recruitment and personnel problems than for the unique contribution that these institutions could make.[35] Although ICA is now conscious of the contribution which universities can make, it is nevertheless still wedded to certain established ways and procedures which have stemmed from administrative regulations and executive orders.[36]

The report's specific recommendations departed significantly from previous official statements by the university community. They were directed not at the Agency, but at NASULGC member universities. The items which were emphasized indicated that some of the Association members, at least, were well aware that the participating universities were partly responsible for the problems that had plagued the program. Specifically, the committee recommended the following to member institutions contemplating participation in Agency programs:

(1) A deliberate self appraisal by the institution of its capability and interest in the project.
(2) Improved internal university organization for dealing with international relations on all fronts, preceded by those activities which make for wide acceptance of such responsibilities by departments and staff members of the universities.
(3) Clarification of the status of staff members on assignment, to the end that their role is understood and appreciated.
(4) Better selection, orientation and preparation of staff members and their family members for overseas living and working.
(5) Longer range planning by the university with active participation in the planning process by those host country, home government, other country and private agencies which are materially involved. The objective is to build a program rather than to follow a prefabricated one.
(6) Effective ways of securing an ongoing appraisal of our effort from people at different levels in the host country and also from our own institutions.
(7) Research activities which will undergird the program and also produce some of the answers needed to questions of critical importance in the host country.[37]

Of course, the Association had no power to enforce compliance with these recommendations. However, it is clear that by the end of this period, influential members of the university community were approaching the program with increasing awareness and sophistication.

Chapter I emphasized the need to differentiate between Agency-university relations at the level of the university community and Agency-university relations at the level of the participating universities. This distinction becomes very useful in attempting to understand the changes which took place during the period of inertia and their significance. Until the end of the Hollister Administration, changes in the relationship at the level of the university community were a reflection of the changes at the operating level. In the period of inertia, however, this pattern changed. The evidence, from both interviews and the official record, points unequivocally to the fact that—although there was a significant improvement in relations at the level of the university community and an increasing focus on substantive, rather than operational problems—the improvement in relations at the level of the participating universities was relatively slight. The conclusion is, therefore, that CIPA and NASULGC activities during the period were not major contributions to the reduction of negative incidents at the operating level. What they did do was to create the *illusion* of such a reduction by generating positive incidents involving ranking university and Agency officials.

This interpretation suggests one of the functions which the CIPA conferences served for the Agency. It is revealing to compare the CIPA conference *Proceedings* with the reports of interviews conducted by Adams and Garraty,[38] Glick,[39] Bronfenbrenner,[40] Weidner,[41] and the Technical Assistance Study Group (TASG)[42] during the same period (1957-60). The conference *Proceedings* reflect cooperative attitudes between the two parties and a concern with solving basic policy problems in order to achieve common goals. The interviews paint a picture of hostile attitudes, misunderstandings and continued disagreements about both operational and substantive issues. Both portrayals are accurate; both viewpoints existed in the Agency and the universities. Among Agency personnel during this period, there were a few strong supporters of the university-contract program (particularly in the offices of Food and Agriculture and Education),

The Period of Inertia (September 1957–September 1961)

a few who opposed university participation in any form, and many who were merely committed to maintaining the status quo. High Agency officials were anxious to avoid the type of pressure from the university community which had led to expression of Congressional concern with the program in 1957, and viewed the promotion of good relations with the university community *as an end in itself*. Thus, there was a tendency to designate the *known supporters of the program* to participate in the CIPA conferences. This would explain why the conferences made so little impact on most other operating personnel in the Agency. Supporters of the contract program attended the conferences, contributed to the discussions, generated positive incidents involving ranking university officials and then returned to the same positions in the organizational structure, holding essentially the same views they had held prior to attending. Most other Agency personnel—who were concerned with higher priority items in the press of daily business—never even heard about the conferences; few read the conference proceedings or understood what had transpired. Personnel who had supported the program continued to support it. Personnel who had opposed it continued to press for its reduction or termination, and the majority continued to maintain the status quo with as little disturbance as possible.

A somewhat similar observation may be applied to the universities. Participation in international programs was not given high priority *at the departmental level* of most universities. Yet this is where many of the problems of lack of commitment originated. That university presidents attended the conferences and participated in the discussions did not necessarily mean that they were prepared or even able to provide the incentives which would lead to the recruitment of first rate personnel for overseas service and home campus backstopping. However, it appears that constraints imposed on international participation by the structure and environment of the universities were not fully discussed with Agency representatives. Probably most university officials attending the conferences were not fully aware of these constraints themselves.

This is not to denigrate the CIPA's contribution to Agency-university relations or the program as a whole. As has been suggested, CIPA established lines of communication between the highest levels of the university community and the Agency at a time when the absence of such lines of communication threatened to destroy the program. In a sense, the first two CIPA annual conferences may be viewed as a safety valve permitting university representatives to let off steam and preventing a major explosion. The later annual conferences were thought-provoking and fruitful enterprises in themselves. The discussions of major substantive issues and the committee recommendations which emerged paved the way for some of the major changes which took place during David Bell's term as Administrator. However, it must not be assumed that the major improvement at the level of the university community reflected a similar degree of improvement at the level of the participating universities.

PUBLISHED STUDIES OF THE UNIVERSITY-CONTRACT PROGRAM
  AND THEIR IMPACT

Before leaving the subject of Agency-university community relations, the appearance of the first published studies dealing with the university-contract program should be noted. A brief discussion of several of these will serve to elaborate the points made above regarding differences between upper and lower organizational levels. Especially significant is the fact that, despite the excellent scholarship which characterized several of these works, they made virtually no impact on the program.[43] This phenomenon provides additional evidence that the label, "inertia," is appropriate for this period.

Three of the studies were essentially statements of what has been called the IIAA/TCA philosophy of technical assistance. Two of these, Philip Glick's *The Administration of Technical Assistance: Growth in the Americas*[44] and Arthur Mosher's *Technical Cooperation in Latin American Agriculture*,[45] were scholarly products of a program of technical assistance research at the University of Chicago which had been initiated at the request of TCA Administrator Andrews.[46] The third study, *University Contracts: A Review and Comment on Selected University Contracts in Africa, the Middle East and Asia*,[47] was written by Andrews himself at the request of the Technical Assistance Study Group. Of the three, the Andrews study, which included—in addition to specific recommendations—a blistering condemnation of Agency administrative, contracting and management procedures,[48] was

The Period of Inertia (September 1957–September 1961) 97

most widely read and also widely criticised. Reaction to the study suggested that even at this late date, the wounds from the "do gooder," "big money boy" controversy were not fully healed. Agency personnel picked at minor factual errors in the report, criticised its "inflammatory tone" and suggested that Andrews was merely trying to justify his own policies during the period that he was Administrator of Technical Cooperation.[49] The substantive recommendations of the report, however, received little attention.

The Adams and Garraty book, *Is the World Our Campus?* evoked a similar reaction. This work was the first analysis in depth which focused specifically on the university-contract program. The purpose of the study was:

> To find out how particular programs operated and to discover their strengths and weaknesses so that the mistakes of the past might be avoided in the future. The underlying motive was to suggest constructive reforms.[50]

Nine case studies of university projects, including one project in agricultural and rural development, formed the basis of the study. The information was collected through depth interviews of more than three hundred persons as well as official documents and reports. The findings of the study were highly negative and criticism was by no means limited to the Agency.

Adams and Garraty did not pull their punches when assessing the contribution which their colleagues in the universities had made in overseas projects. In the conclusion of a chapter entitled "An Editorial," they observed:

> Too many overseas operatives are mediocrities, fed up with the academic routine and in need of extra cash. Having little success at home, they seek status elsewhere. Being alienated in their profession at home, they possess all the frustrations that plague the academic personality—a sense of rejection which grows out of the low prestige accorded the academic priesthood in America. Overseas, such men may find a sense of belonging, a feeling of importance. Once they have had the experience, they cannot get it out of their blood. They hire themselves out to different projects in different universities. They join the growing ranks of a new class—what one professor has called the "expatriate academic bums." They become part of a mercenary army that lacks purpose and morale and zeal . . .

these mercenaries are not representative of American higher education and they should not be sent to represent it abroad.[51]

Their negative statements on this and other subjects were supported by critical references to specific projects and institutions, for example:

> ... [U.S. Institution] was little more than an ICA hiring agent.
> ... The [U.S. Institution] staff, say the Turks, is composed of relatively "unknown men" or "second raters" recruited specifically for the project, men whom [U.S. Institution] regards as "good enough for Istanbul," but not [city in which U.S. Institution is located]
> ... [U.S. Institution] teams are largely composed of American women married to Turks, widows, and the wives of Americans stationed in Ankara. These are not the top level professors the Turks expected to get.[52]

Although the study also included some favorable references, the authors' summary left no doubt about their overall evaluation of the program:

> We found not all foreign assistance is worthy of the nation; that not all American universities (regardless of their prestige at home) are responsible purveyors of technical assistance; that many (perhaps most) professors engaged in overseas projects are far from ideal ambassadors; and that university and ICA or foundation financed contracts are not necessarily effective instruments for helping other countries.[53]

The typical reaction to this polemic was hostility. An Agency official, who had been familiar with the study while it was in progress, stated that, after reading *Is the World Our Campus?*, he called up an official of the institution which had sponsored the research and said, "How could you do this to us?" Mission directors and mission staff associated with the projects examined in the study became familiar with its contents when they were directed to submit their own reports regarding the authors' findings. Naturally, these reports tended to be critical rebuttals. The substantive recommendations of the study, however, were largely ignored. The Agency's reaction was concisely summarized by one official who reported: "We were so damn mad we weren't interested in any of their recommendations."[54]

There is a lesson to be learned from the fate of the Adams and Garraty and the Andrews studies. It is that investigations of

The Period of Inertia (September 1957–September 1961)

Agency programs must be undertaken with great care and in full view of the sensitivities involved. A focus on specific defects of specific projects virtually ensures that the Agency will initiate investigations of the instances involved and, for its own protection, attempt to discredit the studies themselves. Heat, but not light, is generated by this approach.

Paradoxically, there is one justification for using the sharply critical approach which characterized these two studies. *Is the World Our Campus?* and *University Contracts* were at least read by Agency personnel. While one may suggest that the works might have received a more positive reaction from the Agency had they been more positive, one can marshall equally strong evidence for the proposition that there would have been no reaction; that the studies would not have been read at all.[55]

A thorough and restrained study which seems to have met this fate was *The Report of the Committee on the University and World Affairs*,[56] generally known as the *Morrill Committee Report*.[57] This was "a systematic attempt to clarify the international role of American universities and to suggest ways that U.S. institutions of higher learning might perform more effectively in world affairs."[58] Despite its limited impact, it is one of the best studies of this subject ever published.

Although the Morrill Committee was not directly linked with the CIPA, the report was clearly influenced by the CIPA-sponsored dialogue between the government and the university community which took place in the late 1950's. Moreover, it presented a clear statement, backed by men of major stature from government, the foundations, business, and the university community, of the need for deepening university involvement in a carefully planned long-range program of international education.

In examining the university-contract program, the Committee emphasized that "by no means all universities have a sufficient spread of institutional competence to undertake programs overseas" and that even for universities with the necessary resources, programs of international education would only be effective "if there (was) full institutional commitment to selected programs." Specifically, the Committee recommended:

> [The universities] should help to frame the overseas projects in which they participate; undertake only commitments that are within their

demonstrated competence; relate overseas projects to research programs in the same cultural areas and to home-campus educational activities; and make the necessary institutional administrative arrangements to attract the participation of their best faculty and staff members.[59]

To the ICA, the Committee stressed the need for greater emphasis on a cooperative relationship in all phases of project operation and a contract instrument which would provide the "autonomy and flexibility" which such a relationship implied. Particular attention was directed to the need for a long-term commitment by the government to programs involving university participation:[60]

> The Mutual Security Program itself lacks the assurance of continuity essential to planned participation by the universities. Multi-year contracts are necessary to regularize university-government relations and to avoid unreasonable expectations of quick results. No contract can take the place of a climate of continuing mutual confidence and expectation of continuing relations, as the experience of university contracts in the natural sciences demonstrates. Without this climate, there is no assurance of tenure for the scholars engaged on the project (or for the substitutes who take over their teaching duties on the university's home campus) beyond the two or three year life of the contract. In order to achieve it, the Executive Branch should announce and the Congress should accept the proposition that educational development in other countries seeking our help is a continuing United States responsibility and that the universities are an indispensable resource in carrying it out.[61]

The *Morrill Committee Report* was widely acclaimed by the university community. The recommendation to establish "a wholly private organization whose primary concern would be the programs and purposes of the universities in world affairs"[62] was adopted and implemented by the Ford Foundation.[63] However, the report is not remembered as "particularly significant" by Agency personnel,[64] was not widely read within the Agency and had little impact on Agency-university relations. To some degree, this was a matter of timing. The report had the misfortune to appear in December 1960 when the Agency was faced with an uncertain future. In his campaign, President-elect Kennedy had promised a major reorientation in the foreign assistance program and Agency personnel correctly surmised that major changes in personnel and organizational structure would soon be forthcoming. For two years following publication of the report, the staffing, organizational structure and administrative procedures of the Agency were highly unstable. Thus, the report's impact was simply muted by the general confusion and uncertainty. It did not serve as the basis for major initiatives in the university-contract program because such initiatives were organizationally impossible.

Individuals or groups who are considering analyses of the university-contract program or the making of recommendations regarding it would do well to look at these early studies and their history. Most of the sources of negative incidents had been identified and discussed by 1961. Moreover, reasonable solutions had been proposed to most of the outstanding problems. However, the identification of problems and possible solutions at the level of the university community did not lead to a period of harmony. In fact, most of the reports and recommendations of this period were quickly forgotten; both problems and solutions had to be rediscovered in the years following the period of inertia.

Agency-University Relations at the Level of the Participating Universities

The above discussion asserts repeatedly that the change in Agency-university community relations during this period was not accompanied by a commensurate improvement in harmony at the level of the participating universities. Although the ratio of negative incidents to total incidents cannot be measured, all available evidence, from published studies, interviews and university files, points unequivocally in this direction. This phenomenon can be explained by the fact that the major factors contributing to the occurrence of negative incidents during the period of retrenchment remained essentially unaltered.

First, *structural problems* became, if anything, more severe. Although the staffing difficulties in the Office of Contract Relations were resolved somewhat by the end of 1957, procedures had become more complex and the priority of the contract program was no higher. The inability of the succession of directors to deal effectively with Congress increased the uncertainty surrounding the authorization-appropriation process. In the area of *fiscal management,* overhead adjustments and disallowances continued to pose major problems for the universities. Little progress was made in attempting to modify required procedures through legislation.

It might have been thought that *contractual problems* would be alleviated significantly by the adoption of the "standard contract" but this apparently was not the case. The new document had not changed the orientation of the contract specialists who held ultimate decision-making responsibility; furthermore, if there was any mitigation of negative incidents resulting from the adoption of the standard contract, it was counterbalanced by additional negative incidents which occurred when the Agency tried to force the contract on some of the more experienced universities that preferred to retain an earlier format. Finally, there is no evidence of any major reduction in incidents arising from *fundamental conceptual problems* or from the *attitudes* of Agency personnel at the operating level. There was, however, improvement in a few specific programs, notably in India.[65]

Although major problems persisted unaltered, there were a few changes which may have contributed to some slight improvement in relations. First, the administrators who followed Hollister, especially James Smith, generally favored university contracts and may have had some positive influence, however slight. Second, the termination of many of the projects involving direct university relations with host governments eliminated one source of ambiguity and hostile attitudes. One justification for restricting the universities to areas in which they had "special competence," primarily "sisterhood" relationships, was that in these projects, the division between the authority and responsibility of the mission and the university was much easier to establish.[66] Third, despite the paucity of evidence supporting this view, there must have been at least some spillover effects from the discussions at the level of the university community, though substantially less than the participants (and subsequent observers and analysts) imagined. Finally, precedents began to be established in the university-contracting area as contract officers and other relatively inexperienced Agency officials who worked with the universities became more experienced, and corresponding university personnel gained familiarity with Agency procedures. Unfortunately, the chronic instability of personnel in the Agency limited the effects of this phenomenon.

It should also be noted that during the period of inertia, there was an increasing realization among at least some university representatives that the Agency had its problems too; that it was impossible for Agency representatives to alter some of the regulations and procedures which the participating universities found most offensive. This growing tolerance may have reduced the intensity of disagreements between the two parties, even where the issues dividing them remained.

It may seem to the reader that these concluding points, emphasizing positive forces of change, controvert or at least confuse the major thrust of the analysis. This is not the intention. However, these positive aspects deserve mention, especially in light of the organizational paroxysm which shook the Agency in 1961. The period of inertia was as stagnant as that label implies, but there were potential forces for change which might have been mobilized, even in the absence of a major reorganization. Moreover, defects in ICA can by no means be wholly attributed to its organizational structure. Many other factors, especially Congressional pressure and the absence of effective leadership from the top, were at least as important.

CHAPTER VI

The Interregnum (September 1961–December 1962)

A Period of Transition

ONLY BRIEF attention will be devoted to Agency-university relations during the year and three months following the establishment of the Agency for International Development, which encompassed the short tenure of Fowler Hamilton as Administrator. During this period a new national administration proposed and attempted to implement a "major shift of emphasis in the working concepts underlying the foreign aid program."[1] In line with this "shift in emphasis," the Agency was subjected to the most fundamental organizational and personnel changes since the fall of 1953. It is difficult to assess accurately the effects of these changes on Agency-university relations during the first year after their implementation, because the attempts of new personnel to implement new policies through new organizational machinery under a new and inexperienced administrator[2] caused considerable confusion.

The discussion of this period focuses primarily on the organizational and personnel changes during this period and the immediate consequences of these changes. The long-term effects did not begin to become apparent until after the beginning of David Bell's regime.

The Reorganization

The reorganization of the Agency adhered closely to the recommendations of the Working Group on Administration and

Operation of the President's Task Force on Foreign Economic Assistance. The Working Group's published report, *Organization and Functional Statements for the Agency for International Development,* generally known as the *Gant Report*,[3] provided the basis for that portion of the Act for International Development dealing with organizational matters and for the implementing documents which formally established the new agency.[4] The recommendations of the Working Group were based on the conclusion that much of the delay, indecisiveness, and lack of imagination in the administration of the foreign assistance program[5] could be attributed to the multiple lines of authority which characterized ICA's decision-making structure. The *Gant Report* recommended, therefore, a clear line of authority from the mission director to the director of the cognizant geographic area bureau to the Administrator.

In the reorganized Agency, the Administrator was responsible (under the State Department and in conjunction with other cognizant government agencies) for establishing general objectives, standards and policies for the foreign assistance program.[6] The assistant administrators of the regional bureaus were designated as the "principal line officers in the Agency with responsibility for program direction, implementation, planning and reporting within their own respective regions."[7]

One of the most significant changes in the new organization was the decentralization of technical service (functional) responsibilities. Management staff functions (general counsel, management services, personnel administration and controller) continued to be performed by central offices, acting in an advisory capacity, directly under the Administrator. However, the powerful technical support offices, Food and Agriculture, Public Services, Industrial Resources, Contract Relations and Engineering, which had functioned directly under the Deputy Director for Operations were broken up and miniature replicas of these offices were established in each regional bureau under Bureau Directors of Technical Support. Each regional bureau was also assigned its own legal advisor who reported directly to the assistant administrator for the bureau.

The Working Group recognized that the reduction in stature of the technical service offices would lead to the loss of large numbers of senior technical service personnel who had long terms of service and valuable experience in the administration of foreign assistance programs, particularly in the area of technical assistance and institutional development, but who could not feasibly be assigned to the miniature offices within the geographic area bureau technical service divisions. It was hoped that at least some of these men could be retained in the Agency in a nonoperational role through the establishment of the Office of Development Research and Assistance.[8] This office was the grandfather of the Office of Technical Cooperation and Research (AA/TCR) which was abolished in 1967. It was given primary responsibility for "stimulating and supporting research to assure the most effective use of development assistance resources."[9]

As might be expected, there were also major personnel changes. The President's *Report to the Congress on the Foreign Assistance Program for Fiscal Year 1962,* noted that: "A complete review of personnel was made during the transition from ICA to AID and 274 ICA employees were not rehired. New chiefs were appointed for many AID country mission teams, and a completely new administration was recruited."[10] As this report suggests, the turnover was even more extensive than the one following the appointment of Harold Stassen. This was especially true at the upper and middle management level. Although no Agency-wide examination system was introduced, many persons, particularly those who had served in the technical service bureaus, simply resigned rather than accept a reduction in status in a miniaturized regional "tech-service" office or relegation to the "old folks home," which was the name given by Agency personnel to the Office of Development Research and Assistance.[11] Among those who were "not rehired" in the process of "recruiting a completely new administration" was D. A. Fitzgerald, the man who, during the years of indifferent leadership in ICA, had been most responsible for "holding the Agency together."[12]

In a rather bitter valedictory which accompanied his retirement from the Federal service, Fitzgerald observed that "It's time to stop this farcical game of musical chairs with the administration of the foreign assistance program."[13] His comments were a succinct assessment of the immediate post-reorganization period:

> These periodic attempts to shuck off the old and don the new can, in the long-run have only adverse consequences. . . . The United

The Interregnum (September 1961–December 1962)

States foreign assistance program is a difficult and complex one under the best of circumstances. It has a solid record of performance and its future should not be jeopardized by the fanciful contention that brilliant new policies, bright new administrators and a brand new organization are going to vastly improve that performance. The policies will not be brilliant and new, but will largely reflect a shift in emphasis. The administrator, if new, may indeed be bright, but lack for at least a year that vital ingredient of experience. The organization may be brand new, but will take a year or more to recover its morale and achieve the same degree of efficiency the old one had.[14]

A more detailed assessment of the consequences of the reorganization was presented in a perceptive report, *Personnel Administration and Operations of the Agency for International Development*, prepared under the direction of Senator Gale W. McGee for the Senate Committee on Appropriations.[15] The conclusion of the *McGee Report* echoed Fitzgerald's warning:

> . . . It now seems obvious that in the 1961 reorganization, too much was attempted in too short a period of time. The influx of so many key personnel into this large, complex and amorphous, though previously highly specialized organization, at a time when vastly increased responsibilities were being assumed and a radical reorganization through decentralization was being undertaken, had the effect of greatly increasing an existing state of confusion. . . . in other words, the changes made in the Agency, together with its greatly expanded functions, seemingly were too drastic for the organization, such as it was, to take in stride and while it now appears to be rapidly improving it went through a rather agonizing period. . . .[16]

More specifically, the report observed that during AID's first year, there were "instances of long delays" which not only affected progress but made for poor morale in the field. Lack of centralization in the area of contracting was also criticised. "It is almost impossible," the report noted, "for anyone within the Agency to ascertain what is occurring in the contracting field until long after the fact."[17]

What is most interesting about these and other criticisms directed against the new agency is their similarity to the criticisms which had been leveled against the decentralized administrative structures preceeding FOA. Decentralizing had solved one set of problems; but the problems which centralization (in 1953–54) had been designed to solve, began to appear again.

Major Policy Changes Affecting Agency-University Relations

On the national level, major long-term effects were produced by the increased emphasis which the Kennedy Administration placed on foreign assistance to Africa and Latin America. The philosophy underlying the Alliance for Progress was particularly significant in promoting university involvement, though the major expansion of contracting in Latin America did not take place until after 1962. The emphasis on "long-term development assistance" and programs of "self help" in the "working concepts underlying the foreign aid program" suggested increased emphasis on technical assistance, but Administrator Hamilton was oriented toward capital development and not wholly sympathetic to this approach.

Another factor of major significance on the national level was the growing dissatisfaction of Congress with the foreign assistance program. Passage of the foreign assistance appropriation legislation had become increasingly difficult under the skillful attacks of Congressman Passman and others, and the previous administration had failed completely in 1957–60 to gain the "no year" appropriations for certain technical assistance programs (including the university-contract program) which had been desired by the universities and recommended by no less than five major studies of the foreign assistance program between 1957 and 1961.[18] The extent of the changes in both organization and personnel reflected, in part, the view of the administration that a complete break with the past, a total "new look" supported by appealing slogans such as "self help," "assistance in relation to ability," "loans rather than grants" and "well-conceived program plans"[19] would promote the additional Congressional support necessary for the survival of the program. However, Fitzgerald's comments in this regard proved to be prophetic. He observed that while "these maneuvers may temporarily impress the uninitiated, they do not fool the experienced. And among the most experienced by now [1962] are those Congressional committees and their staffs who over the years have handled United States foreign assistance legislation. . . ."[20] Representative Passman and other opponents of foreign aid viewed the new look with no more favor than the old and the "annual minuet"[21] or "annual spring donnybrook"[22] continued, as in the past, to be a debilitating and uncertain enterprise.

Within the Agency itself, there were no immediate policy changes of consequence for Agency-university relations. Fowler Hamilton's background inclined him toward the capital development point of view and this, combined with the elimination of the central technical service offices, tended to lower the priority of all technical assistance programs, university contracts included. However, even this was much less an explicit policy change than an unintended spillover effect resulting from organizational and personal factors. Hamilton should not be compared to Hollister, for example, whose downgrading of technical assistance was quite deliberate.

Patterns of Participation

Minor changes in patterns of participation reflected the changes in emphasis initiated by the Kennedy Administration. New programs were added in Africa, one directly with a government ministry, as additional funds were made available for this region. Additionally, several new contracts were under negotiation in the Latin American bureau, although only one was actually in operation at the end of the Hamilton Administration. There were twenty-nine active contracts in agriculture and rural development at the end of 1962.

Agency-University Relations

University representatives who had to deal with the Agency during this period found that the organizational changes had not produced instant improvement in the Agency side of the contract operation. In fact, as the *McGee Report* suggests, the immediate effects were exactly the reverse of those intended and foreseen by the Working Group on Administration and Operations. A university campus coordinator observed that "it took a year for people

TABLE V

University-Contract Rural Development Projects Initiated and Terminated During the Interregnum

REGION	COUNTRY	U.S. INSTITUTION	HOST INSTITUTION	DATES
Contracts initiated:				
FAR EAST	Thailand	Univ. of Hawaii	Kasetsart University	1962–65*
NESA	None			
LATIN AMERICA	Uruguay	Iowa State Univ.	Universidad de la Republica	1962–Active
AFRICA	Kenya	West Virginia Univ.	Egerton Agricultural College in Njoro	1962–Active
	Tanganyika	West Virginia Univ.	Agricultural College of Tanganyika	1962–Active
	Tunisia	Texas A & M	Department of Agriculture, Govt.	1962–65
Contracts terminated:				
FAR EAST	Vietnam	Univ. of Georgia	National College of Agriculture Animal Husbandry and Forestry	1960–62
NESA	Israel	State Univ. of N.Y.	Hebrew University	1958–62
LATIN AMERICA	None			
AFRICA	None			

Summary Data: (1) Number of contracts initiated   5
             (2) Number of contracts terminated   2
             (3) Number of active contracts   30

Source: AID Statistical Reports
NOTE: Contracts listed as ACTIVE were active as of July 1, 1966.

to find out what they were supposed to be doing and nobody would commit themselves to anything."[23] A NASULGC official reported:

> The consequences [of the reorganization] were chaotic. Nobody who had participated in the planning of the new Agency was retained to operate it. For a while, there was nobody there with whom I had had previous dealings. People from universities would call me to ask with whom they should speak to get authoritative information or a decision and I had to answer frankly that I simply did not know.[24]

It is interesting to note, however, that the increase in negative incidents encountered by some universities did not lead to major manifestations of discontent at the university community level. On the whole, university representatives seem to have been sympathetic toward the purposes of the reorganization and willing to bide their time until the organizational machinery of the Agency began to run more smoothly. The growing experience of the universities, the fact that the reorganization did not coincide with a major expansion in contract operations and the relatively short duration of the interregnum were also, no doubt, contributing factors.

In any case, it is clear that this period constitutes a relatively minor chapter in the history of Agency-university relations, which was quickly overshadowed by the period of harmony which followed.

CHAPTER VII

The Period of Harmony (1963–1966)

David Bell

THE APPOINTMENT of David Bell as Administrator of AID marked the beginning of a period of harmony in Agency-university relations. In view of the fact that the slow building of consensus to support his policies and the very gradual introduction of change were hallmarks of Bell's philosophy of administration,[1] it may seem surprising that there is such agreement, particularly among university officials, that his appointment marked the beginning of a period of greatly improved relations. However, the evidence on this point is clear. In interview after interview statements were volunteered such as: "Under David Bell, there was significant improvement, and things started to work out very well,"[2] and "There has been a general pattern of improvement [in relationships] during recent years. Of course the change has been most significant since David Bell became administrator."[3] It is appropriate, therefore, to begin the discussion of the period of harmony with an assessment of Bell's specific contributions to improved relations.

David Bell's initiatives in the areas of university contracting and rural development were guided by a coherent philosophy. This philosophy was based on his own views, gained from personal association with the university community, and on the experience of such individuals as Leona Baumgartner, Ralph Ruffner and Erven Long. During his tenure, the emphasis on technical assistance increased, and the Agency committed itself to expand and diversify university participation. In undertaking this expansion and diversification, there was an attempt to learn from previous problems which had been associated with this form of technical assistance and to respond to the concerns of the university community in such areas as research support and participation in planning. Finally, there was greatly increased emphasis on communication, both with the university community and, perhaps even more important, within the Agency itself. There were no counterparts to "SSS policies" during the period of harmony. The identification with Bell's philosophy by many Agency personnel, plus the effectiveness and stability of his leadership contributed to a feeling of professionalism and pride in the Agency which contrasted sharply with prevalent attitudes during other periods. Clearly it was not only the university-contract program which benefited from this type of leadership, but it was a major beneficiary.

SPECIFIC INITIATIVES AND POLICIES

Shortly after becoming Administrator, Bell began a series of initiatives in the area of university relations. These provided a concrete demonstration of the change in philosophy and approach which had taken place at the head of the Agency. First, he appointed an advisory committee, consisting of members of the university community, to advise him on matters relating to university contracting. Moreover, he actually took some of the advice when it was offered. Second, he designated a "single point of contact" (Dr. Erven Long) within the Agency as his personal representative for rural development matters, responding to a long-expressed concern of the universities. Later, a liaison office for university-contract matters was established and staffed with a ranking member of the university community.[4] Third (and perhaps most important of all), he commissioned the *Gardner Report*,[5] supported its preparation and endorsed its recommendations. Finally, he encouraged the initiatives which led to the highly successful Conference on International Rural Development and then actively and personally participated in the Conference. Moreover, his activities in connection with these matters and his dealings with individual universities promoted cooperation and good feeling.[6]

Bell's style of administration, however, was a more important factor in the changes during this period than any specific action. His tact and sense of pace contrast sharply with the approach used by his equally dynamic and forceful predecessor, Harold Stassen. The emphasis on downward communication has already been noted. All policy changes were prefaced by careful preparation and discussion. Personnel throughout the Agency were exposed to the rationale behind Bell's policies as well as the policies themselves. In many cases he was able merely to support an existing area of consensus within the Agency or the ideas of others which reflected his own thinking. Sometimes individuals who thought along the same lines as the Administrator were attracted to key positions in the Agency. Thus, he was able to generate support through essentially persuasive measures, rather than attempting to compel it through organizational changes and improved compliance control procedures. In the area of university contracting, he did not try to move too far too fast as Stassen had done. Working within organizational machinery based on the recommendations of the *Gant Report,* he was able, through his method of administration by persuasion, to allow the Bureau Assistant Administrators wide flexibility in planning and implementing their programs while at the same time ensuring that those programs would move in the direction he intended and would reflect much of his own philosophy.

The Gardner Report

In the area of university contracting, specifically, the impact of the *Gardner Report* is most revealing. The background and significance of this remarkable document should be examined in some detail, not only because of the intrinsic value of the report itself, but also because the entire story of the report exemplifies Bell's approach to the problem of improving Agency-university relations.

The discussion of the period of inertia commented on the relatively slight impact that most studies of university participation in technical assistance had made on Agency personnel. From the perspective of this observation, the ubiquitous presence of well-thumbed, blue-covered copies of *AID and the Universities* in the Washington offices of the Agency officials who were interviewed for this study seemed highly significant.[7] Even more striking, in view of the general lack of familiarity with the other literature related to the university-contract program, was the fact that officials frequently quoted passages from the report or pulled out copies to refer to specific points in the course of the interviews. It seems quite clear that the *Gardner Report* was a major contribution to promoting mutual understanding between the Agency and the universities (and therefore, to the reduction of negative incidents resulting from a lack of such mutual understanding) during the period of harmony.

What is different about the *Gardner Report?* Clearly the difference does not lie in the substance of the report. For every substantive statement of fact and recommendation presented, a corresponding statement and recommendation, often more than one, can be found in earlier literature on the university-contract program. This statement is not intended as criticism. Any other situation would have been surprising, given the extent to which university participation in technical assistance had been discussed and written about by governmental officials and members of the university community. To say that the statements or recommendations had been previously set down is not to say that they had become part of the "memory" of Agency and university officials.

Three things set the *Gardner Report* apart from other studies of the university-contract program. One of these, that it was widely read by both Agency and participating university personnel, has already been mentioned. The report's wide audience was a consequence of the other two things which distinguished it; namely, (1) John Gardner wrote it and (2) David Bell endorsed it.

Actually, John Gardner made two important contributions to the report associated with his name. First, he performed the usual function of task-force chairmen, that of legitimizer. As President of the Carnegie Corporation and a highly respected scholar and member of the academic community, he was an ideal person to lend his name to the study regardless of any personal contribution he might make. However, the report which finally emerged after seven months of effort on the part of the task force and its staff was not the Gardner *committee* report or the Gardner *task-force* report, it was the result of Gardner's personal efforts. "By John Gardner" on the flyleaf means exactly what it says and is one of the reasons it stands above other task-force studies of the foreign assistance program. Many reports bearing the names of eminent men simply reflect endorsement of the work of a staff or committee or commission. Usually they also reflect the compromises and diffuseness of style which such preparation entails. They are read because of the reputation of the endorsee, then forgotten. Such was not the case with *AID and the Universities*.[8]

As has been indicated, the quality of the report was not the only reason for its impact. In addition, Bell gave it his strong endorsement. Agency personnel were urged to read the report and in the Foreword, Bell stated:

> The report—as was to be expected—is forthright, lucid and provocative. It seems to me to lay just the right kind of analytical basis, and to set out just the right kind of conceptual guidelines for AID and the universities to use in proceeding to work out practical improvements in our joint undertakings.[9]

Thus, Agency personnel were made aware that this report would serve as an important basis for university-contracting policy henceforth.

It was suggested above that the Agency response to the *Gardner Report* could be viewed as one manifestation of Administrator Bell's "persuasive" style of administration. One official remarked: "There was certainly a high correlation between the report and Bell's ideas. I don't know how much the report was influenced by Bell as opposed to Bell being influenced by the report."[10] The relationship of the report to the policies of the Administrator was probably not a matter of influence—Bell by Gardner or Gardner by Bell. Rather, it was a consequence of Bell's belief that the report would provide a lucid statement of a shared viewpoint before it was ever suggested. This being the case, the *Gardner Report* provided justification and reinforcement within the Agency for policies to which Bell was already committed. At the same time, it provided a means for communicating those policies and their underlying rationale to the Agency with an impact which no directive from the Office of the Administrator could ever have achieved.

Policy Changes Affecting Agency-University Relations

During this period the expansion of contract operations was supported legislatively by the "Humphrey Amendment" to the

The Period of Harmony (1963–1966)

foreign assistance legislation, which specifically directed the Agency to make maximum use of the resources of non-government businesses and institutions and other governmental agencies whenever possible.[11] The expansion of contract operations was also supported by the findings of the *Clay Report*,[12] which noted:

... Experience makes us doubt AID's ability to mobilize the high quality manpower necessary to implement well and supervise properly all of the current technical assistance programs amounting to approximately $380 million annually.

... In this connection, we have noted certain resources whose potential has not been adequately tapped or in all cases adequately offered in the uniform high quality of personnel required. We believe that our nation's universities, particularly the Land-Grant colleges as institutions created for development, possess talent and experience whose adoption should make possible a unique and greater contribution in several fields than is presently the case.

These two external influences were important because they raised the priority of the university-contract program somewhat.

Two restrictive policies were also imposed by the Congress. The "Hickenlooper Amendment" directed the Agency to suspend aid to countries expropriating privately owned U.S. property without adequate compensation and prohibited the granting of assistance to Communist countries except under extraordinary circumstances.[13] A second amendment, which led to several particularly irritating incidents involving university personnel in the field, required all procurement for foreign assistance projects to be undertaken in the United States.[14]

The pattern of lengthy hearings and substantial appropriation cuts continued without significant alteration, despite virtuoso performances before the Congress by Administrator Bell which elicited grudging praise, even from Representative Passman.[15] In 1963, massive cuts in the requested appropriations were imposed, motivated in part by the generally negative tone of the *Clay Report*. In 1964, President Johnson was able to persuade the Congress that the customary "padding" of the legislative request from the Agency had not occurred; and the bill emerged essentially unscathed. In 1965 and 1966, cuts were again imposed, however, and prospects appeared, if anything, less favorable for the future.

As noted above, President Kennedy exerted pressure to expand programs in Africa and Latin America, particularly the latter.

Officials in the Alliance for Progress mentioned numerous instances of direct White House intervention, particularly requests to initiate new projects and "get action" in the Latin American area.[16] Another policy change was in the Kennedy letter of May 1961, which reaffirmed and clarified the responsibility of the ambassador for all programs in his country.[17]

Policy changes within the Agency reflected the Administrator's philosophy and interests. These have been discussed in detail above and a summary of the significant points here should suffice. Specifically, the policies affecting universities which received greatest emphasis were:

(1) Greater use of university contracts, in preference to direct hire personnel.

(2) Greater involvement of university and field personnel in planning.

(3) Greater field responsibility for day-to-day decision-making.

(4) Diversification of the use of universities.

(5) Strengthening of university competence in the area of technical assistance through the initiation and support of basic and applied research, by means of separate research contracts and the inclusion of a research component in technical assistance contracts. These policies, in addition to affecting Agency-university relations, led to significant changes in patterns of participation.

Organizational Relationships and Issues

There were no organizational changes of major consequence during the period of harmony. In fact, it was Bell's policy to oppose such changes, even when there seemed to be some justification for them. He felt that the Agency desperately needed a period of stability and that almost any organization would be better than another reorganization. Because of this, the basic structure established by the *Gant Report* remained virtually unchanged, although there was some effort on the part of the Office of the Administrator to establish more uniform policies and procedures among the bureaus.[18]

As noted above, an attempt was made to meet the demands of the university community for a central point of authority and

The Period of Harmony (1963–1966)

responsibility, high in the Agency's administrative structure, to deal with university-contract matters. In 1963, Dr. Erven Long, a TCR official with a university background, long experience in the Agency, and a sympathetic attitude toward the contract program, was designated by Bell as the central point of contact in the Office of the Administrator to whom "any problems in the broad field of rural development" could be taken.[19] In particular, Dr. Long was to serve as a liaison official between the Agency, the Assistant Secretary of Agriculture for Foreign Affairs and the newly established International Rural Development Office of the NASULGC.[20] The establishment of the Office of University Relations, in TCR, in the fall of 1964 represented a further step toward the establishment of a central point of contact. Dr. Norman Auburn, President of the University of Akron, was appointed Special Assistant for University Relations. Although the office was nominally under the authority of the Assistant Administrator for TCR, Auburn was authorized to communicate directly with the Administrator regarding university-contract matters. This arrangement lasted for only a year. When Auburn departed, no official of comparable stature was appointed to take his place. Instead, the status of the office was lowered, the special relationship with the administrator was eliminated and the title "University Relations Officer" was assumed by Dr. Auburn's deputy.

Neither of these innovations achieved the goal which the universities desired, namely an office with authoritative decision-making power over the university-contract program. Indeed it is difficult to see how the principle of "line" authority within regional bureaus could have been maintained if a central office with authoritative decision-making powers over a substantive area (such as university contracting) had been established. The philosophy of the *Gant Report,* which Bell endorsed, was quite explicit on this point. The function of staff offices was to maintain liaison, advise, and provide staff services upon request[21] to the assistant regional administrators. There certainly was no desire in the regional bureaus to return to the type of organization which had characterized ICA and they zealously protected their autonomy over the operational aspects of their programs. Drs. Long and Auburn served useful, but limited, advisory and liaison functions. Long played a leading role in coordinating the planning of the Conference on International Rural Development within the Agency. Auburn served a similar planning and coordinating function for the working group which drafted the 1965 revision of the standard university contract. However, neither "point of contact" provided a satisfactory basis for handling the "nuts and bolts" operating problems with which many universities were still concerned. The broader issues out of which these problems arose could be perceived at the TCR level with greater clarity than was possible at the level of an individual contract officer or technical officer in a regional bureau. However, TCR officials argued that there was no organizational channel through which this knowledge could be effectively brought to bear on bureau decision-making processes.

The difficulties faced by Long and Auburn can be better understood when viewed from the context of the more general "status problem" with which all TCR officials had to cope throughout the life of this office and its predecessors. This problem was touched on by the *Gardner Report,* which noted there is "conclusive evidence that AID's present organizational arrangements for dealing with educational and human resource development are far from satisfactory,"[22] and specifically, that TCR has been "severely understaffed and never able to command the attention and respect of the regional bureaus."[23] The findings of the *Gardner Report* were confirmed by interviews with both university and Agency officials. Although the rank of the director of TCR was raised to assistant administrator in 1964, obviously to raise the status of the office within the Agency, this did little to improve things. TCR officials were never able to gain the operational control over programs in agriculture and human resource development which they desired. Nor did TCR ever function as a really effective staff office, which was what the Administrator wanted.

Dr. Auburn was much less associated with the fight for power between TCR and the regional bureaus than was Long. In Auburn's case the main problem seems to have been inexperience. The rationale behind the appointment was that the status of the newly created office would be enhanced by the appointment of a prestigious member of the university community. Additionally, it was hoped that the selection of Dr. Auburn would be viewed as evidence of good faith on the part of the Agency by the participating universities. Both of these goals were attained to some

The Period of Harmony (1963-1966)

degree. Auburn was apparently well liked in the Agency, but he had no real power, and this fact was quickly recognized. The fact that he was a university president gained him respect and access, but carried little weight in actual decision-making processes. His position was further weakened by his limited familiarity with the Agency. Because of this he often did not seek out the necessary information to perform a communication and liaison function effectively. One ranking university official summed up a broad consensus on this point with the observation that "Auburn had no real power, but worse than that, he didn't know it." Therefore, it is perhaps not surprising that the change in status of the University Relations Office caused little stir either in the Agency or the university community.

In conclusion, while it is clear that Agency-university relations improved at both levels during the period of harmony, it is equally clear that the organizational arrangements just discussed made only a minor contribution.

Patterns of Participation

As a result of the policy changes discussed above, there were significant changes in both individual and regional patterns of participation. The number of participating institutions increased and the types of activities became more varied. Although "sisterhood" relationships remained the most prevalent type of contract, the policy of limiting participation to this pattern was rejected. As in the early years of the program, there was experimentation with a variety of projects. A second change was the emergence of significant regional differences within the Agency. Both of these changes had consequences for Agency-university relations and need closer examination.

INTER-REGIONAL DIFFERENCES IN PATTERNS OF PARTICIPATION

Because of the organizational structure of the Agency, particularly the degree to which responsibility for program planning was delegated to the regional assistant administrators, considerable differences emerged between the bureaus in the degree to which general policy guidelines regarding university contracts became Agency policies at the operating level.

The policy of expanding and diversifying university participation was most vigorously implemented in the Latin American Bureau. In fact, initiatives in this direction were undertaken during the Hamilton Administration. During 1963 and 1964 university contracts of all types were promoted in a manner reminiscent of the period of proliferation,[24] and universities were encouraged to involve themselves in all phases of country programs. Direct hire personnel were replaced by contract personnel in some instances. In Africa there was also a substantial expansion of contracting, but the attitude of bureau officials was more conservative with regard to diversification and delegation of planning responsibilities to the field and the universities. Changes in the NESA and Far East Bureaus were much less pronounced. There was some diversification but little expansion. In the Far East, in fact, there were, as of September 1964, fewer active projects in the rural development field than there had been at the beginning of 1963.

DIVERSIFICATION IN INDIVIDUAL PATTERNS OF PARTICIPATION

The increasing use of universities to perform a variety of technical assistance and research functions was one of the most significant characteristics of the period of harmony. This diversification was partly a response to political pressure, as it had been in 1953–54, but it also reflected the desires of the university community and the increasing flexibility and sophistication of both parties.

Most contracts still involved the direct participation of universities in technical assistance. However, within this category three new patterns emerged. The first might be called a *broadened sisterhood relationship*. This conformed rather closely to Harold Stassen's concept of an ideal university contract and resembled the multi-purpose contracts initiated during the period of proliferation.[25] Many of the new contracts of this type were in Africa. Cornell University, for example, accepted a contract "to develop the University of Liberia into an institution of more acceptable educational standards so that it might produce trained personnel to fulfill the requirements of the country's economic and social development."[26] A second pattern, direct assistance to one or more

The Period of Harmony (1963–1966)

host government agencies, also had antecedents in the period of proliferation. Contracts of this type were negotiated in both Latin America and Africa, but mostly the former region. A typical example was the Iowa State project in Peru to develop a nationwide program of agrarian reform and credit.[27] With the encouragement of the mission director, the Iowa State team assumed many functions formerly performed by direct hire mission personnel. It is not surprising that the reaction of some "old hands" in the Agency to this type of contract was similar to that of their counterparts in 1954 and 1955. However, the deliberate non-cooperation and intense hostility which characterized the earlier period do not seem to have been present.

A third variant on contracts involving direct participation in technical assistance was the inclusion of an integral "research component." This reflected a long-term concern of the university community which had been supported by the recommendations of numerous studies of the program. The University of Wisconsin was a leader in negotiating contract provisions which would permit on-site research by graduate students for academic credit.[28]

In addition to the contracts involving participation in technical assistance, several contracts involving institutional or multi-institutional research were negotiated. These projects, which were directly administered by TCR,[29] represented an entirely new approach by the Agency to the use of universities.[30] Three of the most significant innovations were regional research and training contracts, departmental research contracts in areas of special departmental competence, and research contracts with groups or consortia of American universities.

An example of the first approach was the Wisconsin Land Tenure Center contract. Under the contract, regional research and training centers were established at Madison and in Latin America. These centers "engaged in the comparative study and analysis of the economic, social, political and administrative aspects of land ownership, land tenure and the agrarian structure."[31] The general objectives of the program were to "build a comprehensive body of knowledge of agrarian reform" and to "train men and women from Latin America and the U.S. who wish to make a professional commitment to economic development in the Latin American countries."[32]

A TCR-administered contract with Cornell provides an example of the departmental research approach. In 1963 the Cornell

TABLE VI

University-Contract Rural Development Projects Initiated and Terminated During the Period of Harmony

REGION	COUNTRY	U.S. INSTITUTION	HOST INSTITUTION	DATES
Contracts Initiated:				
NESA	Jordan	Univ. of Illinois	Ministry of Agriculture, Department of Agricultural Extension	1963–66
LATIN AMERICA	Argentina	Texas A & M	National Institute of Agricultural Technology	1964–Active
	Argentina	Michigan State U.	National Institute of Agriculture	1965–Active
	Bolivia	Utah State Univ.	Ministry of Agriculture	1965–Active
	Brazil	Univ. of Arizona	University of Ceara, Fortaleza	1963–Active
	Brazil	Mississippi State U.	Ministry of Agriculture	1964–Active
	Brazil	Ohio State Univ.	Agricultural College, University of São Paulo	1964–Active
	Brazil	Univ. of Wisconsin	University of Rio Grande do Sul	1963–65
	Costa Rica	Univ. of Florida	Univ. of Costa Rica, and the Institute of Lands and Colonization	1965–Active
	Dominican Republic	Texas A & M	Govt. of the Dominican Republic	1965–Active
	Guatemala	Mississippi State U.	Ministry of Agriculture	1966–Active
	Jamaica	Univ. of Florida	Government of Jamaica	1966–Active
	Paraguay	New Mexico State U.	College of Agriculture and Veterinary Science of the National University of Asuncion	1964–Active
	Uruguay	Iowa State Univ.	Universidad de la Republica Oriental del Uruguay	1962–Active
AFRICA	Regional	West Virginia Univ.	Makerere Univ. College, Faculty of Agriculture	1964–Active
	Nigeria	Kansas State Univ.	Ahmadu Bello University	1963–Active
	Nigeria	Colorado State U.	Ministry of Agriculture	1964–Active

Country	U.S. University	Host Institution	Dates
Nigeria	Michigan State U.	Government of Nigeria	1965–Active
Nigeria	Univ. of Wisconsin	University of IFE	1964–Active
Western Nigeria	Univ. of Wisconsin	Ministry of Agric. and Natl. Resources	1965–Active
Nyasaland (Malawi)	U. of Massachusetts	Agricultural Training Center near Lilongwe	1963–Active
Northern Rhodesia (Zambia)	U. of Connecticut	Monze Agricultural Training Center	1963–Active
Sierra Leone	Univ. of Illinois	Njala Teacher Training College	1963–Active
Somali Republic	Univ. of Wyoming	Govt. of the Somali Republic, Ministry of Agriculture	1965–Active
Uganda	West Virginia U.	Agricultural College at Bukalasa and Arapai, Training Institute in Veterinary Medicine at Entebbe	1963–Active
NESA			
India	Univ. of Illinois	Madhya Pradesh Agricultural Univ.	1964–Active

Contracts Terminated:

Country	U.S. University	Host Institution	Dates
FAR EAST			
Cambodia	Univ. of Georgia	National College of Agriculture, Animal Husbandry and Forestry	1960–63
China	Michigan State U.	National Taiwan University and Taiwan Provincial Chung Hsing University	1960–64
NESA			
Iran	Utah State	Karaj College	1951–58–64*
LATIN AMERICA			
Guatemala	Univ. of Kentucky	University of San Carlos	1957–63
Paraguay	Montana State Univ.	National University of Asuncion	1960–63

Summary Data: (1) Number of contracts initiated   26
(2) Number of contracts terminated   5
(3) Active contracts   51

Sources: (a) *Interim Report* of the CIC-AID Rural Development Research Project, Appendix A
(b) AID Statistical Reports on University Contracts
(c) Participating university files

*Changed to a "sisterhood" relationship in 1958.

NOTE: Contracts listed as ACTIVE were active as of July 1, 1966.

Department of Anthropology negotiated a contract "to accelerate the process of analysis and reporting of results for its long term project on comparative studies of cultural change."[33] The funds provided by AID enabled Cornell investigators to return and carry out updated field research in areas and communities in which they or their colleagues had worked years ago.[34]

The CIC–AID Rural Development Research Project represented an attempt to apply the consortia approach to improving the university-contract program itself.[35] Another project of this type involved several universities in a long-term research program in Nigeria.[36]

At the end of the period of harmony, in mid-1966, it was too early to assess accurately the long-term consequences of these emerging patterns. The new approaches to individual participation represented a significant departure from what had been called the "purchase psychology" of the Agency. In the short run, the effects on Agency-university relations were clearly beneficial. It seemed that continued policies of tolerant and flexible administration on the part of the Agency, and responsible commitment on the part of the participating universities would ensure that these beneficial effects continued.

The consequences of the differences in regional patterns of participation were more mixed. The administrative problems posed by such differences were considerable and had by no means been entirely resolved. It was clear that a continued awareness by both the Agency and the universities of the problems which could arise when such differences existed would be necessary to minimize the occurrence of negative incidents. One only needed to review the history of the periods of genesis and proliferation to be aware of the potential problems. One could not really predict whether or not parties to the relationship had gained sufficient understanding and experience so that a deterioration in relations could be avoided as the use of universities was expanded.

Agency-University Relations at the Level of the University Community

During the period of harmony, it is possible to focus explicitly on the rural development area in examining AID-university relations. A differentiation between rural development and other types of university-contract projects is less meaningful before 1962 because, after the period of genesis, rural development projects were not singled out for special attention.[37] Furthermore, policy, procedural and organizational changes which most significantly affected Agency-university relations do not appear to have had discernibly different effects on different substantive areas.[38] Even at the level of the university community, no such distinction was drawn prior to 1962, in discussions of major issues relating to the program.[39] During the Bell Administration, however, special organizational machinery was established within the Agency, the USDA and the NASULGC for promoting and expediting university participation in the area of agriculture and rural development.

The steps which led to the establishment of this new machinery and, indirectly, to the Conference on International Rural Development began with the concerns of a few high officials in the Alliance for Progress. They believed that the development of the agrarian sectors in Latin American countries posed serious problems and that "successful development of other sectors was unlikely without greatly increased purchasing power on the part of rural populations."[40] These concerns were more fully developed at a meeting of a governmental committee concerned with the Alliance for Progress on February 16, 1962. The committee resolved that:

> The situation obviously requires most urgent attention and can only be improved through an intensive program of institutional development combined with development and expansion of agricultural research and extension services. Positive action on this problem will require technical assistance and training on an unprecedented scale. Without such technical advisory and training assistance, financial assistance (will) be relatively ineffective in furthering agricultural development.[41]

Accordingly, it was concluded that "the resources of the Land-Grant universities and the USDA and the private foundations should be enlisted to supplement an enlarged effort on the part of the Agency's own staff."[42] These conclusions provided the impetus for a series of developments involving the Agency, the NASULGC and the USDA which profoundly influenced Agency-university community relations. These developments were: (1) the September 1962 meeting of the Alliance Steering Committee on

Rural Development, (2) the establishment and subsequent activities of the International Rural Development Office of the NASULGC, and (3) the 1964 Conference on International Rural Development held in July.

THE ALLIANCE STEERING COMMITTEE
ON RURAL DEVELOPMENT

The February meeting of the Alliance for Progress committee led to a series of informal consultations with university representatives which culminated in a request from Alliance Director Moscoso to NASULGC President, Dr. John T. Caldwell, to appoint a five-man committee to represent the Association on an Alliance Steering Committee on rural development. The Committee was to lay the foundation for new policies of joint participation in the rural development area. In addition to the representatives from the university community, participants were also included from the USDA, the Ford, Kellogg and Rockefeller Foundations, the American International Association, and an "observer" from the U.S. Department of the Interior.[43] The Committee met on September 6, 7, 8, 1962, with Dr. Erven Long, Agricultural Chief of the AID Office on Educational and Social Development, acting as chairman.

The discussions focused on ways in which USDA, Land-Grant university and Foundation contributions to the Alliance rural development assistance programs could be increased and integrated. The need for such contributions was emphasized by Administrator Hamilton,[44] who made the introductory address at the meeting. The Committee's conclusions and recommendations, adopted after three days of deliberation, illustrate the scope of the discussions. These included:

(1) A statement of activities in which AID should assume responsibility.

(2) A check list of resources available to AID programs from the USDA, the Department of the Interior and the Land-Grant colleges and universities.

(3) A statement by the NASULGC regarding mechanisms and scope for potential participation.

(4) A statement by the USDA proposing establishment of permanent working committees to advise AID on country programs.

(5) A statement by the USDA on the relationship between technical assistance and development loans in rural development.

(6) A statement on areas of rural development where research might be needed.[45]

The first three statements deserve special attention: the first because it explicitly delineated the areas in which there was reasonable agreement that the Agency's authority could not be delegated; the second because it defined the areas of "special competence" of the universities; and the third because it proposed the establishment of a new liaison organization to represent the university community in rural development matters.

The statement, "Activities in Which AID Should Take Responsibility," reflected the fact that "AID is charged by Congress with certain responsibilities which cannot be delegated or contracted; and a function of responsibility is the determination of policies of AID and policy relationships with other countries." The activities in the listing related to the university-contract program included the following:

> ... (b) Establish policies and guidelines for U.S. AID country missions in development of programs and activities with countries. (c) Participate in the recruiting of contract agencies, services or individuals for performing specific projects; and for some projects be the sole implementor for contract services. . . . (f) Prepare good project plans that call for capital and/or technical assistance help. (g) Engage in direct hire of personnel for services not contracted and for those services necessary until a contracting party takes over. (h) Follow closely and participate in the work, progress and results of project tasks under contract as necessary to meet its obligations of responsibility and policy determination.[46]

In the "Check List of Resources Available to AID Programs," the following areas of special competence were ascribed to the state universities and Land-Grant colleges:

(1) Development of educational programs from elementary level up to and including graduate education and development of institution building.
(2) Research in specific countries (both basic and applied research)
    (a) Emphasis on adaptive research in the natural sciences.
    (b) Emphasis in social science on research that will contribute to economic development.

(3) Training local people for managerial and technical assistance to farm families.

(4) Development of an agricultural extension system in cooperation with USDA.

(5) Combination of the teaching, research and extension function.

(6) Short term assignments on specific problems.[47]

The statement of the NASULGC representatives, in the form of a recommendation to the Association, indicated the "readiness and willingness [of the Land-Grant universities and colleges] to undertake an expanded role in overseas programs, including technical assistance." The representatives also recommended establishing a "specific coordinating instrumentality . . . to provide a more concerted pattern of assistance from the Land-Grant universities and colleges to the overseas programs of AID, with special emphasis on programs of agricultural education, research, and extension."[48] This recommendation ultimately led to the establishment of the International Rural Development Office of the NASULGC.

The NASULGC representatives also presented a statement of policy regarding Agency-university relations "in an effort to define problem areas and establish an objective position for the Land-Grant universities and colleges in coping with the problems." Because of its relevance to the major concern of this study, this statement is worth quoting at some length:

> If the Land-Grant universities and colleges are to contribute most effectively in the coming years, it is essential that the fiscal relationship between them and the AID . . . permit them the maximum degree of flexibility and freedom. The best management practice is that authority must accompany responsibility. If the universities are to have responsibility for carrying out these programs, they must have the authority to make decisions rapidly and to allocate resources as in their judgment will bring optimal results. First class work cannot be done under any other operating philosophy, and the Land-Grant institutions will naturally be increasingly hesitant at entering into agreements which will hamstring them and impair the quality of their efforts.

> The Land-Grant institutions have had a long history of highly satisfactory fiscal relationships with the Federal government (e.g. USDA), and this type of relationship should be emulated in joint efforts of the Land-Grant institutions and the government in future overseas programs. The movement toward more simple and flexible fiscal

relationships which has taken place in recent years between universities and government in many areas has resulted in better results for all concerned.[49]

This statement summarized many of the major concerns of the university community which had been presented to the Agency in previous statements and recommendations. It also suggested the degree to which operating problems were still viewed as a major impediment to a satisfactory relationship.

Before considering the establishment and subsequent activities of the NASULGC International Rural Development Office, it is important to re-emphasize the degree to which this meeting was an exclusively Latin American Bureau effort. The concerns expressed by the Agency representatives did not reflect the concerns of the Agency as a whole and no representatives from the other regional bureaus attended. In fact, although the meeting had Agency-wide significance for Agency-university community relations, the approach of the Alliance for Progress to the areas of contracting and rural development was viewed with some disfavor by the other regional bureaus.[50]

THE INTERNATIONAL RURAL DEVELOPMENT OFFICE OF THE NASULGC

The recommendation of the Alliance Steering Committee regarding the establishment of a Rural Development Office of the NASULGC in Washington was endorsed by the International Affairs Committee[51] and Senate of the Association at the 1962 Annual Convention. Following this endorsement, foundation support was solicited and procured for a three-year trial period.[52] Dr. I. L. Baldwin was appointed to serve as director on a part-time basis. The office began full operation in April 1963.

The success of the new office was greatly enhanced by the interested and cooperative attitude of Bell and other high Agency officials. The Administrator quickly became involved in the activities of the office by meeting with the Agency, NASULGC and USDA officials who were most concerned to express support for the liaison arrangement, inform himself about the functions which the office could be expected to serve and establish machinery which would enable the Agency to cooperate more effectively with it. He emphasized that the Agency as a whole, not merely the Latin American Bureau, would work closely with the new office.[53] As noted above, Dr. Erven Long was designated as the "central point of contact" in the Office of the Administrator for rural development matters.

Following this meeting, a policy statement on AID/USDA/Land-Grant university relations was circulated to the Agency. This statement, *AIDTO Circular LA 190,* emphasized the need for increased involvement of NASULGC and USDA representatives in project planning. An important section of the statement dealt with new coordination procedures to be followed by the Agency in relations with participating universities and the NASULGC Rural Development Office. Dr. Long's new responsibilities were outlined, and each regional assistant administrator was also directed to designate a "single point of contact" who would be responsible for "obtaining and channeling decisions" at his respective level. In keeping with Bell's philosophy, the circular emphasized that relations between the new office and the regional bureaus would "be kept as direct as possible."[54]

During the first fifteen months of its existence,[55] the energy and tact of Director Baldwin and the cooperation of the Agency enabled the office to perform a variety of functions which both contributed to and reflected improved Agency-university community relations. A review of the activities of the office, summarized by Dr. Baldwin in his concluding report to the Association as Director, suggests the degree to which the office was able to effectively promote the interests of the university community and communication between the Agency, the university community and the participating universities.

The bulk of Dr. Baldwin's activities involved liaison and communication with government agencies and member universities. In the first months after the office was established, he met almost weekly with Dr. Long and Dr. Roland Rennie, Assistant Secretary of Agriculture for International Affairs, to discuss university-contract matters. Often other USDA and AID officials would also participate in these informal meetings.

In the Latin American region, the office assisted in establishing a number of country planning committees consisting of AID, USDA, and NASULGC representatives. There were also numerous contacts with regional bureau staffs dealing with such matters as contractor selection, project planning and occasionally specific issues of difference which had been brought to Dr. Baldwin's attention by either Agency or university personnel. Usually, however, basic operational problems continued to be resolved at the individual project level.

Of course, there was a great deal of communication with member institutions. The office tried to collect and keep on file information about the international activities, interests and desires of individual universities. This enabled Dr. Baldwin to be a more effective source of information for governmental agencies. In addition, he would also respond to requests for judgment regarding tentative AID proposals in such fields as research activities or contract revisions. In his role as spokesman for an important segment of the university community, Dr. Baldwin attended several conferences on rural development matters.

The office was not equally involved with all of the Agency's regional bureaus. Dr. Baldwin later observed that over half of his time was devoted to matters relating to the Alliance for Progress.[56] Contact with officials of the Far East Bureau was relatively infrequent. This observation provides additional evidence of the differences in regional bureau policies with regard to the utilization of universities.

Dr. Baldwin also assumed the duty of NASULGC coordinator for the planning of the July 1964 Conference on International Rural Development. Because of its importance for Agency-university relations, it will be useful to discuss certain aspects of this conference at some length.

THE CONFERENCE ON INTERNATIONAL
RURAL DEVELOPMENT

The 1964 Conference on International Rural Development is rightly viewed as a landmark in Agency-university community relations. Along with the *Gardner Report,* it provided a vehicle for forcefully expressing the concerns of the university community to the Agency. At the same time, largely due to the impression made by Administrator Bell, the Agency was able to make substantial progress toward convincing the university community of its desire for a relationship based upon the principle of "equal partnership." As the published *Proceedings* have been widely distributed, there will be no attempt to summarize the events here. Rather, the focus will be upon those characteristics of the conference which distinguished it from its predecessors (the conferences sponsored by the CIPA) and contributed to its greater impact. Four such characteristics seem particularly significant.

First, *the initiative for holding the conference came from within the Agency. Moreover, it was jointly sponsored by the Agency, USDA and NASULGC.* The idea of holding a conference involving university presidents is generally attributed to Deputy Administrator Frank M. Coffin; however, the origins can be traced further back to the recommendations of the Alliance Steering Committee. For it was out of these recommendations and the weekly meetings of Baldwin, Rennie and Long which followed the establishment of the NASULGC International Rural Development Office, that the basic issues underlying the conference were raised for consideration.[57] In the course of these weekly discussions, Dr. Baldwin made it clear that there was a need for fundamental changes in the way that the Agency operated in the contracting area and presented specific suggestions and recommendations for policy and organizational changes. The major concerns of the university community were presented by Drs. Long and Baldwin to Deputy Administrator Coffin. Mr. Coffin proposed holding a conference which would permit interchange between Agency and university personnel on these important questions. All agreed that careful preparation would be necessary if anything significant was to be accomplished, and it was decided to designate working groups to submit recommendations to a conference which would be attended by university presidents and ranking Agency officials. The idea was approved by Administrator Bell and President Kennedy, and plans for the conference proceeded with Dr. Long, Secretary Rennie and Dr. Baldwin acting as coordinators for their respective agencies. At the suggestion of Chancellor Hardin of Nebraska, it was decided that the chairman of each working group would be an Agency representative. Following the death of President Kennedy, the conference was endorsed by President Johnson, who agreed to lend status to the enterprise by receiving conference participants at the White House. Thus, throughout the planning period, high government officials demonstrated their commitment to this enterprise.

Second, *Agency representatives participated in the working groups which prepared reports and recommendations for conference consideration.* Chancellor Hardin's suggestion to have the chairmen of the working groups be Agency representatives contributed to the beneficial "feedback" effects of the conference. Although, as in the CIPA conferences, strong supporters of university participation were appointed to the working groups, Agency personnel did not feel that the recommendations were being forced upon them by an outside group.[58] Mutuality of concern was emphasized in conference preparations as well as in conference discussions.

Third, *Administrator Bell and other high officials participated actively in conference discussions.* This point has already been discussed above. Clearly Administrator Bell's attendance at every plenary session of the conference particularly impressed university representatives with the importance which he ascribed to the conference discussions.

Finally and most important, *Agency representatives, and Bell in particular, made it clear that they viewed the working group and conference recommendations as a basis for initiating policy change within the Agency.* Bell made this point specifically both at the beginning and at the close of the conference. In his introductory presentation, he stated:

> We are prepared to accept these [working group] reports without significant qualification. If this conference, after considering these reports and modifying them as it may wish to do, sees fit to adopt reports along the lines of these drafts, we will be prepared to accept them as working guidelines and proceed to put them into effect so far as that lies within our competence.[59]

In his concluding remarks, he re-emphasized the Agency's commitment to following up the conference recommendations:

> I can promise you that we will follow up on these matters in an orderly and systematic fashion. We will need, as you will all recognize from the reports of the committees, to review and modify a number of our methods and our attitudes....[60]

Bell's promise was more than mere rhetoric. Following the conference, the *Proceedings* were analyzed by Agency officials and over seventy specific recommendations were excerpted. A committee was appointed to review these recommendations and initiate Agency action in appropriate areas. However, it is clear that the major impact of the conference did not derive from this enterprise. Indeed, in interviews with officials who served on or were associated with the conference follow-up committee, it was impossible to determine exactly what concrete changes within the Agency resulted from the recommendations and the follow-up procedures.[61] The impression of both Agency and university officials is that the concrete changes were relatively few; that most of the recommendations had not been implemented for one reason or another. However, two years later, the conference was still viewed in a very positive light.

Changes in attitudes, rather than changes in procedures, were the significant consequences of the conference. Most of the high university administrators who attended came away convinced that the Agency was firmly committed to the establishment of relationships based on the principle of "true partnership." Agency officials came away with a better understanding of the concerns of the university community and more important, an awareness of the degree to which their Administrator was committed to responding to them. Thus, a high degree of communication and mutual understanding had been established at the level of the university community.

Agency-University Relations at the Level of the Participating Universities

It is impossible, as yet, to view the period of harmony in perspective; however, the interviews indicate that the continued improvement in Agency-university relations was accompanied by a marked improvement in relations at the level of the participating universities. The influence exercised by David Bell was crucial to this development. However, it remains to be considered specifically how his initiatives and style affected the major problems contributing to negative incidents.

Bell's most important contribution was to raise the priority of the program. This was particularly important in reducing negative incidents resulting from structural problems, but it had beneficial effects in other areas also. Because of the Administrator's concern, university contracts became more closely associated with other goals of importance to Agency personnel.[62] Changes in personnel were also important. Persons with close ties to the university community gained influential positions in the Agency and were listened to by the Administrator.

A growing body of standardized procedures and greater familiarity of both parties with each other tended to reduce contractual problems and especially financial management problems. Although a high rate of personnel turnover has been as endemic to the Agency as organizational change, there were at least some individuals with experience in dealing with universities in the contracting and auditing branches. Similarly university business officers were becoming more sophisticated in their dealings with the Agency. Furthermore, the mechanism of joint Agency-university participation in periodic contract revisions seemed fairly well established.

Specific changes in regulations and procedures also helped to eliminate potential sources of negative incidents. Passage, after long delays, of legislation modifying the troublesome overhead procedures was particularly important in this regard. Requirements for security clearance of university personnel serving overseas were modified in 1965, implementing a recommendation of the *Gardner Report*. The modification of publication clearance regulations was another product of consultation between the Agency and the university community.

Despite the impact of the *Gardner Report* in informing Agency personnel about the concerns of the university community, at the level of the participating universities there was no fundamental change in attitude towards university contracts. This generalization would apply especially to the contract and technical officers most responsible for day-to-day decision-making in the contracting area.[63] However, there was little of the overt hostility characteristic of the period of retrenchment and procedural improvements plus the higher priority of university contracts tended to smooth the operational aspects of contract administration.

The years from 1962 through 1966 were not only years of relative harmony, they were also years of optimism on the part of both Agency and university officials. It seemed as if the university-contract program had "come of age" and that this improvement was likely to continue.[64] However, there were a number of reasons why this optimism needed qualification.

First, many of the problems which the program had faced arose outside of the Agency, especially in Congress and in the universities themselves. The structure and dominant values of these institutions were unlikely to change rapidly, regardless of transient developments in the Agency. Second, at the end of the period of harmony, there was nothing to indicate that the high priority of the university-contract program and other more diffuse aspects of Bell's philosophy had been institutionalized in the Agency. Clearly, many of the favorable conditions for Agency-university relations could be altered by an administrator with different views. This leads to the third point. Bell was succeeded by his deputy, a respected practitioner of foreign aid with long experience in the Agency. Mr. Gaud apparently shared Bell's philosophy to a considerable degree, though the two men differed in personal style. However, there was certainly no valid reason for predicting that future administrators would be respected by the university community and favorably disposed towards university contracting. Conditions leading to the appointment of a conservative administrator like Hollister, a flamboyant administrator like Stassen or a passive administrator like Smith or Riddleberger could easily be imagined.

The improvement in relations during the period of harmony was probably not a "natural" consequence of the developments which preceded it. Nor was there any reason to believe that deterioration might not again occur in another period of retrenchment.

PART II

Persistent Issues, Environmental Constants and Behavioral Patterns

AN ANALYSIS OF STABILITY AND CHANGE IN AGENCY-UNIVERSITY RELATIONS

CHAPTER VIII

Persisting and Unresolved Issues

HISTORIANS AND philosophers often state that there is nothing new under the sun. Qualified support for this aphorism may be found in the history of Agency-university relations. As other observers have noted, sixteen years of day-to-day activity in university contracting have produced discernible patterns, but they tend to be cyclical rather than evolutionary. The analogy between the university-contract program and a maturing organism, which is suggested by many scholars and participants, has been greatly overdrawn.

It will be useful, initially, to review the findings with respect to changes in Agency-university relations from 1950 to 1966. Agency-university relations at the level of the university community changed considerably during the different periods; however, there was no direct or necessary relationship between these changes and changes at the level of the participating universities. During the period of inertia for example, relations at the university community level improved greatly. Communications between Agency officials and high university administrators increased and each side became more aware of the problems and concerns of the other. However, the effect on actual project operations was relatively insignificant. Few of the basic issues discussed at the CIPA conferences were actually resolved; in fact, Agency personnel who participated had little power to change the direction of Agency activity. Deterioration during the interregnum was slight, primarily because the period was relatively short and new initiatives undertaken in university contracting did not reach the level of actual project operations.

A particularly striking phenomenon is the points of similarity which exist between the period of inertia and the period of harmony. These similarities provide the basis for the rather gloomy prognosis at the end of Chapter VII. To be sure, a gifted and personable administrator was able to promote rapid improvement in relations at the university community level and, by informing his subordinates and raising the priority of the program, to promote improvement at the level of the participating universities as well. However, it was surprising to examine reports and talk to low level Agency and university personnel during this period and find that the same old problems continued to be raised for discussion. By the end of the period of harmony, Agency and university personnel had, in many instances, established better working relationships, seemed to understand one another's problems and were simply able to get along better. But it was apparent that there had been little progress toward resolving certain basic divisive issues which had led to negative incidents, especially at operating levels, over the years. The few issues which had been completely resolved involved irritating, but peripheral "boilerplate" matters.

The persistence of these basic divisive issues is surprising, even puzzling, when one examines the history of the university-contract program. For there has been an awareness of their existence and the need to resolve them since the very early years. The statements and recommendations of the NASULGC in 1953, the CIPA in the late 1950's and the International Rural Development Conference in 1964 differ in tone and in scope, but all are addressed to essentially the same concerns. The ubiquity of these concerns is one of the most significant patterns to emerge from this study. Moreover, a focus on these persistent, but unresolved issues leads to other highly stable but latent characteristics of the program which have been of great significance in determining the form of Agency-university relations.

Before turning to these characteristics, however, the issues themselves must be examined in detail.

Five Persisting and Unresolved Issues

The basic divisive issues of the university-contract program share a common concern, in brief, the question of *who shall decide*. The participating universities have argued for considerable autonomy with regard to the conduct of their projects. This view has been based on the deeply felt belief that the Agency has no "right" to "interfere" where the university has "special competence," especially in matters involving "academic freedom." Furthermore, proponents of the university "side" have maintained that when the Agency does retain decision-making authority over detailed aspects of project operations, its personnel frequently make the wrong decision or, for long periods of time, make no decision at all. The Agency position has been based on the belief that the university should not have final authority to make decisions affecting U.S. foreign policy interests or national security. Some Agency officials would go further and add that university personnel would act irresponsibly were they given the autonomy which they desire. Indeed, some justification may be found for this viewpoint in the history of the university-contract program. Agency officials also maintain that they are constrained by legislation regarding the latitude which they can grant to a contractor and that frequently the requests of university representatives fail to take this into account. In examining the more specific issues with which this study will be concerned, it is helpful to keep this very basic difference between the two parties in mind.

The Issue of "Equal Partnership"

"Equal partnership" is one of the slogans used to describe certain aspects of the program since the early days of university participation. Moreover, the development of equal partnership has been a central and often expressed concern of university representatives. However, when one gets down to specifics (as Agency representatives are fond of saying), the concept becomes very difficult to define. Perhaps the closest definition is: *a relationship similar to that which is perceived by university officials to exist between the Land-Grant universities and the Department of Agriculture under the provisions of the Morrill Act (and supporting legislation).* This somewhat cumbersome explication expresses the longing of the university officials for the simpler problems, closer personal ties and more flexible financial arrangements which have characterized their very productive domestic programs of research and extension supported by USDA.

The idea of fair play (in terms of the values of the academic community) is also incorporated in the partnership idea. In the interviews for this study, the ideal of equal partnership was often invoked by university personnel when they were criticizing an Agency policy or set of activities which particularly displeased them. An example from a discussion of contracting procedures during the period of retrenchment illustrates this point:

> The university [representatives] felt, particularly as a result of meetings when campus coordinators would get together and compare notes, that the Agency tended to act quite capriciously in their dealings with the universities. The universities had just to go in and each get the best deal for themselves. *This was not the idea of equal partnership.* The university [representatives] felt that both parties to the contract should want to do what was right and fair and the universities should not be subsequently penalized because they had failed to read some portion of the small print on their contract.[1]

High Agency officials have also occasionally invoked "equal partnership," usually in speeches or presentations before the university community when they were attempting to promote favorable attitudes towards the Agency. For example, David Bell, in his highly successful address before the International Rural Development Conference, spoke of a *partnership* between AID, USDA and the universities as "essential to develop a solid program" and expressed his hope that a *"true partnership* might gradually evolve."[2] Similar passages may be found in the speeches of Henry G. Bennett, Harold Stassen, James Smith and others.

Personnel at lower levels of the Agency, however, use this term with great reluctance and observe, with good reason, that it seems to mean whatever the universities want it to mean. If partnership means equal participation in decisions, as Bell and others have implied, it is still necessary to specify the areas of decision-making to which this principle is to be applied, and who, representing the university community side of the "partnership," will participate. It is in this process of specification that difficulties arise. The primacy of the Agency in certain areas is generally accepted by the universities. Legislation defines its primacy rather specifically in other areas. Thus, the persistence of the "equal partnership" issue is primarily a manifestation of university dissatisfaction with specific problems which can be discussed more usefully in other terms. If these problems could be resolved, it is probable that "equal partnership" would become a dead issue.

The Issue of University Autonomy Versus Agency Control

This is the aspect of the "who will decide" question which particularly applies to day-to-day project operations. The point of contention is the kind of decisions for which each party should be responsible. Should the Agency merely define the "broad goals" of the project and allow the university complete autonomy in determining the means by which they are attained? Should it exercise rigid control in some areas (e.g., financial management and personnel selection) where it has special responsibilities and not in others (e.g., advising on curricula for the host institution) where the university has "special competence?" These kinds of questions are not easily resolved and broad guidelines, agreed upon by the Agency and the university community, have often provided little real guidance in specific instances.

Herbert Simon's concept of a "hierarchy of goals and means" is useful in thinking about this problem.[3] A hierarchy of goals includes one relatively broad goal (e.g., improve the quality of education at university A . . .), and a set of intermediate goals which link the specific activities to be performed to the broad goal. If the high level goals in the hierarchy are defined in operational terms, then the elements of the hierarchy will be closely linked together: the higher level goals (ends) will determine the lower level goals and activities (means). In abstract terms, the problem of autonomy versus control is simply this: If control is exercised over the implementation of lower level goals without due regard for higher level goals, decisions are likely to result which are harmful for the latter. This is exactly what happens, university representatives argue, when the Agency involves itself in relatively low level decisions which the universities are better able to carry out themselves (or so they claim). As shall be seen, however, Agency representatives often view the problem in very different perspective. It must be remembered that they are governed by different broad goals than the university personnel. Thus their requirements for "control" are based on a somewhat different set of premises. Moreover, usually neither set of broad goals is very clearly defined. Thus, when brought down to specifics, this issue has often proved to be frustrating and virtually intractable.

It must be emphasized that the *idea* of university autonomy has not been opposed within the Agency. In fact, many Agency officials, including almost every administrator from Bennett to Bell, have endorsed it, at least in principle. But this type of endorsement has not resolved the very real problems with which operating personnel have had to deal.

The history of university contracting, almost from the beginning, reveals the pervasive, long-term character of this issue. The desires of university officials for autonomy and their objections to close control have been documented in project reports, published studies and *Proceedings* of CIPA and NASULGC conferences. Readers will recall from Chapter III that as early as 1953, the Agency was advised by the NASULGC Senate that "overconcentration of administrative control by federal agencies in the field has resulted in delay, frustration and inefficiency."[4] Eleven years later, a working group of the International Rural Development Conference focused on exactly the same issue, though the university viewpoint was expressed in somewhat more positive terms:

> AID should not contract with a university unless it has confidence in not only the university's integrity but also in its administrative ability to carry out agreed upon project responsibilities. Given confidence, maximum administrative responsibility should be vested with the university in the field. The mission should encourage this basic principle and be prepared to use its administrative resources to serve and complement those of the university. . . .[5]

Another statement illustrating this issue comes from a 1956 project annual report which summarized clearly the prevailing view that the university should be responsible for determining the means by which broad project goals would be attained:

> . . . from the educational point of view, a far more effective job could be done by the Contractor if he had greater freedom of action. . . .
>
> Would it be unreasonable to suggest, even at this late date, that ICA/Washington eliminate its present close controls, especially in the case of educational decisions and limit its efforts to the selection of reputable institutions to render the desired educational services

and to the approval of a suitable contract governing the proposed operations. Where sufficient care has been given to the selection of the institution should the university be hampered by Washington decisions concerning matters of an educational nature.[6]

Perhaps the *Gardner Report* is correct in its somewhat ambiguous statement that "the nearest we can come to . . . a formula [for resolving this conflict] is the assertion that universities functioning overseas should enjoy the maximum *reasonable* degree of autonomy."[7] Mr. Gardner maintains that since "sensible" officials have demonstrated that they *can* agree as to the meaning of "reasonable," the solution, in the long run, will depend on "a systematic attempt to staff AID field missions with men of high professional caliber, well equipped by background and training to deal with the universities and a similar attempt by universities to ensure that senior members of field parties be of proven judgment and stability as well as professional competence"[8] rather than on changes in doctrine. There can be no doubt that stable, professionally competent individuals will be better able to cope with difficult situations than individuals deficient in these qualities, all other things being equal. But highly competent officials may disagree more bitterly than incompetent ones when they are basing their positions regarding an issue on fundamentally different premises. Thus, in order to resolve the issue of autonomy versus control the underlying factors which have contributed to its persistence may require alteration. Many of these factors have nothing to do with the competence of the personnel involved. Chapter X will discuss the reasons why the resolution of this and other issues requires much more than having the "right man in the right place at the right time."

The Issue of Contractual Form

Undoubtedly, the greatest number of disagreements between the Agency and the participating universities have been focused on the contract itself. The fundamental question involved is: through what type of a legal instrument can the relationship between the Agency and a university be most appropriately formalized and institutionalized. Concerns related to the financial management aspect of project operations have been the major complicating factors. Universities need money to perform their technical assistance functions; the Agency needs to predict, control and justify its expenditures.

Of course, the issue of contractual form cannot be neatly separated from the issue of autonomy versus rigid control. In a sense, the problems related to the first issue are simply one aspect of those related to the second. However, the contractual issue is more closely related to questions of legal procedures while the autonomy issue is more closely related to what might be called the basic doctrine of technical assistance project operations. In examining contractual matters, it is also necessary to differentiate between questions relating to the contract itself, and questions relating to the organizational arrangements within the Agency for dealing with contract actions. Considerable attention has been devoted to the history of this issue above; hence a brief summary will serve to recall the major points of the discussion.

During the early years of the program, there was little in the way of an established form for the contract document. Even the parties to the contract differed for different projects. In general, TCA-negotiated contracts were patterned after those which had been used in IIAA and OFAR technical assistance projects.[9] ECA–MSA contracts tended to closely resemble ECA contracts for administering projects in Europe involving major capital construction work by U.S. commercial organizations.[10] Following the reorganization of August 1953, FOA contract officers tended to negotiate contracts which conformed more closely to the ECA–MSA format; however, no attempt was made to alter the form of the contracts previously written by other agencies. There was no Agency-wide contracting doctrine or central office for dealing with contract matters. Contracts were negotiated on an ad hoc basis for each project.[11]

The difficulties resulting from this arrangement have been discussed in Chapter IV. Some universities felt that they were not receiving "equal pay for equal work" and that the Agency officials were behaving in a "capricious" manner with regard to their contract negotiations. Agency negotiators, on the other hand, who often had little familiarity with the rather unique folkways of university administration, felt that they were merely carrying out their responsibility to "protect" the government.

The development of a "standard" university contract was mostly a consequence of university dissatisfaction. A concurrent development, the establishment of the Office of Contract Relations, reflected more general Agency-wide concerns. Both changes created almost as many problems as they solved. If the Office of Contract Relations had been properly staffed, and if the university-contract program had occupied a somewhat higher priority during the first year that the office was in existence, the hostility which developed between university representatives and Agency contracting officials could have been lessened. However, certain basic areas of disagreement would have arisen, regardless of the organizational arrangements within the Agency, so long as "contract specialists" were assigned decision-making responsibilities for contract-related matters. It will be useful to quote from some of the studies which have explored the contractual issue, in order to examine the problem in a little more detail.

The reader will recall that the development of the 1957 version of the "standard contract" was a cooperative effort initiated by CIPA. A committee of university business officers evaluated the new instrument as ". . . a workable document that places responsibility for our programs precisely where it belongs, squarely on the contractors." "Many of the problem areas which we believe have been resolved," the committee reported, "have existed since the first contracts were negotiated back in the early days of ECA."[12] However, several years later, university representatives and other observers were still directing some of their bitterest criticisms against the contract itself (which by this time had undergone several revisions). Stanley Andrews reported in 1961 that:

> The contract itself is totally unfitted and unsatisfactory as an arrangement to promote the maximum use of resources, people, imagination and initiative upon the part of universities as institutions and the people who work in them are concerned. The present contract is a simple purchase order, designed, it seems, to buy so many packages of pencils or man hours to go through so many motions and bring forth predetermined results which can be recorded by a government auditor and an IBM machine. This, of course, is the sheerest sort of misconception of what the contract system is all about.[13]

Andrews concluded his assessment with the observation that "most of the trouble on the contracts is American made and American exported."[14]

The *Glick Report* (1961) was specifically concerned with the administration of contract projects involving both universities and commercial organizations. It noted a number of specific defects ranging from salary approvals to procurement procedures.[15] Again, the emphasis was on the delays caused by rigid procedures. The report observed that "the 'standard provisions' create needless problems and delays by requiring numerous written prior approvals before the contractor can take action." The report also commented on the air of mutual hostility which seemed to characterize negotiations between contractor representatives and Agency contract specialists.[16]

There is ample evidence to indicate that this issue was not resolved by the 1961 reorganization. Indeed, following the abolition of the Office of Contract Relations, the problems with which that office had been created to deal began appearing again. The reader will recall the comment of the *McGee Report* that "because the contract operations of the Agency are decentralized throughout four regional bureaus and a contract division at the Washington headquarters, it is almost impossible for anyone within the Agency to ascertain what is occurring in the contracting field until long after the fact."[17] Following the issuance of the *McGee Report*, the powers of the central office were again increased. But two years later, the *Gardner Report* observed that "conflicts resulting from contract administration have been the most persistent irritants in the AID-university relationship"[18] and a year after that, the topic of "Contractual Arrangements" was one of the four major concerns to which the International Rural Development Conference addressed itself.[19]

Following the conference, there was another round of committee work and discussions, this time directed by Dr. Auburn's Office, which produced still another revision of the standard contract. Both university and Agency personnel reacted favorably to the new document. However, when the history of the program was viewed in perspective, it seemed unlikely that issues would be fully resolved or that this would be the last revision.

Why Not A Grant?

One body of opinion argues that it is impossible to develop any sort of a contract instrument which will meet the operational requisites of Agency-university technical assistance projects. Individual scholars, university representatives and special committees, usually representing the "university side" have repeatedly recommended that university technical assistance projects be funded on a grant rather than a contract basis.[20] The procedures of USDA, the National Science Foundation and the Atomic Energy Commission are pointed to as examples. Agency representatives have, in general, opposed this arrangement, arguing that overseas programs are fundamentally different from the grant-type programs cited as examples.

It is doubtful whether the foreign assistance legislation, as it is presently written, would permit an arrangement such as is envisioned by proponents of this idea, even if sufficient support could be generated for it within the Agency. Whether the instrument through which funds for university projects are provided is called a "contract" or a "grant" is not going to make much difference with regard to specific questions of financial management and administrative control. The Agency representatives who discussed this question maintained almost unanimously that it was essentially a "dead" issue. Probably, specific concerns of legal form and procedure can be discussed more meaningfully in other terms; however, there is little doubt that there are concerns in this area which still remain, in a very real sense, open questions.

The Issue of Project Length

How long should a project continue? When and under what conditions should it be discontinued? Whose viewpoint should carry the heaviest weight in making these decisions, and why? These are some of the questions relating to the length of projects over which the Agency and participating universities continue to have major disagreements. Although there are instances in which a university has discontinued a project over Agency objections, this has been a relatively infrequent occurrence.[21] The major cause of negative incidents has been the divergent views in those situations where Agency representatives discontinued, or attempted to discontinue a project over the objections of the participating university.

The Agency is not empowered to negotiate contracts for a longer period than three years.[22] The complex budgeting and programming cycle is, of course, an annual one. Certain decisions *must be made* every year or every three years by the responsible personnel in the Agency. The persistent character of this issue is explained, in part, by this situation.

It will be useful to illustrate the types of problems which arise and the typical arguments which are presented by each side with two examples, project A and project B. Project A was a "sisterhood" relationship between a U.S. university and a small "Land-Grant model" institution. The host institution was founded as a result of the project which, by the end of the period of harmony, had run almost fourteen years and was still in operation. In general, the performance of the U.S. university was regarded as highly satisfactory. Competent team members had been provided, mostly from the home campus faculty and smooth working relationships existed between team members and host country faculty and officials. In 1966, the project was still regarded by some observers as one of the most successful in the program.

However, during the periods of interregnum and harmony, the pressures from the Agency to discontinue the project became increasingly severe. The facts of the situation were that despite the length of the project, U.S. faculty members were still taking an active role in the day-to-day functioning of the institution rather than just acting as advisors. Moreover, the institution had been slow to develop its own faculty; many graduates and participant trainees had taken more lucrative positions in government or commercial enterprises rather than accepting teaching positions. Thus, in one sense at least, the institution was clearly not self-sustaining. On the basis of these facts, Agency officials urged that the project be discontinued. The presence of U.S. faculty members had prevented the host institution from "standing on its feet," they argued, and thus the U.S. institution had not attained its primary objecive. The cessation of assistance would make host country personnel assume responsibility and would also free funds for more valuable enterprises. The university officials (supported by host government officials) accepted the premises of the argument (i.e., that the institution was not self-sustaining) but reached exactly opposite conclusions. Reasonable progress had been made, they argued, given conditions in the host country, but the needs for further assistance were still great. Moreover, it was just silly to think that a university could be created from scratch in a few years. Without further assistance, not only would existing needs not be met but much of the investment of past years would be lost.

Project A was not discontinued. However, its continuation was due to the fact that regional bureau and mission personnel were repeatedly overruled, primarily because of political considerations. Obviously this did not change the opinions of the officials concerned, nor did it increase the friendliness of their attitudes toward the U.S. university.

In project B, a multi-purpose "sisterhood" arrangement between a major Land-Grant university and a somewhat similar institution in the host country, the Agency was successful in its efforts to discontinue assistance. The project's life was about eight years, and the reaction of the U.S. university was quite bitter. Typical arguments for continuing assistance were presented in the campus coordinator's final report. First, it was alleged that continued assistance would be necessary to consolidate progress already achieved:

> ... [U.S. university] advisers in their final reports have pointed out without exception that substantial progress has been made to date in all contract fields but that further assistance is desperately needed if the gains which have been made under the contract are to be consolidated. This point of view seems to be shared by the officials of the [host university].[23]

The U.S. university also argued from a broader perspective, claiming that alternative uses of funds would be less productive than continuation of the project:

> ... [Host country] at present has substantial unemployment. Construction projects and other types of economic aid might assist in relieving this situation to some extent. However [host country] lacks an adequate supply of individuals trained to the professional level in critical areas of agriculture, engineering, medicine and public administration. The [U.S. university] is convinced that only through further assistance to higher education can this deficiency be overcome.[24]

Agency officials in the field mission and in Washington took a very different view. Obviously the university would like to continue its work, they observed, but when viewed in broader perspective it was clear that discontinuation would better serve the total needs of the host country and the host university. The

Agency's position was summarized in a letter from a high official to the academic vice president of the U.S. university:

> Maintenance of a large scale technical assistance program of an essentially indefinite duration, as seems implied by [campus coordinator's] thinking might well,—in the light of our extensive experience with university programs and in our judgment now—have a counter-productive effect. The mission in [host country] with full ICA Washington suport, is making a renewed attempt to press for the assumption of increasing initiative by [host country citizens] and [host country] institutions with respect to all joint U.S.-[host country] programs. It is important to our larger purposes in this respect, and to the lasting success of the [host institution] project itself that the university look to the consolidation of its gains.[25]

Four years later, there still was no valid way of comparing the merits of the two cases to evaluate the decision which was made. The host institution had encountered serious problems, but was slowly resolving them (partially with foundation support). On the other hand, the over-all program of aid in the host country had been highly successful.

Two rather typical examples of situations which have actually occurred were chosen because an attempt to describe the number of incidents where this issue has arisen in general terms would probably confuse rather than clarify matters. However, two tentative general observations regarding project length are suggested by this study:

(1) Viewed from the perspective of the individual project and assuming that the performance of the U.S. university has been satisfactory according to the standards developed by the Agency for measuring such performance, projects should in general be permitted to run for a relatively long period of time, probably ten or more years. The literature dealing with technical assistance is nearly unanimous on this point. Several experienced persons interviewed for this study expressed the opinion that in order for a project to "take hold" in a country, assistance should be planned for twenty or more years. The "university side" tends to argue for projects of relatively long duration. Furthermore, Agency officials seem generally sympathetic to this point of view, at least in private.

(2) The status of the individual project is usually a minor consideration in the Agency's decision to discontinue it. Agency

officials must consider factors which are usually relatively unimportant to the representatives of the participating university including the total level of funding for a country, the attitudes of Congressional committees and the claims of competing projects. As a project continues over a period of time, the very fact of its duration appears to lower its priority in comparison with other concerns. Agency representatives have argued that once a project has been initiated, it is extremely difficult to close it out, regardless of the actual situation in the field. It would appear, however, that this characteristic, which of course tends to be prevalent in all bureaucratic enterprises, is mitigated by the three-year limit on the length of contracts and the requirements of the budgetary cycle. Often the administrative costs of extending a contract are far greater than those of discontinuing it.

There is still another factor which can lead to complications. Sometimes, ranking university officials associate continuation of a project with the prestige of their institution. While this is less important than many Agency officials believe, cases have occurred where political pressure was brought to bear on the Agency to continue a project even where the university's own field team supported the Agency position. When this prestige factor is operative, the resolution of divergent views on the length of a project becomes even more difficult.

To the degree that these observations are correct, they suggest some of the reasons why this issue has often been perplexing and irritating and why it has persisted for so many years. There is simply no common frame of reference for decisions about the length of projects. Agency and university officials frequently "talk past" one another because of their different values and objectives. Where this situation exists, only an exceptional level of communication and mutual understanding can prevent the occurrence of negative incidents, characterized by real bitterness and ill feeling.

Personnel Clearance: A Partially Resolved Persistent Issue

In 1964, John Gardner observed that "there is no issue more sensitive than that of personnel clearance. It generates as much or more controversy than any other question in the university-AID relationship. There are two aspects of the problem that concern the universities and AID—security clearance and professional clearance."[26]

Since that observation was made, the problem of security clearance, which Gardner regarded as the more difficult, has been largely resolved. Manual order 610:2, "Security Clearance for Contractors and Contractor Personnel Under AID-Financed Contracts" issued in December 1965, designated all overseas contract employee positions as "non-sensitive" with the exception of chiefs of party and other employees requiring access to classified material. Since this change, usually the chief of party has been the only university representative who must submit to the long, detailed background investigation. Thus a major source of friction has been eliminated, at least for the moment. The reimposition of more stringent requirements by Congress must, of course, always be considered a possibility.

The other problem, professional clearance, has two aspects. The first is the delays involved in the clearance process. In a 1967 survey numerous university officials reported this as a major "relationship problem" with AID.[27] Even with the most exceptional candidates, a process which requires clearance from AID officials, both in Washington and in the field, and host government officials is inevitably a tortuous one. When delays do occur, the fulfillment of planned commitments is often impeded, and the persons involved become irritated about bureaucratic "red tape." Probably little can be done to correct this since it is unlikely that any of the parties to the contract is going to relinquish all "clearance" authority.

The second and more fundamental aspect of the problem arises when the Agency exercises its authority to reject a potential university appointee. Such action, viewed with extreme disfavor by universities, rarely occurs simply because of the sensitivities involved. However, experienced Agency officials have observed that they would like to control the selection of team members more closely than they do. They argue that while there is no question that the university should be the sole judge of the *professional* competence of its team members, this is not really the point at issue. The qualifications which make a superior member of a university department are not necessarily those which lead to success overseas. Unfortunately the Agency has not been able to develop a well-documented set of criteria defining such qualifications. On the other hand, university officials tend to reject the Agency's right to exercise control over personnel selection as a matter of principle. Once again, vaguely defined criteria and conflicting values and objectives seem to be the heart of the matter.

Conclusion

The persistence of the *same* issues of controversy between the Agency and participating universities has been amply demonstrated. What has not been demonstrated is why this should be the case. Unfortunately, each side has tended to suspect the motives, competence and in some cases even the honesty of the other. The history of Agency-university relations suggests, however, that the causes of these disagreements have had little relationship to specific projects, universities or individuals. They have been caused by factors which were essentially outside of the control of the individuals who were most immediately involved. The remainder of this study will be concerned with identifying these factors and assessing their significance.

CHAPTER IX

Historical Patterns and Individual Behavior: A Framework for Analysis

WHY HAVE divisive issues persisted despite policy, personnel and organizational changes, and the recommendations of analytic studies specifically aimed at resolving them? Why have the best efforts of competent and dedicated men in the Agency, the university community and the participating universities been so frequently unsuccessful in eliminating disharmony? As has been seen, a number of factors seem related to this phenomenon, for example, Congressional attitudes, the dominant norms and values of the university community, the lack of concrete knowledge about technical assistance and the characteristics of the budgetary process. However, the connections between these factors and the activities of the many individuals who have participated in the contract program—Agency officials, faculty members and university administrators—are often unclear.[1]

Historical Patterns

The type of historical patterns which have been identified (i.e., persisting issues) are merely abstractions which categorize the activities of large numbers of individuals over time. It is said that a pattern exists where it is discerned that many different individuals acted in a similar way when presented with certain problems or decision-making situations. For example, despite organizational changes, the involvement of diverse individuals and the idiosyncracies of projects and participating universities, the behavior of Agency contract officers regarding certain issues of contractual form was usually very different from that of university representatives. Indeed, this is essentially what is meant by a persisting and unresolved issue.

What are the reasons making it possible to associate particular types of behavior with particular organizational ties? Why did particular patterns emerge as individuals in different situations chose among possible alternatives? Of course, the reasons for a particular individual's particular decision in a given situation cannot be identified using the approach of this study. It seems reasonable to assume, however, that if a large number of individuals have behaved in essentially the same way in an organizational setting, many of the factors influencing that behavior were non-idiosyncratic. But if explanations are to be presented in these terms, it must also be assumed that individuals *in general* tend to behave in the same way in the types of settings and situations under investigation. This assumption provides the necessary linkage between the external factors which seem to lead to patterned behavior and the behavior itself.

Individual Behavior in Organizational Settings

Before looking at common behavioral attributes, it will be useful to formulate a general way of describing the setting or environment in which behavior occurs.

In this framework, the setting of behavior comprises two basic elements, *decision or task situations* and *goals*. For an individual a situation arises whenever in the course of his official duties, he must choose among alternatives or undertake a set of activities to accomplish a given task. The alternatives which are posed for his consideration by external sources or which he chooses to consider are also part of the situation. So is the information which he has about the different consequences of alternatives. Of course, any individual in an organization may face a multiplicity of situations during his daily activities. However, it is possible to focus on a relatively small number of these for purposes of analyzing a particular phenomenon.

Attributes of Goals

The goals which influence behavior in a setting will require a little more discussion because the relationship among different types of influential goals is crucial to this analysis. A goal is a desired outcome or state of affairs. But individuals are rarely affected by just one goal. In a given situation they will most often have to choose not only among alternatives, but also among goals. In order to understand the conditions and consequences of choice in situations where there are several, not necessarily complementary goals, it will be useful to define certain general attributes of goals which can be used to draw distinctions between them.

The first attribute of goals which will be defined is *level of generality*. This notion ties in with the idea of a hierarchy of goals which was introduced earlier. The reader will recall that the elements of a hierarchy of goals are a very general goal at the top of the hierarchy and increasing numbers of more specific goals at lower levels. At the bottom of the hierarchy are activities which are actually performed, or could be performed. Specifically, the level of generality of a goal refers to the number of different types of activities which are relevant to its attainment. Within a single relatively simple and relatively well-defined hierarchy, the generality of goals can be compared fairly easily. As things become more complicated, comparisons become more difficult but also less important. For example, the goal to improve the faculty at university X would be more general than the goal to improve the faculty in the department of poultry science at university X. The second goal would be an intermediate goal or sub-goal in the hierarchy of goals defined by the first.

The second attribute of goals is *specificity*. A goal is specific to the degree that a valid indicator exists for determining whether or not the goal has been (or is being) attained. The degree of specificity, then, is the degree of validity of the indicator.[2] For example, in business enterprises, indicators of the degree to which the goal, "profitable operation," is being attained are usually valid and reliable. Certainly this goal is more measurable than most of the goals governing university-contract operations such as "institutional viability" or "promotion of agricultural development."

The third attribute of goals is *operationality*. Abstractly, this refers to the clarity with which the linkages in a hierarchy of goals are specified. However, this definition is not very helpful in looking at the university-contract program. More concretely, a goal is operational for a particular individual to the degree that he knows how it can be attained. Given a considerable degree of knowledge, he will be able to choose the best alternatives or course of action in a particular situation quite easily. If the goal is less operational, the choice will be more difficult. In the area of technical assistance, the general goals which govern many projects are not very operational.

The final attribute is *importance*.[3] For any individual in a setting, some goals will be more important than others. His behavior will be an indication of this when he has to choose among alternatives which affect different goals in different ways. However, often the relative importance of goals will be less significant in determining choice than might be imagined. In terms of a given set of alternatives, goals will often be non-comparable, that is, not equally operational. Under these conditions, the relative operationality of goals becomes much more significant than the relative importance.

In a choice situation with multiple goals, the goals can be either *complementary, conflicting* or *neutral* with respect to one another. This is probably quite clear intuitively; however, because of the importance of these distinctions, they will be examined in more detail. When goals are complementary, the choice of alternatives contributing to the attainment of one goal contributes to the attainment of complementary goals as well. Another possibility would be *negative complementarity,* where the consequences of one or more alternatives would affect both goals adversely. Goals are conflicting when the choice must be made among alternatives which have beneficial consequences for one goal and adverse consequences for another. Goals are neutral when the choice of alternatives having beneficial consequences for one, has no discernible effects on the other.

It must be emphasized that it is only possible to talk about the relations of complementarity, conflict or neutrality among goals with regard to particular alternatives. If different alternatives are considered, the relationships among a given group of goals may be quite different. In fact, one important aspect of effective administration is the ability to choose alternatives which maximize the complementarity of relevant goals (or minimize the conflict). Obviously, this is also an important consideration in designing organizations.

Behavioral Characteristics

The discussion to this point has presented certain general characteristics of the settings in which behavior occurs. To complete the picture some general behavioral attributes must be considered. Before proceeding, however, it should be remembered that the justification for this approach is that patterns have already been identified. Thus, the assumption that the individuals concerned followed a more or less common set of rules in making their choices is not only a necessary link between similar settings and similar activities, it is also an intuitively reasonable approach.[4]

In this discussion, the major assumption about behavior is that it is purposeful, or in other words, intendedly rational.[5] For example, an individual, given several alternatives in a setting and several relevant goals, will try to choose the alternatives which seem best in terms of relevant goals. He will not deliberately choose alternatives which affect important goals adversely if other possibilities are available. However, his choices must often be made on the basis of incomplete information under serious time pressures. In the foreign policy area especially, decisions made on the basis of incomplete information often seem much better than no decisions at all. *Satisficing behavior,* a term initially developed by Herbert Simon, will be used to describe the way that individuals cope with this type of problem.[6] The term satisficing was coined to emphasize the difference between assumptions made by Simon regarding administrative behavior and the assumption of rationality which is used by economists.[7]

An individual who satisfices chooses alternatives which are satisfactory or "good enough." He makes his choices using a simple picture of the situation that takes into account only the few factors that he regards as most relevant and crucial.[8] Simon draws two implications from the idea of satisficing which are particularly relevant for this discussion. He summarizes these points as follows:

Historical Patterns and Individual Behavior 163

(1) High level goals provide little guide for action because it is difficult to measure the degree of their attainment and because it is difficult to measure the effects of concrete actions upon them. The broad goals . . . are thus not operative.

(2) Decisions tend to be made, consequently, in terms of the highest level goals that are operative—the most general goals to which action can be related in a fairly definite way and that provide some basis for the assessment of accomplishment. The operative goals provide the kernel around which the administrator's simplified model of the world crystallizes. He considers those matters that are reasonably related to those goals and discounts or ignores others.[9]

Simon's description of satisficing behavior does not use the terminology employed here to describe attributes of goals and the relationships among goals. However, two propositions regarding behavior which do use this terminology can be inferred.

(1) All other things being equal, the more operational goals are the goals which guide satisficing behavior. In other words, if an alternative in a decision situation is viewed as contributing to the attainment of an operational goal, the fact that there may be a less operational conflicting goal affected by that choice will rarely be considered.

(2) The relative importance of conflicting goals will enter into consideration in the decision process only if the goals are equally operational, or nearly so. Otherwise the less operational goals will be perceived as neutral with respect to the more operational.

If, as has been suggested, the choice of alternatives is influenced most strongly by the most operational goals, then the patterns of complementarity, neutrality and conflict among relevant goals are crucial in analyzing the outcomes of organizational activity over time. For the purposive or collective goals of an organization are not the only goals which influence typical choice situations. Individuals will also be influenced by *personal goals* and *organizational maintenance goals*. Often these goals will be both more operational and more important than the specific task objectives which have been promulgated as official policy.

The meaning of personal goals should be intuitively clear. It is assumed that objectives of personal advancement, prestige, security, and remuneration are more or less relevant for every individual, and that they will be taken into account where alternatives seem to affect them in one way or another.

Organizational maintenance goals may require a little more clarification. These goals are important because it is by attaining them that an organization (or organizational unit) maintains a favorable relationship with its environment. A favorable relationship is one which ensures the success, stability and prestige of the organization.[10]

Two further points should be made about personal and organizational maintenance goals. First, though these goals will tend to be complementary, operational and important, they will certainly not be the determining factors for all or even most of the choices which are made. In many task situations, these goals will be neutral; in many others, complementary with organizational goals. Indeed, as has been observed, this is the desirable situation. However, situations will arise where conflicts exist. Here personal and/or organizational maintenance goals will often act as constraints or parameters excluding certain alternatives from consideration. Where severe conflicts exist, i.e., where all of the possible alternatives which seem to contribute to the attainment of the organization's collective goals affect the other types of goals adversely, it is quite possible that an alternative will be chosen which has neutral or even negative consequences for the organizational goal or goals in question.

The second point which should be emphasized is that the observation regarding the importance of personal and organizational maintenance goals is not in any sense intended as a value judgment. Indeed, to assume that an organization could function for very long without a high degree of complementarity between its task objectives, the outcomes which permit it to maintain itself with respect to its environment, and the personal goals of its members seems most unrealistic.

In addition to the conflicts which can arise between the types of goals already identified, conflicts among collective organizational goals may also occur, especially if the organization is a large and complex one. For example, contract specialists were frequently compelled to choose between the objectives of promoting harmony in Agency-university relations and conforming to established interpretations of Federal contracting regulations. Since the university-contract program is a low priority program with rather non-operational goals, it is not surprising that where conflicts have existed, both in the Agency and the universities, other goals have been more influential in shaping the decision process.

One final factor, which will be called a *parameter*, may also influence decision-making in specific situations. A parameter is a rule or procedure—either formal or informal and accepted as authoritative by an individual decision-maker—which specifies that certain alternatives may not be chosen regardless of their relationship to organizational goals. Although other goals may also act in this way, a parameter is unique in that it will probably have no status in any hierarchy of goals which is relevant for the individual. Many of the legislative restrictions imposed on the foreign assistance program by Congress have this characteristic.

Conclusion

It may be useful to outline briefly the way that the framework summarized above is used in Chapter X to analyze the "statics and dynamics" of Agency-university relations. First, the framework directs attention to the goals of the program, especially those intermediate goals most relevant to Agency-university relations. The types of questions raised are, for example: How operational are these goals? How specific and how important are they in comparison with the other goals of the Agency and the universities? What patterns of complementarity and conflict exist with other important goals? What parameters have been imposed which have affected the decision-making process? Clearly the persisting and unresolved issues identified in Chapter VIII have resulted from situations where the objectives of the university-contract program conflicted with other more operational and important goals. Often the complementarity between the organizational maintenance goals of the Agency and the university-contract program has been very low. Similarly there has been a lack of complementarity between the personal goals of university personnel and the university-contract program.

The remainder of the analysis is devoted to identifying the other long-term factors which have contributed to these situations of conflict and lack of complementarity. It should be clear by now that the conclusions are not simple ones, nor do they lead to simple solutions of the problems which the Agency-university relationship has encountered over the years. However, it is believed that this approach does provide a basis for a better understanding of certain aspects of the program which have puzzled participants and analysts alike, especially the phenomena of persisting and unresolved issues.

CHAPTER X

The Statics and Dynamics of Agency-University Relations

DESPITE THE title, this chapter, which attempts to draw the threads of the analysis together, neither achieves, nor even claims to achieve, the type of precision which these physical-science terms might imply. On the other hand, utilization of the framework presented in Chapter IX has resulted in the identification of a number of significant variables and relationships.

The analysis begins by looking again at the university-contract program itself, this time in very broad perspective. The focus is on the operationality, specificity and importance of the goals which have defined the program's objectives and provided guidance for day-to-day decision-making. The procedures for selecting participating universities and the effects of parameters (rules or procedures) are also examined. The program goals have clearly been relatively non-operational and unspecific and have had a low priority in the Agency. Restrictive parameters and ad hoc selection procedures for the participating universities have also affected the program. Moreover, these characteristics have not changed very much during the life of the program. They are the most proximate contributory factors to the persisting and unresolved issues identified in Chapter VIII. However, explanations in terms of institutional and environmental factors would be more interesting. Linkages between these factors and the persistence of disharmony can be established by treating the proximate causes as intervening variables which have themselves been influenced by characteristics of the Agency and the universities. The environments in which these organizations have operated must also be examined.

In Part I, it was noted that organizational and personnel

changes have been endemic in the Agency. Moreover, many of the universities have also altered their administrative structures to cope with international involvements more effectively. But these changes did not significantly reduce the occurrence of negative incidents. Nor did they alter the fact that the operational goals influencing Agency and university personnel were often quite different. This suggests that the factors which determine these conflicting goals have also been relatively stable over time. Environmental characteristics have been particularly significant in this regard.

Many unvarying characteristics of the universities and even the Agency can also be identified. As shall be seen, these characteristics have been the crucial factors in shaping the Agency-university relationship at the level of the participating universities.

Program Goals and Procedures: Proximate Factors Contributing to Disharmony

Five long-term characteristics of the program will be examined under this heading. It will be helpful to begin the discussion by briefly outlining them.

(1) The objectives of university-contract projects have been very vaguely defined, or numerous (and sometimes conflicting) objectives have been defined at very low levels of generalization.

(2) No adequate performance criteria have been established in terms of which the activities of participating universities in the field can be evaluated or one project can be compared with another. There have been no indicators of progress which relate to general goals and are widely accepted.

(3) In comparison with most other Agency activities, university-contract projects have had an extremely low priority. There has been little complementarity between the program and the collective, organizational maintenance and personal goals of Agency personnel.

(4) University-contract projects have been affected by numerous restrictive rules and procedures. These parametric constraints on the decision-making process have excluded alternatives from con-

sideration which might have contributed to the attainment of project goals.

(5) The procedures for selecting participating universities have been, for the most part, ad hoc and unsystematic. The criteria of selection have often had little relation to the requirements of technical assistance projects or the capacity of the particular institution to meet them.

Each of these characteristics (except the last) is suggested by the framework presented in Chapter IX. The use of this framework will be clarified by the more detailed discussion which follows.

Non-Operational Project Goals

The definition of an operational hierarchy of goals for a task or project is the major objective of the planning process. Operational goals not only specify ends to be achieved, they also provide a basis for determining what alternatives (or activities) will be the most appropriate for doing so. Moreover, operational goals provide a reference point in terms of which day-to-day decisions regarding the task or project can be made. Unfortunately, the goals of university-contract projects have been notably deficient in performing these functions.

In the early years, the originators of the university-contract program were guided by the belief that the "Land-Grant experience" could in some way be duplicated overseas. A second objective was simply the recruitment of more competent personnel for technical assistance projects. It was recognized that many highly competent individuals would be unwilling to resign from their university positions to work directly for the Agency, but could be persuaded to participate in technical assistance programs if they could retain their status as university faculty members. Of course, neither of these general objectives, which incidently are still mentioned by Agency and university personnel, provide a sufficient basis for undertaking a particular project or defining its relevant hierarchy of goals. Specific projects have been initiated for a variety of reasons. Sometimes the desires of the host country have been predominant; in other cases, Agency, or U.S. university officials have promoted projects overseas. Projects have been initiated on an ad hoc basis or as elements in a country program. In any case, the implicit goals leading to the negotiation of university contracts have, in general, been highly indeterminate and have provided very little concrete basis for determining what was actually going to happen in the field.

The only place where the goals of a project are given concrete expression (i.e., written down) is in the "objectives" and "operational plan" of the contract. Some Agency officials, particularly technical specialists, have argued that the stated objectives are of little value if one is interested in discovering what actually occurs in the field. Despite the accuracy of this observation, it is nevertheless clear that the statements in the contract do provide the basis for some decisions of particular consequence to Agency-university relations; namely the decisions of officials (especially auditors and contract officers) in the Agency's Washington office.

The problem which arises when "project objectives" are used as a basis for decision is that, although they represent an agreement between the Agency and a participating university about certain low level goals and procedures, they do not reflect a consensus about the project's long-term, high level goals. Since the values and long-term objectives of the Agency and university personnel are often fundamentally different, it is perhaps unrealistic to presume that such consensus could be achieved. However, Agency doctrine requires that some statement of objectives and an operational plan be set forth in detail. Accordingly, the gaps between Agency and university philosophy and objectives are papered over with vague generalities about goals and "agreements" about specific low level activities which do not make relationships to more general goals explicit. For example, a university contract written in 1952 stated:

> In carrying out its obligations under this Agreement the College will:
> (1) Give assistance to the Government of [host country] in the establishment and operation of a college of agriculture.
> (2) Give assistance to the Government of [host country] in the establishment and operation of a country-wide system of agricultural extension services to the people of rural areas.
> (3) Give assistance to the Government of [host country] in the establishment and operation of agricultural research stations.
> (4) Administer such other specific projects and operations and give such other assistance to the government of [host country] in related fields pertaining to the economic development of [host country] as the TCA may request and the College may accept.[1]

In recent years, contracts have become somewhat more detailed in stating what is to be done. However, the goals are still not very operational. For example, a contract written in 1960 stated:

> The general objectives are to expand and strengthen the overall educational program and related operation of the [host university] to meet the rapidly increasing need and demand for professional foresters and trained forestry technicians and to permit the university to provide those services which are expected at a major center of forestry education.
>
> With this general objective as the ultimate goal, this contract seeks specifically to outline procedures and assign responsibilities for the purpose of:
> (1) Modernizing the curriculum
> (2) Improving teaching methods
> (3) Planning and carrying out a policy designed to give increased emphasis to the professional degree course.
> (4) Stimulating research and increasing the number of professional graduates.
> (5) Developing a groundwork for a sound graduate program.
> (6) Enlarging the physical plant.[2]

The difficulty, from the standpoint of making decisions with reference to these "objectives," is that they specify *a process to be performed over time* rather than an *end to be achieved*. This type of statement does not provide a very useful reference point for the behavior of either Agency or university personnel with respect to crucial issues. Consequently, the decisions and activities of both university and Agency personnel tend to be greatly influenced by more operational goals. When they disagree, the degree of difference between the two sides is a reflection of the differences between *these* goals, which may very well have little to do with the specific project.

As has been suggested earlier, disagreements over the length of projects provide particularly relevant examples of this type of problem. Since there is no consensus regarding the end to be achieved (and no statement about such an end in the contract), there is no way of determining whether a contract should run for three, five or twenty-five years which relates specifically to the project itself. University officials, who identify closely with academic goals related to the particular project and may also be motivated by the goal of having *some* project for their institution, will always be able to devise perfectly valid reasons why more should be done. Agency officials, on the other hand, are able to devise equally good reasons, in terms of their perspectives, why more should not be done. If the opposing sides are strongly committed to their points of view, each will perceive the position of the other as "irrational" or worse and real hostility is likely to develop.[3]

Both Agency and university personnel have been aware of the need for careful planning, mutual agreement, and operational goals. In fact, these concerns were specifically considered in the report of Working Group II to the Conference on International Rural Development which was jointly prepared by Agency and university officials.[4] The report emphasized that for a project plan to be meaningful, "it must be cooperatively developed and accepted by [the] concerned parties, be as precise as possible and when implemented through a project agreement, commit performance by the agreeing parties as specified by the plan."[5] The report concluded:

> To the extent that the project plan, thus mutually agreed upon, is precise and accurate in its estimate of requirements and capabilities and is specific in its plans for time phasing and in its proposed magnitude of contributions of efforts, performance by host country and associated administering agents can be evaluated and compliance meaningfully enforced.[6]

Obviously, these recommendations reflected the familiarity of working group members with the disagreements which had arisen in areas where detailed responsibilities, procedures, etc. were not specified, and a desire to avoid the reoccurrence of such disagreements in the future. However, there is some question as to how realistic the group was in its approach to planning requirements. The difficulty lies in the fact that as yet there is no valid theory or model of development process. Knowledge about educational development is especially fragmentary. It seems quite possible that high level project goals are likely to be non-operational by the very nature of the enterprise. If this is the case, regardless of how much attention is devoted to specification of low level tasks and procedures, divisive issues are still likely to arise unless there is a greater degree of complementarity between Agency and university goals in general. Another possibility would be to develop an organizational mechanism which would somehow insulate project operations from some of the more operational and important goals which seem to have detrimental effects. In any case, it is clear that more detailed work plans will not solve the fundamental problems arising from non-operational goals.

Performance Criteria and Evaluation

It has been noted above that relatively general goals may be both non-operational and quite specific. However, the goals related to educational development and institution building do not seem to have this characteristic. The way in which project objectives have been defined has not been conducive to the development of performance indicators which would be accepted as valid by both university and Agency officials.

Part of the difficulty stems from the fact that neither the Agency nor the universities have ever developed effective evaluation procedures for technical assistance projects. The *Lincoln Report*, "Improving AID Evaluation," has studied this problem in detail. Lincoln defines evaluation as "the examination of our experience to provide guidance which can be utilized to improve program execution and to improve program planning."[7] His conclusions (which are confirmed by the interviews for this study) emphasize that there is little utilization of the numerous reports which flow from the field to Washington "to improve planning and execution."

In the program's early years, inadequate feedback and evaluation procedures were a consequence of non-specific, non-operational goals. Later, it might also be said that poor evaluation, by both the universities and the Agency, has contributed to these characteristics. In this regard, Lincoln observes:

> The problem of AID's memory has long been belabored. There always seems to be one or more studies of the problem underway. Every observer takes the position that significant improvement is necessary. The limited progress made to date suggests that either we do not believe that the gains from improvement will be worth the time and effort or that the problem is hopelessly intractable or both.[8]

The lack of effective evaluation is a long-term, indirect cause of divisive issues in a variety of ways; however, a more direct cause is the procedures which the Agency does utilize to check up on contractor performance. Clearly some measure of contractor performance is necessary to "justify" project operations and prove that the Agency is getting its money's worth for contract dollars expended. Congress and the General Accounting Office require this kind of hard data. So do the internal regulatory staff offices of the Agency (Controller and General Counsel) whose procedures are geared to Congressional and GAO concerns. In the absence of specific high level goals, performance criteria are derived from those aspects of project operations which are sufficiently specific to permit some sort of measurement. Consequently, *compliance control* (checks for compliance with legislative and administrative requirements) rather than "evaluation" becomes the basis for measuring contractor performance. Emphasizing this point, the *Bell Report* observes:

> When inadequate technical criteria exist, there is a tendency to substitute conformity with administrative and fiscal procedures for evaluation of substantive performance.[9]

Stanley Andrews puts it even more strongly:

> There is a tendency to evaluate progress in the institution by the number of buildings erected, commodities brought in, and the number of trips made or persons seen. This heavy emphasis on detailed figures on everything from lead pencils to scrap paper, not only takes an inordinate amount of time, but completely misses the point that the building of people in the institution is far more significant than the equipping of buildings. There appears to be no criteria for judging programs in terms of the building up of the competence and the stature of the host country people who will man the established institution once the contract people move on.[10]

The question of evaluation is closely related to the issue of autonomy. Because of the necessity to measure *something* which the contractor is doing, Agency personnel are most reluctant to assent to demands for "flexibility" in those relatively specific areas where performance criteria can be established. Furthermore, the need to make regular reports regarding these matters means that greater emphasis is placed upon them than on those less specific but, in the eyes of the university representatives, more important aspects of project operations about which reports are not required. It is not surprising that for Agency officials the "goals" of a project become *those things which can be measured.* However, university faculty members often see things very differently. So long as the Agency is required to produce "measurable" results, and the hierarchies of goals related to educational development and institution building are relatively non-specific, the differences of viewpoint between Agency and university personnel regarding performance criteria and evaluation are likely to persist; so are the negative incidents which result from these differences.

The Low Priority of the University-Contract Program

Although there have been minor fluctuations in the relative importance of the university-contract program in comparison with other Agency activities, throughout its history it has been a low priority concern. Only the period of proliferation is an exception, and even Harold Stassen did not devote anything like a major portion of his time to university-contract matters. Regardless of official pronouncements, this situation is not going to change unless the U.S. foreign assistance program is altered fundamentally. It is difficult to relate low priority to any specific issue or incident, but probably no single factor has been a greater underlying cause of disagreements between Agency and participating university personnel.

Given the fact that foreign assistance is a large and complex operation and that accordingly, the Agency is a large and complex organization, the reasons for the significance of the priority factor are not difficult to see. All of the goals and activities associated with the diverse programs under the Agency's purview are, in one sense, conflicting and competitive. Each makes demands on a finite amount of resources, time as well as money. As suggested above, the degree of complementarity with organizational maintenance goals is important in determining priority. This consideration is often neglected by university personnel when they make demands on the Agency. However, it can never be forgotten by the often harassed and over-worked Agency personnel. They are reminded of it every year during the annual authorization/appropriations process. Particular emphasis was placed upon this point in the discussion of the inordinate (from the standpoint of the universities) delays in contract-related decision-making which occurred during the periods of retrenchment and inertia. However, the observations about these periods are applicable, although perhaps to a lesser degree, to the Agency's entire history.

The matter of priority is especially relevant to the central issue of university autonomy versus Agency control. From the perspective of Agency personnel, granting the autonomy which the universities demand means doing things differently, departing from established norms and procedures, seeking additional information rather than merely accepting that which is provided in the course of day-to-day operations. All of these things take time and are, in this sense, costly for the Agency. In the past, the returns for these "costs," in terms of the Agency's important goals, have been small.

The matter of personnel competence is also significant. It has often been observed that "good people" are more important than "good organization" in operating programs effectively. The Agency has had many "good people," but never enough. In the competition for the time of competent personnel, the university-contract program, because of its low priority, has often come off second best. From the Agency's standpoint, any other allocation of resources would have been irrational. This problem, incidentally, is not unique to the Agency. In many universities, overseas projects have also been matters of low priority. The consequences have been similar, especially in the competition for the time of competent individuals.

The low priority of the university-contract program, with its adverse effects on Agency-university relations, will not be resolved by simply recommending to the Agency that the priority be raised. Actually, few of the factors which determine the priority of a particular enterprise are under the control of Agency personnel. Instead, the priority-determining factors are part of the environment to which Agency personnel must respond.

Restrictive Rules and Procedures

Administration of the university-contract program has been complicated by a large number of rules and procedures designed to achieve objectives other than those associated with particular projects. The major, although by no means the only, source of these parameters is Congress. Although deplored by many observers, the situation appears to have gotten worse rather than better in recent years. Parameters limit the choices which may be made by Agency personnel, irrespective of the goals of a particular

The Statics and Dynamics of Agency-University Relations 177

project, the desires of a participating university, and the situation in the field.

In general, the legislative requirements established for the foreign aid program are designed to make aid more effective and to insure, insofar as possible, that the taxpayers' money is not wasted on unproductive projects. For example, before initiating a program, the Agency is required by law to examine such factors as (1) the capacity of the recipient nation for self-help; (2) the availability of financing from other free-world sources; (3) the economic and technical soundness of the activity to be financed; (4) whether or not the activity gives reasonable promise of contributing to the development of the country's economic resources or productive capacities; and (5) the consistency of the activity with other ongoing development projects.[11]

The term parameter, however, is used not to refer primarily to this type of requirement but to refer to those regulations which have been imposed to achieve either domestic or foreign political objectives essentially unrelated to the high level goals of foreign assistance. In the Act of 1964, for example, domestically oriented provisions included sections 602, requiring notification to U.S. small businesses of AID-financed procurement; 603, requiring that fifty percent of all tonnage procured under provisions of the Act for shipment overseas be transported in U.S. flag carriers; and 604(a), limiting procurement in general to the United States.[12] There were also a series of provisions "designed to prevent aid from going to countries whose current aims are deemed politically unacceptable or are acting improperly with respect to U.S. private investors or other U.S. interests."[13] For example, aid was excluded from "any country dominated or controlled by the international Communist movement" (section 620b), from any country which had expropriated property of a U.S. citizen and then failed to discharge its obligations under international law (section 620e), and from any country selling or furnishing assistance to Cuba (section 107 of the Appropriations Act).[14]

Not only specific provisions of this nature, but also the procedures and organizational units established to ensure compliance with them increase the number of clearances required and the general complexity of administrative processes. The "inflexibility" of Agency officials in matters relating to some of these provisions (for example, small business, U.S. procurement and security) has exasperated university personnel when enforcement appeared to delay or detract from the achievement of project goals as they perceived them. However, especially with a low priority program, the flexibility of the Agency officials themselves is severely limited.

The matter of contractual form and interpretation provides another important case of disharmony resulting from restrictive parameters. Agency procedures in this area are specified in detail by Federal contracting regulations. Most of these regulations are oriented towards contracting with commercial contractors where, presumably, the government needs to be "protected" against excessive profit taking. The problems which have arisen in the financial management aspects of university contracts (especially audits and overhead) have been a consequence of this orientation. Strong sentiment has developed over the years—in the Agency as well as the universities—in favor of altering some of the particularly inappropriate provisions, especially those relating to conflict of interest, exchange of personnel, and overhead, to reflect more closely the requirements of university contracting. The "provisional overhead" requirement was finally modified in the Act of 1961. The requirement relating to the use of the same contractor in a pre-contract survey and the project initiated as a result of the survey recommendations has also been modified in the case of the universities. However, "campaigning" for the modification of such provisions is a time-consuming and costly activity for the Agency.

The reason Agency contract officers behave in ways which are sometimes incomprehensible to university representatives and became a "lightening rod" for criticism[15] becomes clearer when viewed from this perspective. In the interviews for this study, one contract officer stated: "my job is to see that the universities conform to the regulations in the contract." This is a correct "job description" for all contract officers. An Agency contract officer is responsible for between thirty and fifty contracts. Under present procedures, contract officers do not "specialize" in different substantive areas of contracting as they did from 1957 through 1961. At no time in the Agency's history has the contract officer had time to familiarize himself in detail with the substantive aspects of the projects for which he is responsible. Nor is it necessary that he do so. His function is to determine *what is permissible,* not what will best achieve project goals. He identifies with the interests of

The Statics and Dynamics of Agency-University Relations 179

the government (as he perceives them) not with the concerns of individual projects. Naturally this does not lead to the kind of "flexibility" which university officials would like. Indeed, it has often been observed that contract officers exercise an inappropriate "policy-making function" with respect to university contracts. Technical service personnel within the Agency are as vehement on this point as university officials.[16] However, this function is exercised only in situations where regulations specify that "policy" must be legally authorized and in accordance with contractual provisions.[17]

Selection Procedures

How is a university selected to participate in a particular project? The *Gardner Report* notes that "in the past, selection of contractors has too often been haphazard and based on chance encounters. There has been no adequate philosophy or strategy governing the choices."[18] Moreover, Agency officials have discovered through sad experience that the reputation of a university in the United States is not always an accurate predictor of its performance in the field. The result of poor selection has been poor performance in the field; and poor performance has led to attempts by the Agency to exercise greater control over project operations. Because of the Agency's size and complexity and the sensitivity of its officials to criticism, rules, when instituted, have been made to apply to the "lowest common denominator" of university competence. More rules have inevitably been followed by more clearance requirements, more "bureaucratic red tape," and (on the university side) more demands for flexibility. The most extreme instances of university performance which was mediocre or worse occurred during the period of proliferation. University officials accepted contracts and even sought them out with little appreciation of the requirements of overseas projects or their ability to meet them. Some institutions sent none of their own staff members overseas. Graduate students were designated as campus coordinators, and once the project had been initiated, the interest of top administrative officials became negligible. Agency officials with negative attitudes toward university contracting can usually remember specific projects of this type and the difficulties that they caused.

When a university performs badly in the field—inadequate

backstopping, neglect of participant trainees and failure to provide competent personnel for the field party seem to be the most frequent offenses—there are "spillover effects" which go beyond a particular project. Agency representatives have developed impressions from such projects which have affected their behavior towards all universities. Furthermore, as noted above, new rules designed to compel the universities to carry out their obligations in the future have resulted from these experiences. The regulations specifying that sixty percent of all overseas staff members must be recruited from the home campus of the participating university and that the minimum tour for regular staff members shall be not less than two years are examples of such rules.

Recently, the university community seems to have become more aware of this problem and has urged its members to be more realistic and self-conscious about accepting contracts. The successive directors of the International Rural Development Office have been particularly concerned with this area and have occasionally aided the Agency in the matching of projects and institutions. However, Agency officials cannot realistically expect that the university community will objectively police itself and rate one institution against another. The customs and values of academic life do not favor this type of activity, especially when the rating is being done for a government agency. University community officials may assist in the selection process, but ultimately the decisions must be made by the Agency. So long as the selection procedures described in the *Gardner Report* persist, occasionally a university is going to be selected which will not do a very good job in the field. This will contribute to the persistence of disharmony between the Agency and all participating universities.

Environmental "Constants"

Some of the recommendations for improving the university-contract program have either not been implemented or led to unforeseen consequences because the perspective upon which they were based was too narrow. Before recommending that a change should be made in the structure of the Agency or in some specific procedures, it is important to ask: "what influencing factors *outside* of the Agency contribute to making things the way they are?"

If such "variables" have not been taken into account, it is unlikely that things will turn out as the recommender envisioned. Usually, the recommendation will not be implemented at all, although it may be given "lip service." Examples of this in the history of the university-contract program are too numerous to mention.

Two "environmental" factors appear to be particularly significant; namely, (a) the characteristics of the "settings" in which project activity actually takes place (i.e. less developed nations) and (b) the activities of the U.S. Congress. The domestic environments of the participating universities should also be examined.

THE "SETTINGS" OF UNIVERSITY-CONTRACT PROJECTS

There is, of course, an entire literature dealing with this subject.[19] However, the points to be made here can be summarized as follows:

(a) No two less developed nations (or host universities) are exactly alike. (Most are not even much alike.)

(b) The situation in any single less developed nation (or host university) is likely to change considerably over short periods of time, independently of the activities of U.S. personnel.

(c) Not very much is known, even after fifteen or more years of technical assistance activity, about the processes of planned social change which AID is trying to promote. Furthermore, there is little agreement about what or how much is known.

If the above observations are accepted as premises, it follows that the "goals" of university-contract projects, however specifically they are stated, will necessarily be non-operational (i.e., it will be difficult or impossible to predict what low level goals and activities will effectively attain them). This characteristic underlies the arguments for "flexibility" which appear in the literature.

Mr. Bell emphasized, in his introductory address to the Rural Development Conference, that "hard experience has demonstrated that . . . what works in Bozeman may not work at all in Bolivia."[20] Hard experience has also demonstrated that what works in Bolivia may not work in Peru; and that what works in Bolivia in 1964 may not work in 1965. Furthermore, the probability that what "will work" in any given situation can be specified in advance is not very high.

Given the present function of operational plans in the Agency, this raises considerable doubts about the desirability of long-range planning, such as has been recommended by the Conference on International Rural Development, at least from the *perspective of the individual project and field setting*. A long-range plan which specifies the behavior of the participating parties in fairly minute detail assumes that (a) there are no outside factors which will alter the conditions envisioned by the plan and that (b) the behavior specified will produce the results predicted by the plan. However, experience suggests that exactly the opposite assumptions are the correct ones for technical assistance programs. Detailed specification of low level goals and activities does serve a variety of needs, very important needs in fact; *but these needs are largely unrelated to the social development goals of university-contract projects*. They are needs which inhere in the *domestic* political setting of the Agency and are thus closely related to organizational maintenance goals.

Disagreements arise because once a plan is institutionalized in the form of a project implementation order (PIO/T) and a contract, it is very difficult administratively to change it. Furthermore, the "frozen" reality of the plan rather than the extremely fluid reality of the situation becomes the source of decision premises for the Agency. The decision-making problem is compounded, of course, by parameters which are supposed to apply uniformly to all settings at all times. Often the relationship between these rules and the characteristics of any individual setting is only a matter of coincidence.

Unfortunately the lack of specificity of high level project goals tends to preclude the granting of flexibility. If accepted performance indicators were agreed upon, then perhaps the universities could be allowed greater latitude. However, from the perspective of Agency officials, "flexibility" is synonymous with vagueness, or nearly so. Moreover, it must be remembered that uniform planning and implementation procedures have a much greater degree of complementarity with the organizational maintenance goals of the Agency, at least in the short run, than flexible ones.

CONGRESSIONAL INFLUENCE

It was suggested above that one of the ways in which Congressional influence is exerted on the university-contract program is through the imposition of parameters. The parameters themselves may be considered part of the "environment" of the Agency. In other words, they affect the behavior of Agency personnel, but are essentially beyond their control.

Equally significant, however, is the influence which Congress exerts in determining the relative priority of Agency activities, particularly through the annual appropriation-authorization process. Because of the obvious importance of this process to the "survival" of the Agency, *the attitudes of certain influential Senators and Representatives become, to a considerable degree, the organizational maintenance goals of Agency personnel.* Only from this perspective can certain persistent characteristics of the Agency which have direct bearing on the university-contract program be fully understood.

The requirement for annual authorizing and appropriating legislation is the touchstone of Congressional influence over the Agency. It is a requirement which the Congress, as a whole, has been most reluctant to abandon, even though numerous studies of the program, including some sponsored by Congressional committees,[21] have recommended modifications to enable the Agency to make commitments for longer periods of time. The authorization-appropriation process provides the Congress with an annual, institutionalized opportunity to impose parameters and make its values known to the Agency. The process can also be used to influence aspects of foreign policy-making which are less subject to direct legislative control.[22] Furthermore, the annual hearings *in themselves* constitute a significant mode of influence over the Agency, especially with regard to the determination of priorities. These hearings, which involve separate presentations before four Congressional committees,[23] are correctly viewed with respect and some apprehension by Agency officials since the scope and form of Agency activity for the coming year depends largely upon committee recommendations. Two especially important aspects of the hearings are the time devoted to them by Agency officials and the way in which they influence the form of the Agency's budgetary requests.

The major expenditure of time is devoted to preparing the "Congressional presentation," a process described by F. M. Coffin:

> Planning for submission of the year's program begins nine months in advance. From January to mid-March, hundreds of officials in the Pentagon, the Department of State and the Agency for International

Development spend thousands of hours in writing and editing a bookshelf of volumes on the proposed military and economic aid programs. The Agency for International Development alone submits six large printed looseleaf books, replete with charts and statistical tables running well over 2,000 pages.[24]

Obviously the time allocated to the Congressional presentation is important because it can not be devoted to other Agency activities, and low priority activities are the most likely to suffer.

In addition to preparing the presentation, Agency administrators are called upon to make supporting verbal presentations and are often questioned about selected aspects of their programs in exhaustive detail. They must testify at four hearings covering essentially the same material. With regard to the amount of time devoted to this activity, Coffin observes:

> It is safe to say that from April through August, one fourth to one third of the time of the senior executives responsible for administering overseas programs of economic and military assistance is devoted to the Congressional hearings. The actual time spent in testifying is but the visible part of the iceberg to the submerged bulk.[25]

The emphasis in the hearings is on "justification" of expenditures in terms of those things the legislators believe important and on "showing results." This explains in part the emphasis within the Agency on evaluating performance in terms of specific goals, whether or not these are meaningful in terms of the project and the field setting.

Many observers have noted that Congressional dissatisfaction with the Agency has increased in recent years. Why should we continue the "giveaway" program, opponents of foreign assistance argue, when after fifteen years, the nations which we have assisted are no more politically stable or friendly to the United States than they were when foreign aid began. While the outright opponents are a minority and their statements should not be equated with the position of Congress as a whole, the growing dissatisfaction has been manifested in delays and cuts in appropriations, and increasingly restrictive parameters to compel Agency personnel to make the program do the things that the legislators think it ought to do. From the perspective of the history of university contracts, it appears that this dissatisfaction has had, over the years, the effect of a self-fulfilling prophecy. The situation can be represented by a paradigm, which is rather depressing for supporters of aid.

THE PARADOX OF CONGRESSIONAL DISSATISFACTION

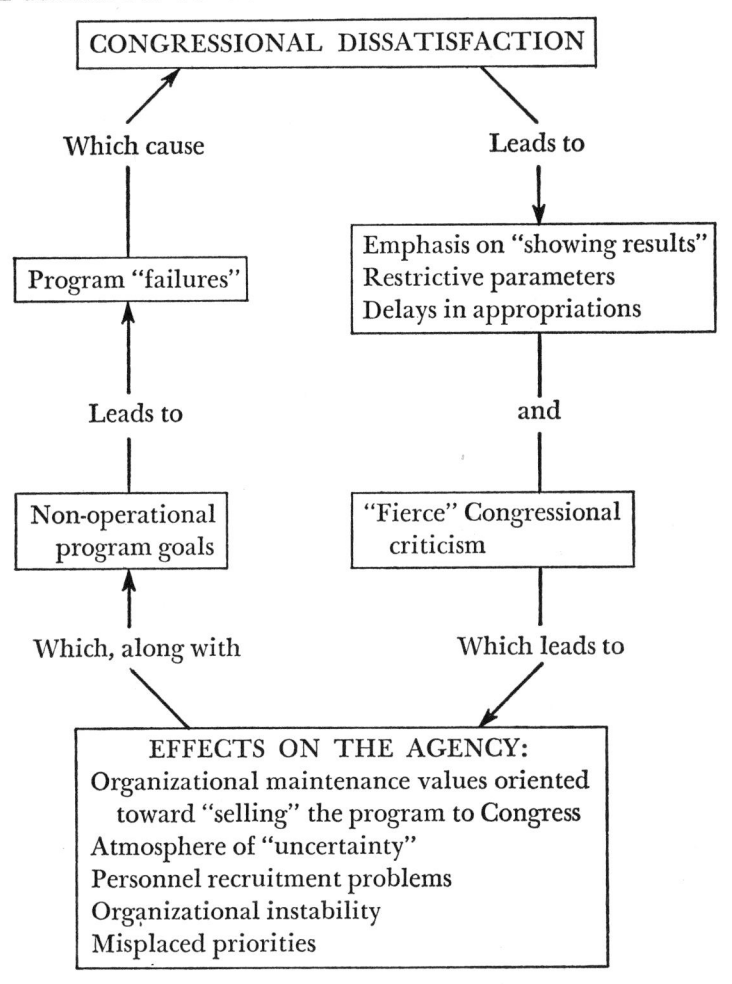

```
                    CONGRESSIONAL DISSATISFACTION
                    ↗                            ↘
            Which cause                      Leads to
                │                                │
                │                                ▼
                │                   ┌─────────────────────────────┐
         ┌──────────────┐           │ Emphasis on "showing results"│
         │  Program     │           │ Restrictive parameters       │
         │  "failures"  │           │ Delays in appropriations     │
         └──────────────┘           └─────────────────────────────┘
                ▲                                │
                │                                │
             Leads to                           and
                │                                │
         ┌──────────────┐           ┌─────────────────────────────┐
         │ Non-operational│         │ "Fierce" Congressional       │
         │ program goals │          │ criticism                    │
         └──────────────┘           └─────────────────────────────┘
                ▲                                │
                │                                │
         Which, along with             Which leads to
                  ↘                         ↙
         ┌────────────────────────────────────────────┐
         │         EFFECTS ON THE AGENCY:              │
         │  Organizational maintenance values oriented │
         │     toward "selling" the program to Congress│
         │  Atmosphere of "uncertainty"                │
         │  Personnel recruitment problems             │
         │  Organizational instability                 │
         │  Misplaced priorities                       │
         └────────────────────────────────────────────┘
```

This paradigm suggests what is meant by the "self-fulfilling" consequences of Congressional dissatisfaction. The "failures" which are perceived in foreign assistance programs are, all too often, real enough. However, Congressional reaction to previous failures is a major contributing factor to their reoccurrence. As noted above, this reaction has taken the form of "fierce" criticism directed at Agency personnel, and the imposition of restrictive parameters. The effects on specific projects of specific regulations written into legislation are relatively easy to discern. The more general effects which Congressional criticism has had on the Agency over the years is less readily identifiable but equally significant.[26]

A discussion of all of the varied ways in which Congressional influence affects the Agency goes far beyond the purview of this report. However, it must be emphasized that talking about raising the priority of the university-contract program or eliminating parameters or, in fact, making any changes in the Agency, becomes a rather academic exercise if this factor is neglected.

STATE LEGISLATURES

It should not be forgotten that the universities have their own environmental concerns and organizational maintenance values, some of which, in the case of Land-Grant universities at least, are determined by state legislatures. Obviously, the situation is not analogous to the position of the Agency *vis a vis* Congress. (If university participation in overseas projects depended upon appropriations from state legislatures it is highly unlikely that there would be any university-contract program at all.) This does not mean, however, that the views of local legislators are not important considerations.

An overseas contract can constitute a serious drain on the resources of a university, particularly if it attempts to staff the field team entirely from its own faculty. In a time of soaring enrollments and budgets, this activity must be justified in terms of the university's primary mission, service to the people of a particular state. Agency administrators and university presidents have recognized this fact since the early years of the program, but it has been difficult to incorporate this recognition into specific contracts. One of the reasons for a lack of "total university involvement" in a project has been the fact that this conflicted with other more operational and more important domestic goals.

Some Agency personnel have failed to give sufficient weight to this environmental variable in their dealings with the universities. Disputes over the form and administration of contracts have resulted. The acrimonious disagreements involving disallowed costs and provisional overhead provide particularly good examples of this situation. Clearly Agency-university relations will be more harmonious if project goals and goals dictated by a university's domestic environment are complementary rather than conflicting.

Institutional Variables: Persistent and Changing Patterns in the Agency and the Participating Universities

An investigation of institutional variables, the organizational structure and important goals of the Agency and (to the degree that generalization is possible) the participating universities, will complete the analysis of static and dynamic factors affecting the Agency-university relationship. Part I provides considerable evidence that the effects of these institutional variables have been more proximate and more easily identifiable than the effects of environmental "constants." However, many important institutional characteristics have been determined by environmental factors.

Once again, the analysis focuses on those characteristics which have persisted throughout the program's history and are associated with persisting and unresolved issues. In addition, some of the major changes in structure and personnel which have been identified will be examined and their consequences assessed.

THE AGENCY: UNCHANGING BEHAVIOR AMIDST ORGANIZATIONAL INSTABILITY

One of the most interesting phenomena noted in the interviews was the limited recollection of the many policy and organizational changes which a study of the relevant documents reveals. At the participating university level, it does not seem to have made much difference whether the Agency was called FOA, ICA or AID, whether it was organized along geographic or functional lines or, during most periods, who was the administrator. The perceived outputs from the Agency were about the same.

Five persisting structural characteristics of the Agency identified in Part I provide a partial explanation for this. Since most of these characteristics have been emphasized earlier, a brief summary should be sufficient to remind the reader of points made previously and relate them to the discussion here.

(1) *Scope and heterogeniety of activities:* Throughout the program's history, the universities have had to deal with an organization which was responsible for a large number of varied activities in equally varied settings. The procedures, doctrines and administrative structure of this organization have inevitably represented compromises between the requirements of all of them. The activities having the highest priority have, of course, been most influential in determining what form specific compromises would take.

(2) *Overload:* As is true with most governmental organizations, there never seems to have been enough people to do everything properly, or at least enough "good people." The activities of high officials have necessarily been devoted to high priority concerns.

(3) *Organizational instability:* The structure of the Agency has been characterized by perpetual change, even during the relatively stable periods of harmony and inertia. As Coffin aptly observes, "Instead of pulling up the weeds, we have repeatedly pulled up the flower to see why it wasn't doing better."[27] In many instances these changes seem to have simply reflected a feeling that there was a need to "do something" in the face of continued "failures" and mounting Congressional criticism.

(4) *Personnel instability:* The *Gardner Report* notes that "AID and its predecessor agencies have experienced consistent difficulty in recruiting and retaining men of appropriate qualifications.... despite over fifteen years of activity in foreign aid, the government still lacks any adequate personnel system in the field."[28] This instability has existed at all levels of the Agency. It has placed a premium on the time of competent, experienced personnel.

(5) *Feedback and memory:* A system of feedback and "organizational memory" is almost totally absent. The frequently heard statement that "AID has no memory" has been documented in Col. Lincoln's report and numerous other studies of the Agency. To some degree, issues persist because the conditions leading to their occurrence have simply been "forgotten" by the organization. Decisions relating to low priority projects continue to be made on an ad hoc basis.

As has been emphasized repeatedly, these characteristics are largely determined by environmental factors. They will not be altered merely because of recommendations and internal policy changes. There have been enough of those already to make this point clear. If one is concerned with projecting the future of an

Agency-administered university-contract program, these characteristics should probably be taken into account as "constants."

Nevertheless, there have been some changes in the Agency which have influenced the university-contract program, at least temporarily. In perspective, these changes seem less significant than they appeared to be when they occurred. However, it should be noted how and why the university-contract program was affected by them, in terms of the framework used in this study. The changes to be examined are (a) changes in the administrator, (b) changes in "emphasis" on university contracting, (c) changes in patterns of participation, and (d) changes in the organizational structure of the Agency with respect to geographic versus functional concerns.

Changes in the Administrator

An administrator is "powerful" to the degree that he can make his own goals important and operational to Agency personnel. This can be done through personal techniques and qualities of leadership which persuade subordinates to identify with him as an individual, and through administrative practices which cause subordinates to associate his goals with their own personal and organizational maintenance goals. A third determinant of an administrator's power is the way in which he exerts control over the flow of information within the Agency (both the substance and volume of communications are included in this category).[29]

The Agency has had three relatively powerful administrators, Stassen, Hollister and Bell. They affected Agency-university relations by influencing patterns of participation and the priority of university-contract projects in relation to other Agency activities and by the degree of their personal participation in university-contract decision-making. In terms of the above discussion, it might be said that they attenuated (or in the case of Hollister, increased) the effects of environmental and structural variables with respect to university-contract projects.

The primary consequence of Stassen's tenure was a change in patterns of participation. A major increase in the volume of university-contract decision-making related to crucial divisive issues did not occur until the beginning of Hollister's tenure. Because of this, as well as because of his interest and energy, Stassen could cope personally with the most troublesome problems which arose.

It is doubtful, given the demands on the administrator's time, that even Stassen would have been able to continue to exercise the role of personal mediator in the face of the multiplying problems which were caused by proliferation in 1955 and 1956. However, had he remained, the lines of communication to the university community would certainly have been kept open and the hostility which developed at this level during the period of retrenchment would have been less pronounced.

The major consequence of Hollister's tenure was to lower the priority of the university-contract program. Unfortunately (from the standpoint of improving Agency-university relations), the change in administrators occurred at the worst possible time, just as the crucial divisive issues were becoming particularly salient. The consequences have been discussed in detail in the analysis of the period of retrenchment.

Under Bell, the priority of the program was increased somewhat. However, Bell's most important contribution to Agency-university relations was to alter the substance and volume of communications within the Agency relating to university-contract projects. His "persuasive" activities had the effect of making the goal of "improving Agency-university relations" more operational for lower echelon Agency personnel by making low-cost information readily available regarding the means by which this might be achieved (i.e., the *Gardner Report*). Furthermore, he appears to have exerted the sort of leadership which enabled his subordinates to identify with his goals because of personal identification with him as an individual.

"Emphasis" on University Contracting

"Emphasis" on university contracting refers to the degree of pressure, within the Agency, to initiate university-contract projects. It is important to differentiate between emphasis and priority. During the period of genesis, for example, university contracting was not emphasized as an Agency activity. However, the priority of individual projects was extremely high. The emphasis variable is characterized by what might be called a delay feature. Because of the time necessary to negotiate contracts and the fact that the major divisive issues often do not occur until after the first few months or even the first year of project operations, the effects of a period of emphasis on the Agency are not fully apparent immediately.

From the standpoint of harmonious Agency-university relations, the ideal situation is a low emphasis program, with a very high priority placed on each individual project. Presumably, in this situation (all other things being equal) only the most competent universities would be asked to participate, they would conduct project operations in an exemplary manner, and their concerns would receive immediate and sympathetic consideration within the Agency. The closest approximation to this situation occurred during the period of genesis.

The worst possible situation is, obviously, a high emphasis, low priority program. This is the situation which occurred during the period of retrenchment. During the periods of inertia and the interregnum, the priority of the program was relatively low, but emphasis was also relatively low. This situation contributed to a slight improvement in relations (or at least to not making things any worse). During the period of harmony there has been a marked increase in emphasis and a moderate increase in priority.

The degree of diversity in patterns of participation is also related to the emphasis variable. If emphasis is low, most of the projects will conform to the "sisterhood" relationship pattern. As emphasis increases, patterns of participation tend to become increasingly diverse.

Patterns of Participation

The changes in patterns of participation which have been most significant for Agency-university relations have been changes in the degree of diversity (or heterogeniety) of university activities.

In examining the significance of this variable, the focus will be primarily on changes in the degree of diversity of individual patterns of participation. As noted above, "sisterhood" arrangements between a U.S. and a host university have been by far the predominant pattern of individual participation. During the periods of proliferation and harmony, however, in conjunction with an increase in emphasis, there was a considerable increase in other types of projects. In each case, university personnel began to assume increasing responsibility for tasks which were not directly educational and which, more often than not, had previously been performed by direct hire personnel. During the period of proliferation, this change occurred on an Agency-wide basis. During the period of harmony, it was restricted primarily to the Latin American region. Consequently, during the latter period, interregional differences also became more pronounced.

This study suggests that any change in patterns of participation in the direction of increasing diversity is likely to intensify divisive issues. Two problems associated with this phenomenon contribute to disagreements between Agency and university personnel.

(1) *The "appropriate role" problem:* Although problems of autonomy will arise in any project, a "sisterhood" relationship tends to clarify the boundaries between the authority of the university and the Agency. The roles performed by university personnel in the field tend to be quite similar to those which they perform at home and the distinction between them and direct hire personnel is relatively easy to maintain. However, as the roles of university personnel become more and more similar to those of direct hire personnel, this distinction becomes, at least from the standpoint of the Agency, less and less meaningful. It does not, however, become less important to participating university officials or to the personnel themselves. Issues revolving around the norm of "academic freedom" provide a particularly good example of the problems which can arise. A good case can be made for applying this norm to a university professor acting as advisor to the chairman of the department of agricultural economics at a host university. However, suppose that he is acting as advisor to the Minister of Agriculture. Should he be any more "academically free" than his predecessor, a direct hire official who performed the same function? University representatives are likely to argue that he should, by virtue of his position on the staff of the university. Agency mission directors and chiefs of division are likely to argue that he should not. Of course, depending on the individuals involved, it is often possible to resolve such disputes. However, the probability of disagreement is increased when the functions of university and direct hire personnel begin to overlap.

(2) *The "threat" problem:* Whenever the functions of universities have been expanded and diversified, there has been a concomitant contraction in the responsibilities of direct hire personnel. The direct hire personnel have, quite naturally, developed a certain amount of resentment towards the intruders. Obviously,

these feelings have not contributed toward harmonious working relationships between Agency and university personnel. The negative attitudes toward the initiatives undertaken in Latin America, both within the Alliance for Progress and in other bureaus, are explainable in part by this concern. The hostility toward universities was even greater among lower echelon Agency personnel during the period of proliferation.

It does not necessarily follow from this discussion that university-contract projects should be restricted to a "sisterhood" relationship. It does follow that, *all other things being equal,* a deterioration in relations is a probable consequence of deviating from this pattern.

Geographic vs. Functional Organization

The Agency has cycled between a geographically and a "functionally" oriented organizational structure. A high degree of functional orientation occurred during ICA's later years. The 1961 reorganization of the Agency which established a geographically oriented structure reflected the belief that many of the problems associated with the program derived from this characteristic. Since then, AID has been gradually drifting back towards a more functionally oriented structure, although these tendencies are vigorously opposed by the regional assistant administrators.

Insofar as can be determined, these rearrangements have not affected Agency-university relations to any significant degree.[30]

THE UNIVERSITIES: LIBERAL IDEALS AMIDST INSTITUTIONAL CONSERVATISM

To generalize about that complex entity labeled "the Agency" over a fifteen-year period is difficult enough. To do the same for "the universities" verges on the impossible. Yet there are some characteristics of universities in general which merit attention and will serve to make the analysis a little more balanced. As has been noted, a major cause of negative incidents has been fundamental differences between the goals or values of Agency and university personnel. Here, some of the reasons for this on the university side will be examined.

The key to the university side of Agency-university relations is three areas of decision-making activity, namely (1) the making of commitments to overseas project activity by university officials and the goals and values which underlie those commitments; (2) the structure and patterns of administration affecting the recruitment and backstopping of field personnel; and (3) the motivation and effectiveness of personnel in the field. Before turning to more detailed examination of these areas, however, some general comments about the administrative structure of universities and the professional goals of university faculty members will provide a background for the subsequent discussion.

Superficially the administrative structure of a university looks much like any hierarchically structured organization with the president at the top, deans and department heads somewhat lower down, and individual faculty members near the bottom. In practice, things work quite differently. The term "layered" could appropriately be used to describe university organizations, since there is a great deal of autonomy and independence at each level. This is especially true at the departmental level. Members of a department owe allegiance not only to the university, but to a particular academic discipline. It is primarily in comparison with other departments in the same discipline that a given department gains its reputation and status. Moreover, it is from the members of their own discipline that faculty members tend to derive prestige and professional reputation.

Although there are exceptions, there is usually a high degree of complementarity between the personal and professional goals of a professor and the organizational maintenance and professional values of his discipline. Indeed, the incentive system of the university reinforces this complementarity by using professional reputation as criterion in determining salary and promotion within the university. Rightly or wrongly, research and published articles, especially in discipline-sanctioned professional journals, are the primary indicators in terms of which such judgments are made. In addition, the prestige of a department is usually determined by the number of prestigious people within it. Thus, control of ranking administrators over the goals which influence their faculty members is limited. Moreover, the "academic freedom" of individual professors (especially tenured professors) is jealously guarded. In most circumstances, however, the system works quite well because there is a high degree of complementarity between institutional, discipline, departmental and individual goals. The

Land-Grant universities, in which the goals of academic excellence and community service are harmonized, provide a superb example of just how effective and productive this type of system can be. However, when programs are undertaken without a clear recognition of the need for complementary goals, especially where conflicting goals exist, the system is not likely to work at all well. In many universities, contract projects provide an example of less than "total commitment" because their goals are conflicting or neutral with respect to the important and operational goals of the institution. Investigation of the areas of commitment, structure and motivation mentioned above will make this point more explicit.

Overseas Commitments and Institutional Goals

University presidents and high administrators define the reasons for undertaking projects in a variety of ways. However, they may be generally classified under the headings of (a) patriotic commitment to national service, (b) desire to build an "international dimension," (c) desire to enhance institutional prestige, and (d) humanitarian concerns.[31] Obviously these goals are not necessarily in conflict, but neither are they necessarily complementary. The failure to recognize this contributed to great difficulties in the periods of proliferation and retrenchment. For however patriotic and humanitarian an administrator's goals may be, his patriotism and humanitarianism are not, in the long run, going to provide the foundations upon which successful projects are built.[32] Nor will the goal of institutional prestige by itself provide such a foundation, though several institutions have grown from little more than parochially oriented "cow colleges" to internationally recognized institutions through participation in overseas programs. The need for complementarity of project and institutional goals has been increasingly recognized by the university community and by university administrators with experience in international programs. It is no accident that the institutions which have had the most successful projects are also the ones which have fought the hardest for such things as supplementary research funds, faculty overstaffing, and graduate student training in their contracts. Unfortunately these provisions have often been opposed by Congress and by some government agencies—such as the General Accounting Office—which have been concerned with the "justification" of project expenditures. Equally unfortunate have been the cases where university presidents and deans made commitments for their institutions which they could not keep because of the nature of the contracts which were agreed upon and the character of their institutions.

Administration of Recruitment and Backstopping

Once a contract has been granted, the university still retains a large degree of flexibility regarding personnel recruitment and project backstopping. A variety of approaches have been tried over the years. In general, institutional involvement in international programs has been broadened and the administrative mechanisms of home campus support and coordination have been enlarged considerably. During the early days of the program, project administration would often be the collateral responsibility of a vice president, dean or associate dean. Frequently a junior faculty member or part-time graduate assistant would perform most of the actual duties related to project administration. Now, most of the larger universities have full-fledged deans of international programs. These positions are often manned by individuals with high professional status in international agriculture, plus experience in overseas project operations and Agency-university relations.[33] However, in many institutions, even those with considerable international experience, a serious problem of conflicting goals has arisen between the departmental level and the level of the office of international programs.[34] Part of the problem is lack of communication. Deans of international programs have been known to recruit faculty members for overseas projects without consultation or prior knowledge of the department heads involved. Moreover, in many universities, few tangible benefits accrue to the departments from faculty member participation in such projects. Funds are not provided for a replacement, the ongoing research of the participant is interrupted, and, consequently other staff members are overloaded. In addition, returning participants often fit into the department much less well than they did when they departed. As a result of their experiences, they have new interests which may not be at all consistent with the "slot" which the department head had planned for them to fill. Participant trainees pose another kind of problem for the department head. First, they require more attention on the part of staff members—usually senior staff members—than the average graduate student. Second, the kind of research in which they are interested does not usually fit within the context of normal departmental research activities. Often no funds are available to support this type of research.

All of these factors contribute to a phenomenon which was noted in many institutions by a research group of the CIC-AID project.[35] Department heads are often indifferent or even hostile towards overseas projects. Naturally this situation, where it exists, affects recruitment and the overall quality of project performance. This leads to the final area to be examined, the motivation and quality of performance of personnel in the field.

Personal-Professional Goals and Project Participation

One does not have to subscribe to Adams and Garraty's observation that many overseas participants are "expatriate academic bums" to recognize that throughout the program's history, many universities have faced serious recruitment problems in meeting their contractual obligations. Either projects have not been staffed to agreed manning levels, or individuals have been recruited from off campus or inexperienced or retiring faculty members have been sent overseas. When this has occurred or when an obviously mediocre individual has been assigned to a project, Agency officials have used this as evidence that the universities should have less, not more autonomy and flexibility. Part of this problem lies within the universities. When the program was initiated, many staff members suffered directly from participation in terms of lower salary and less rapid promotion. Now these obvious problems have mostly been corrected. However, there is still an impression among many university personnel that participation, though justifiable on moral and humanitarian grounds, is a professional and personal sacrifice. In some institutions, the hostile attitude of department heads contributes to this impression; however, the main problem seems to be that there has been little attempt to make project participation professionally attractive. Participation in projects involves "advising" at relatively general levels and often there are considerable administrative responsibilities. For the most part, this type of activity does not contribute to professional growth as much as a similar period of service at home or participation in a foundation or Fulbright program would do. This problem is not entirely correctable by the universities. University administrators are constrained by the professional values of the disciplines to which faculty members belong. In this area the process of change is very gradual. Moreover, part of the fault lies within the Agency and the domestic environment in which it operates. There has been a curiously negative attitude towards activities by team members which enhance their professional competence but have no other "justifiable" output. The strictures against participation in professional meetings by team members provide a good example. Whether or not activities of this nature are "right" or "wrong," the regulations against them clearly complicate the recruitment problem. The discussion of this subject might be summarized by the observation that outstanding scholars who have participated in university projects have often paid a price. But for poor or mediocre scholars little or no sacrifice has been required.

In conclusion, it is clear that many universities have become more aware of the requirements of overseas programs and better able to cope with them. The ones that have done the best are those that have not forgotten their own institutional goals when negotiating contracts. Certainly there is still room for considerable progress. The Agency can contribute by providing for a strengthening of the resources of participating universities in their contracts. Some definite steps in that direction have been taken by Congress; even more should be taken if the university-contract program is to continue.

Increased university competence is always desirable, but the assumption that the degree of university competence and the degree of harmony of Agency-university relations are always positively associated should be guarded against. In the past, outstanding universities, totally committed to their projects, have been the ones which have most vigorously asserted their prerogatives. In fact, as the international competence of participating universities increases, there must be an increase in the competence of Agency personnel as well. A failure to recognize this may lead to the alienation of the resources which are most necessary for a successful program. In particular, Agency and other governmental officials must be sufficiently far-sighted to realize the need for complementarity between project goals, institutional goals, and the professional goals of U.S. participants.

Summary

This chapter has been devoted to identifying a number of factors or variables associated with the persistence of divisive issues. Also identified are a limited number of "variables" which appear to have contributed to changes in the degree of importance of these issues (i.e., the number of negative incidents devolving from them). Implicit in this analysis is a set of propositions in terms of which these variables can be related to one another. For example, it might be said that (all other things being equal) the issue of university autonomy tends to become more salient for any given project as more restrictive parameters are imposed. It might also be said that, all other things being equal, the saliency of the "contract form" issue is negatively associated with the operationality of project goals. Each of the four variables mentioned in these two propositions are also related in other ways, for example:

(1) The saliency of the "contract form" issue is positively associated with the saliency of the "university autonomy" issue, and vice versa.

(2) The number of imposed parameters is positively associated with the determinacy of project goals, but not vice versa.

(3) The saliency of the "university autonomy" issue is negatively associated with the operationality of project goals, but not vice versa, and so forth.

The problem in attempting a meaningful summary of this study is not uncommon in studies of macro-social phenomena. First, despite stating that "all other things are assumed to be equal" for any given relationship, in reality "all other things" are never equal at all. Unless the effects of the "other things" believed to be important are known, the propositions are neither very interesting nor useful. Second, the degree of intercorrelation among variables, even within the categories of variables which have been considered, is extremely high. The priority of a given project is positively associated with the degree of operationality of its goals, for example. Thus, this analysis leads not to a few propositions, but to a number approaching infinity. What exists, in fact, is an exceedingly complex matrix of intercorrelations. The conclusions should, ideally, describe the structure of the matrix in some way rather than merely focusing on a few of the most obvious relationships. A mathematical representation is precluded by the nature of the data. Nevertheless, despite the self-evident inadequacies and inaccuracies inherent in this approach, an attempt will be made to relate some of the most important variables in the form of a matrix.

SUMMARIZING THE ANALYSIS: A MATRIX OF RELATIONSHIPS

First the variables will be summarized. Here they are stated in such a way that they can be thought of in terms of an ordinal (or relational) scale of measurement. Of course, the variables have not been specifically operationalized in these terms, but this representation will make the matrix clearer and more useful. The variables have been grouped into five categories, as follows:

A. *ISSUE VARIABLES:* Degree of saliency of the issue of
 (I- 1) Equal partnership
 (I- 2) University autonomy vs. Agency control
 (I- 3) Contractual form
 (I- 4) Project length
 (I- 5) Personnel clearance
B. *INTERVENING VARIABLES* (Characteristics of the university-contract program)
 (V- 6) *Project goals:* operationality.
 (V- 7) *Project goals:* specificity.
 (V- 8) *Performance criteria:* degree of relatedness to substantive project goals.
 (V- 9) *Priority:* relative priority in relation to other Agency activities.
 (V-10) *Parameters:* degree to which project-related behavior is free from restrictive parameters.
 (V-11) *Selection procedures:* degree to which selection procedures are based on project-goal related criteria and knowledge of university competence.
C. *ENVIRONMENTAL VARIABLES*
 (E-12) *Field setting:* degree of uniformity/predictability with respect to the temporal dimension (i.e., over a period of time).

The Statics and Dynamics of Agency-University Relations 201

(E-13) *Field setting:* degree of uniformity/predictability with respect to the spatial dimension (i.e., among countries).
(E-14) *Congressional influence:* degree of dissatisfaction.

D. "STRUCTURAL" CHARACTERISTICS OF THE AGENCY
(A-15) *Activities:* number of activities and degree of heterogeniety (assumed to be positively associated).
(A-16) *Stability:* degree of organizational stability.
(A-17) *Personnel:* level of competence.
(A-18) *Feedback-memory:* degree of effectiveness.

E. OTHER CHARACTERISTICS
(O-19) *Administrator:* degree of support for university contracts.
(O-20) *Emphasis:* degree of emphasis on university contracts.
(O-21) *Patterns of participation:* number and degree of heterogeniety (assumed to be positively associated).

The relationships among these variables suggested by this analysis are presented in Figure I. From this matrix it is possible, in a rough way, to derive the propositions which are implicit and explicit in the analysis and to make some judgment about significant patterns of inter-relationship. For example, the importance or intensity of the project length issue has been strongly affected by the operationality and specificity of project goals, and moderately affected by the priority of the contract program, differences in field settings, Congressional dissatisfaction, the degree of organizational stability and the support of the administrator. The operationality of project goals has been strongly affected by the characteristics of the field setting and affected somewhat by the priority of the program, Congressional dissatisfaction, the scope of agency activities, etc. Of course, the matrix can also be used to assess the effects of particular variables. For instance, the priority of the program has had a moderate effect on the importance of the issues of autonomy, contractual form and project length and on the effectiveness of selection procedures and freedom of projects from restrictive parameters. It has also had some effect on the clearance issue, the operationality of project goals, and the relationship of goals and performance

FIGURE 1

"Independent" Relationships: Entries in the cells denote that a change in a variable on this dimension will tend to have an effect on other variables.

"Dependent" Relationships: Entries in the cells denote that a change in a variable will tend to be "affected by" changes in other variables.

	I-1 PARTNERSHIP	I-2 AUTONOMY	I-3 FORM CONTR.	I-4 TERMINATION	I-5 CLEARANCE	V-6 GOALS (SP)	V-7 GOALS (O)	V-8 CRITERIA	V-9 PRIORITY	V-10 PARAMETERS	V-11 SEL PROC	E-12 FIELD (T)	E-13 FIELD (S)	E-14 CONGRESS	A-15 ACTIVITIES	A-16 STABILITY	A-17 PERSONNEL	A-18 FB/MEMORY	O-19 ADMINISTRATOR	O-20 EMPHASIS	O-21 PATTERNS
I-1 PARTNERSHIP	—	H	H	H	H							l	l	L	M	l	l	l	l	L	M
I-2 AUTONOMY		—	M	M	M		m	l	m	h		l	l	M	M	l	l		l		L
I-3 FORM CONTR.	M		—				l	l	m	h			m	M	L	l			m	L	L
I-4 TERMINATION	M	M		—		h	h	l	l	m				L	l	m	l	l	m		l
I-5 CLEARANCE	H	M	H	M	—		l		l	m				L	l	l			l		
V-6 GOALS (SP)						—	M		L			H	H	O	O		O	O		O	O
V-7 GOALS (O)							—		L	M		H	H	l	l		l	l	L		l
V-8 CRITERIA						L	H	—	L		L	M	M	m	l	L	L	L	L		l
V-9 PRIORITY						L	L	L	—			l	L	O	m	L	L	L	L	l	l
V-10 PARAMETERS							L	L	M	—		l	L	h	l	l			M	l	l
V-11 SEL PROC							L		M	M	—		l	l		l	L	L	L	m	l

E-12 FIELD (T)				l		l	L	L
E-13 FIELD (S)			l		l	l	L	L
E-14 CONGRESS				l		l		
A-15 ACTIVITIES					l			
A-16 STABILITY		m	m					
A-17 PERSONNEL			1		M	l		
A-18 FB/MEMORY								
O-19 ADMINISTRATOR							l	
O-20 EMPHASIS			2					
O-21 PATTERNS								l

EXPLANATION OF SYMBOLS

(1) Capital leters (H, M, L) denote that the two variables to which they refer tend to be positively associated, (i.e. that an increase in the "independent" variable is associated with an increase in the "dependent" variable). Small letters denote negative association.

(2) A *relatively great* degree of association is denoted by "H" or "h".

(3) A *moderate* degree of association is denoted by "M" or "m".

(4) *Some* degree of association is denoted by "L" or "l".

(5) "O" denotes that the direction of the relationship depends on other factors.

NOTES

1. Occasionally, Congressmen will intervene directly in the selection process in favor of a particular university.

2. Congress can also affect the emphasis on contracts directly, as in the case of the Humphrey Amendment.

3. Obviously, the degree of association is, to a large degree, determined by the influence of the administrator. The values noted are for a relatively great degree of influence (i.e., Bell or Stassen).

criteria. Numerous propositions can be drawn from the matrix in a similar manner. Although no additional precision is introduced by this mode of presentation, it is useful in summarizing the most obvious factors which have been considered and suggests the complexity of the phenomena which the discussion has tried to simplify.

In conclusion, it seems appropriate to examine briefly the major policy implications of this study. Perhaps the most significant finding to emerge is the degree to which the persistence of divisive issues in Agency-university relations must be attributed to the factors which have been labeled "environmental variables" and to the structural characteristics which have been caused by these factors. Unless there is a considerable increase in the knowledge about technical assistance and development or a major shift in Congressional attitudes, it is difficult to see how there can be a significant, long-term change in Agency-university relations. Moreover, policy changes which attempt to alter the "intervening variables" without altering the factors which influence them are likely to be no more effective in the future than they have been in the past. An exceptional administrator, such as David Bell, may be able to affect some moderate improvements for a short time but these are likely to be no more than transient phenomena.

This conclusion leads to a second important finding regarding the changes which have occurred. From the standpoint of the university-contract program, these might almost be called chance occurrences for the goals of the program have not been influential premises for the key decisions which were made. Whether or not a particular decision had unintended effects, good or bad, on the university-contract program was simply not a major consideration in the decision-making process by which administrators were selected and major Agency policies were determined. For example, there is no evidence to suggest that David Bell's favorable attitude toward university contracting and unique ability to communicate with university officials was a factor which led to his selection as administrator. Nor for that matter was John Hollister's disinterest in university projects and inability to communicate with university officials a significant factor affecting his selection. Moreover, considerations related to the university-contract program were rarely taken into account in the major organizational changes which have occurred. Thus, to understand what has happened and not happened to Agency-university relations during the past seventeen years, it is essential to recognize that the university-contract program has been a very small frog in a rather large and often turbulent puddle.

Recently there has been an increasing awareness that many significant factors affecting Agency-university relationships are outside of the direct control of either the Agency or the universities. Dorothy Jacobson, in her address to the Rural Development Conference, made the point quite bluntly: "No matter how much we improve our contracts and our procedures and no matter how much we develop new and better working relationships, the programs we seek and their success depends upon public understanding and support."[36] Even more interesting is that Mrs. Jacobson concluded with a specific plea to the university community:

> ... in the State Universities and Land-Grant Colleges we find some of the most powerful forces for moulding public opinion that exist in this nation. I would like to suggest, therefore, that as we dedicate our efforts to the programs and goals we have discussed here; and as we devote energy and talent to these efforts, we do not forget to dedicate some energy and some talent to the task of building public understanding—public understanding of the reasons for the United States policy of assistance in rural development in the less-developed countries; public understanding of the importance of the programs involved.[37]

The reader may remember that when the decision to expand university participation was made, Harold Stassen conceived of the universities as a potential "constituency" for foreign aid programs which would create a new level of public awareness and even support for the Agency's proposals in Congress. There is little evidence that the universities have been successful in this role; indeed, there is little evidence that there has been any significant attempt to undertake this task. Yet, this analysis supports the contention that by increasing levels of public awareness and by mobilizing this awareness to support the foreign assistance program when it comes before the Congress, the universities could effect fundamental improvements in technical assistance programs.

John Gardner has also recognized that simply tinkering with the contracts and procedures will never be sufficient. In the concluding chapter of *AID and the Universities* he implies that some of the problems are so intractable that new organizational forms are necessary before the United States can effectively employ the talents of the universities in technical assistance programs.

He proposed that "sometime in the reasonably near future, there be created a semi-autonomous government institute to handle certain aspects of technical assistance, particularly those aspects dealt with by the universities."[38] The justification for this recommendation reflected a concern with what this analysis has called "structural" and "environmental" variables:

> The chief factor that leads us to propose this is the absolute *necessity* that certain technical assistance activities be relieved of the pressures for early termination that Congress and the public impose on other aspects of foreign aid. . . . We believe that if Congress and the American people were given the opportunity to see certain technical assistance activities in an organizational setting somewhat apart from the rest of the foreign aid package, they would readily grasp the essential long-term character of these activities. . . .
>
> AID officials may be correct in believing that neither Congress nor the American public would approve such continuing relationships as a part of the normal AID program. But we believe that Congress might take a different view if asked to create an instrumentality apart from the regular AID program, an instrumentality designed specifically to handle long-term relationships. . . .
>
> . . . The Institute . . . would provide for the first time in government a vital center for thinking, planning, research and action on the critically important long-term problems of technical assistance. It would provide a base for imaginative and pioneering approaches to the problems of educational and human resources development—problems that lie at the very heart of all economic development, all political maturing, all modernizing of social structure.[39]

Mr. Gardner's concerns go far beyond those considered here. However, the principle underlying his proposal gets to the heart of some of the more persistent of the problems that have manifested themselves throughout the entire history of the university-contract program. It may be that the structural characteristics of the American government place such severe limits on intelligent and dedicated men in both the Agency and the universities, that a truly effective, harmonious relationship is impossible.

This proposal should not be viewed as a panacea, however. The semi-autonomous agency proposed by Mr. Gardner would not make an effective contribution to foreign assistance unless its operations were closely coordinated with the operations that remained in AID. Such a level of cooperation would not be automatic and might even be plagued by more intractable versions of many of the problems identified in this report.

Throughout the program's history, men have struggled to find ways in which U.S. universities could realize their full potential as contributors to technical assistance programs. Many of them have been intelligent and dedicated. The notable successes achieved by some projects suggest what a powerful instrument of foreign assistance a university harnessed with AID in a cooperative arrangement can be. That there were failures, even when intelligent men of good will worked hard to avoid them, indicates the importance of basic structural features of the American system of government which cannot easily be modified. The problem of realizing the full potential of AID-university cooperation is much more than that of simply having the "right man in the right place at the right time." The alternatives open to that "right man," the communications which inform him, the values which guide him and the goals which motivate him must also be "right" for the time and place. Failure to recognize this can only lead to frustration.

Like its many predecessors, this study will now become part of the Agency's history. To be of real value, however, it must become part of the Agency's "memory" as well. An understanding of the program's history and of inherent problems and issues is essential to assessing its impact both at home and abroad. It is crucial that such assessments be made, not with the idea of attaching blame for failure or praise for success to one side or the other, but with the idea of improving the mechanisms for attaining shared goals. Hopefully, policy-makers and others concerned with this objective will find this analysis useful, if not comforting.

Notes

CHAPTER I

1. Stanley Andrews, *Technical Assistance: Case Reports on Selected Projects in Nine Countries* (East Lansing: Michigan State University, mimeo., 1961), p. 12.
2. Interview, TCA official.
3. Andrews, *op. cit.*, p. 4.
4. Interview, USDA/ECA official.
5. See *Table I*, p. 18.
6. "AID Financed University Contracts as of December 31, 1965." Report submitted for the record by the Agency for International Development in connection with the testimony of David E. Bell before the Subcommittee on Foreign Operations of the Committee on Appropriations, U.S. House of Representatives. *Hearings* on Foreign Assistance and Related Agencies' Appropriations for 1967, Part 2, pp. 71–75.
7. Two of the more critical published studies are Andrews, *op. cit.*, and Walter Adams and John A. Garraty, *Is the World Our Campus?* (East Lansing: Michigan State University Press, 1960).
8. In this study, the term "Agency" means "AID and predecessor Agencies which have been responsible for the administration of the foreign assistance program." The specific name of the Agency (FOA, ICA, etc.) is used only when it is of direct relevance to the discussion.
9. Of course, the first incident might also be of some consequence for Agency-university relations at the level of the university community while the second, in all probability would not. Some readers who have been closely associated with university contracting may feel that this assumption is nonsense. However, hopefully they will read further before making up their minds.

CHAPTER II

1. Inaugural Address, 1949. President Truman outlined his objectives as follows: ". . . More than half the people of the world are living in conditions approaching misery. Their food is inadequate. They are victims of

disease. Their economic life is primitive and stagnant. Their poverty is a handicap and a threat both to them and to more prosperous areas.

For the first time in history, humanity possesses the knowledge and the skill to relieve the suffering of these people. . . . The material resources which we can afford to use for the assistance of other peoples are limited. But our imponderable resources in technical knowledge are constantly growing and are inexhaustable.

I believe that we should make available to peace loving peoples the benefits of our store of technical knowldege in order to help them realize their aspirations for a better life. . . .

Our aim should be to help the free peoples of the world through their own efforts, to produce more food, more clothing, more materials for housing and more mechanical power to lighten their burdens. . . .

Such new economic developments must be devised and controlled to benefit the peoples of the areas in which they are established.

. . . What we envisage is a program of development based on the concepts of democratic fair dealing.

Greater production is the key to prosperity and peace. And the key to greater production is a wider and more vigorous application of modern scientific and technical knowledge."

2. Interview, TCA official.
3. Ross E. Moore, address before the Division of Agriculture, Convention of the Association of Land-Grant Colleges and Universities, November 13, 1950, in Carla S. Gelband, *University Contract Programs: Educational Support to Developing Nations* (American Council on Education, Committee on Institutional Projects Abroad, mimeo., 1961), p. 1. (Hereafter cited as the *Gelband Report*.)
4. Circular letter No. 11, Association of Land-Grant Colleges and Universities, January 1949. *Gelband Report*, p. 3.
5. Education and World Affairs, *The University Looks Abroad* (New York: Walker & Co., 1965), p. 53. The differences between the Land-Grant philosophy and more traditional philosophies of education were outlined by former NASULGC President Ellis in his address to the Conference on International Rural Development in 1964. President Ellis pointed out that the Land-Grant College Act had three new concepts. These concepts were:

(1) "Colleges to serve all people and not just a few learned professions.
(2) Colleges to concern themselves with all aspects of nature and all fields of endeavor 'in order to promote the liberal and practical education of the industrial classes . . .'.
(3) provision of federal finance for education under a broad general grant without any accompanying federal control of education."

He went on to emphasize that "though there were many false starts and failures in the early days of Land-Grant colleges, *their goal did remain.* Farmers by 1900 had no doubt as to the worth of the colleges. Soon other groups began to appreciate the flow of engineers, technicians and applied scientists that were coming from the classrooms. The Land-

Grant philosophy which dignified physical effort and work on practical problems had begun to produce a stream of social dividends. Gradually, the concept grew that the colleges were of service to all the people. The concept that the state is our campus became popular. President David Henry [of the NASULGC] a few years ago, wrote as follows: 'What has been unchanging about the Land-Grant institutions has not been their external form or method of organization. The chief persisting elements in the family resemblance have been faith in the efficacy of learning by the many vigorous applications of the democratic idea to educational service, adaptability in meeting each new task to as best to serve the welfare of the State, loyalty to the high mission of the university in any setting at any time, the advancement of knowledge and the search for truth'."

6. Fitzgerald, Holmgreen and Andrews were all interviewed in connection with the preparation of this report. Information on the views of Dr. Bennett was gained from several persons who were closely associated with him during the period when he was administrator of the Technical Cooperation Administration. (Dr. Bennett was killed in an airplane crash in December 1951, while on an inspection tour of TCA missions.)

7. Interview.

8. Martin Bronfenbrenner, *Academic Encounter: The American University in Japan and Korea* (Glencoe: Free Press, 1961), pp. 11–16.

9. *Final Report,* Cornell-Los Baños contract, 1952–60, p. 3.

10. Interview, Former government employee closely associated with the Utah State–Iraq project.

11. Interview, Former government employee closely associated with the Arkansas–Panama project.

12. The Smith–Mundt Act, enacted in 1948, provided funds for a limited world-wide program of technical assistance primarily involving the exchange of technical personnel. Smith–Mundt projects tended to be patterned after IIAA projects in Latin America.

13. Interviews with government officials closely associated with the Utah State project; also, *Completion Report for Project 265–AC–11–AA.*

14. *Memorandum of Agreement between the Technical Cooperation Administration and Oklahoma Agricultural and Mechanical College,* May 16, 1952. A second document relevant to the history of this project is the *Agreement for a Cooperative Agricultural Education Program Between the Imperial Ethiopian Government and the Government of the United States of America,* June 16, 1951.

15. The different organizational arrangements through which technical assistance projects were administered during this period are discussed briefly below. For more detailed discussions, see Arthur T. Mosher, *Technical Cooperation in Latin American Agriculture* (Chicago: University of Chicago Press, 1957) and Phillip M. Glick, *The Administration of Technical Assistance: Growth in the Americas* (Chicago: University of Chicago Press, 1957).

16. For a detailed discussion of *Servicios,* see the works cited in note 15, above.

17. Information on the Arkansas project was obtained from interviews with both government and university officials.
18. Interview, Former government official closely associated with the change in policy cited and with the Cornell–Los Baños program.
19. *Contract between the Agricultural College of the University of the Philippines at Los Baños and Cornell University,* July 1, 1952. That the contractual arrangement was between the two participating institutions rather than between the Agency and the U.S. institution is of little consequence to the discussion which follows. The significance of differences in contractual form will be considered in a later chapter. The formal agreement between Cornell and the Agency was *MSA Letter of Commitment No. 92–2,* July 23, 1952.
20. *Ibid.* The contract goes on to specify the substantive areas in which specialists were to be provided. The reader is invited to compare this definition of objectives with the definition of objectives for the Oklahoma–Ethiopia project.
21. The directors of the Food and Agriculture division during this period were D. A. Fitzgerald and E. N. Holmgreen. Holmgreen continued to direct the bureau throughout the life of the Cornell project.
22. This is one of the most interesting characteristics of the administrative structure of MSA and its successor agencies, FOA and ICA, which followed essentially the same organizational pattern. On technical matters, the mission technical bureau chief could appeal "over the head" of the mission director to his own bureau chief in Washington. In such instances, the differences had to be resolved through negotiations between the technical bureau chief and the cognizant geographic area bureau chief. Such appeals became more frequent in the later history of the Agency and were a continual source of irritation to mission directors and geographic area bureau chiefs. This is discussed in greater detail below.
23. It should not be assumed, however, that all TCA-administered contracts oriented toward a "sisterhood" relationship between a participating U.S. and host country institution were characterized by the expansion of function noted above. In Iraq, where the TCA mission was large, the agricultural development program extensive, and the contractual relationship defined in more detail, the program of the University of Arizona at the Iraq College of Agriculture at Abu Ghraib did not expand beyond the initially envisioned relationship. (Information on the Iraq project was gained from two former government officials closely associated with it and from the terminal report of the University of Arizona, *The Iraq College of Agriculture: Its History and Development, 1952–1959: Collaboration in Agricultural Education.*)
24. Herbert A. Simon, "Birth of an Organization, The Economic Cooperation Administration," *Public Administration Review,* XIII, No. 4 (Autumn 1953), 227–236.
25. For a brief but well-presented discussion of compliance control, the maintenance of conformity to regulations in organizations, see Col. George A. Lincoln, *Improving AID Program Evaluation* (Washington: AID, 1965), p. 11. (Hereafter cited as the *Lincoln Report.*)

26. The background of IIAA is summarized in a "Memorandum Study of the Servicio" (Washington: ICA, 1957, mimeo.), prepared for an ICA evaluation team. See also, Mosher, *op. cit.*, and Glick, *op. cit.*
27. "Memorandum Study of the Servicio." IIAA was established following negotiations initiated at the Panama Conference of 1939 and legislatively supported by the Pittman Act of 1940.
28. Interviews, FOA officials.
29. Mosher, *op. cit.*, p. 71.
30. Interview, Former official closely associated with OFAR programs.
31. Title IV of the Foreign Economic Assistance Act of 1950.
32. See note 12, above.
33. TCA was under the administrative control of the Department of State during this period; ECA was not.
34. Thailand, the Philippines, Burma, Taiwan and Korea were all assigned to MSA.
35. One official associated with the program during this period referred to this as "the two worlds concept."
36. Interview.

CHAPTER III

1. For a detailed discussion of these points, see Chapter X.
2. Actually, Stassen headed the Mutual Security Agency for a short period of time. FOA did not succeed this agency until August 1953.
3. Interview, NASULGC officer.
4. Proceedings of the NASULGC Sixty-Seventh Annual Convention, Columbus, Ohio, November 1963, General Sessions, "Technical Service Overseas" by Harold E. Stassen, Director, Foreign Operations Administration.
5. *Ibid.*
6. The discussion of Stassen's philosophy is based on a lengthy interview.
7. It is not accurate, however, to characterize Stassen's initiatives in the area of university contracts as merely a continuation of the early pilot program. According to Stassen, the experience with the early TCA and ECA contracts did not significantly influence either his philosophy or his decision to undertake a major expansion of university-contract operations.
8. See note 6, above.
9. A minor but interesting manifestation of this change in approach was a directive, originating with Under Secretary of State Walter B. Smith, which strongly discouraged the use of the phrase "Point Four" in official documents and correspondence.
10. The most searching and consequential investigations were conducted by the Committee on Appropriations of the House of Representatives and the Committee on Government Operations of the Senate.
11. Stassen stated that he did not personally favor this provision but did not strongly oppose it because of other more important aspects of the program which required his personal intervention to gain Congressional support.
12. More significant than any specific legislation resulting from the McCarthy investigations was the development of extremely cautious and conservative

attitudes with respect to matters of security among many personnel in the executive branch.
13. Interviews, FOA officials.
14. Interview, Harold E. Stassen.
15. It is interesting to note that this exact phrase was used by five former FOA officials with whom this period was discussed.
16. Authority for the reorganization was included in the Mutual Security Legislation of 1953. The implementing document was Presidential Reorganization Plan No. 7 of August 1, 1953. The reorganization followed, to a considerable degree, the recommendations of the International Development Advisory Board, directed by Nelson Rockefeller.
17. Interview, FOA official who was closely associated with the University-Contracts Coordinator. This position should not be confused with the very powerful one held by Edward E. Kunze as Director of the Office of Contract Relations after 1956.
18. The operation of this part of the system was described by an official associated with the Office of Personnel Security and Integrity during this period. After the examinations and evaluations were completed, the information on each individual was assembled in a folder. Each morning, during the personnel reduction process he would bring a pile of folders into the Director's office. In the afternoon he would go to the office and pick up two piles of folders. In one pile were the folders of the people who were to be retained in the Agency; in the other, the folders of the persons who were to be eliminated. Stassen used the examination scores and evaluations as a basis for judgment, but made his own decisions.
19. Interview, Harold E. Stassen.
20. Interview, TCA official.
21. In making these generalizations, we do not wish to overlook the many individuals, from both the universities and the Agency, who worked closely and cooperatively together. Nevertheless, we believe that the picture presented correctly characterizes the climate of opinion which prevailed in the Agency regarding university contracts during this period.
22. Interview, FOA official.
23. In one of the projects of this type, the concept of a "university team" did not even exist. A chief of party was not designated and the university recruitees were supervised *as individuals* by mission personnel.
24. This analysis uses the conceptual framework developed in Chapter I.
25. Interview, Harold E. Stassen.
26. In preparing this study the complete chronological files of eighteen university projects were examined in detail. These files included quarterly, annual and terminal reports, special studies and reports and in some instances, correspondence between the university and the Agency.
27. Often, these individuals were outsiders who were not members of the regular university staff.
28. University files.
29. University files.
30. Interviews, Agency and university officials.

31. The following statement was included in the Minutes of the Senate at the 1953 NASULGC Convention: "Overconcentration of administrative control by federal agencies over details of operation has resulted in delay, frustration and inefficiency."
32. The account of the *Gelband Report* regarding this period differs substantially from this interpretation. Gelband states (p. 4), "By 1954, each side had come to regard the other as enigmatic, obscurationist and stubborn when it came to the actual negotiation and operation of the contracts. Despite Mr. Stassen's avowed intention to leave decentralized implementation of the work to them, the universities believed that they were being mistrusted, too heavily supervised, directed by non-professionals and in general not being given sufficient discretion and responsibility to do a proper job. Despite university talk of 'sacrifice,' the government believed the colleges expected special treatment, wanted the program to be conducted according to their own rules and were unwilling to relinquish even a bit of their traditional autonomy to the national interest. Recognizing the seriousness of this dispute, representatives of the NASULGC, the Department of Agriculture and the Foreign Operations Administration met to discuss what steps might be taken to ameliorate the rapidly worsening situation." The *Gelband Report* correctly states that these discussions preceded the request to the American Council on Education which resulted in the establishment of the Committee on Institutional Projects Abroad. In our opinion, however, the worsening of relations between the Agency and the participating universities was a consequence of the expansion of contracts, it did not precede this expansion. The first articulation of the policy to "get contracts" did not come until early in 1954 at a meeting between Director Stassen and USOM Chiefs in Lima, Peru. The expansion of contracts did not begin in earnest until mid-1954.
33. Interview, NASULGC official.
34. American Council on Education, *President's Annual Report,* 1953–54.

CHAPTER IV

1. *Overseas Economic Operations:* A Report to the Congress by the Commission on Organization of the Executive Branch, Herbert Hoover, Chairman, June 1955, p. 39.
2. *Ibid.*, p. 63. The Commission report stated: "The task force estimates that if their recommendations are adopted, a minimum of $360,000,000 per annum could be saved from the mutual aid, non-military programs without prejudice to the programs."
3. Unfortunately it was impossible to interview Hollister personally. The description of his philosophy comes mostly from other interviews.
4. Interview, ICA official.
5. *ICA Policy Directive No. 6,* dated April 4, 1957.
6. The directive noted that "Project undertakings of imprecise or indefinite duration usually stem from one of the following two conditions: (1) Insufficient planning of quantitative project goals. (2) Insufficient or un-

realistic planning of project elements to ensure accomplishment of project objectives."

"It is therefore my policy," the statement continued, "that no project, either new or continuing, will be approved in the future without adequate definition of specific and, whenever possible, quantitative goals and realistic termination dates."

7. Regarding these points, the directive stated, "Many offices are responsible for the development, review and approval of projects. Each office will verify that these determinations [of quantitatively defined goals and realistic termination dates] are made and documented in the related project proposal."
8. This phrase was used in several interviews.
9. See Executive Order 10610, dated May 9, 1955 and State Department Delegation of Authority 85.
10. President's Task Force on Foreign Assistance: Working Group on Contracting, *Positive Contracting for AID: Marshalling and Strengthening the Nation's Resources for International Development,* 1961, p. 29. (Hereafter cited as the *Glick Report.*)
11. "Delay in Answering Correspondence," Information submitted for the record by the International Cooperation Administration to the Committee on Foreign Relations, United States Senate, May 29, 1957, in connection with the testimony of John B. Hollister. *Hearings Before the Committee on Foreign Relations, Eighty-Fifth Congress, First Session, on the Mutual Security Program for Fiscal Year 1958,* pp. 72–73.
12. Interview, Agency official.
13. Disallowances are discussed on pp. 63 ff., below.
14. Interview, ICA official.
15. "The University Contract Process," Information submitted for the record by the International Cooperation Administration to the Committee on Foreign Relations, United States Senate, in connection with the testimony of John B. Hollister. *Hearings,* Eighty-Fifth Congress, First Session, pp. 97–98.
16. "Summary of Actions Taken by ICA to Improve Administration of its Programs: New Personnel Policies and Procedures," Report submitted for the record by the International Cooperation Administration to the Committee on Foreign Relations, United States Senate, in connection with the testimony of John B. Hollister. *Hearings,* Eighty-Fifth Congress, First Session, pp. 89–91. The report stated, "although recruitments exceeded separations by 250 during calendar year, 1956, about 460 unfilled positions remained at the end of the year, approximately the same as at the close of 1955."
17. A *contract action* is, roughly, any decision regarding contract matters, usually contract negotiation or contract interpretation.
18. Interviews, Agency and university officials. This point is also touched upon in many published studies and reports dealing with the foreign assistance program. See, for example, F. M. Coffin, *Witness for AID* (Boston: Houghton Mifflin, 1964), Chapter 4.
19. Interviews, Agency and university officials. For a general comment on

overhead problems, see John W. Gardner, *AID and the Universities:* A Report For Education and World Affairs in Cooperation with the Agency for International Development (New York: Education and World Affairs, 1964), p. 28, EWA Edition. (Hereafter cited as the *Gardner Report.*)

20. In 1961, the Agency secured legislation specifically exempting university contracts from Federal contracting regulations with regard to the payment of indirect costs and permitting the negotiation of fixed overhead rates.

21. The actual clause in the contract was usually similar to the following:

    Overhead

    An allowance [is made] to cover the Contractor's indirect expenses at the rate of [ ] per-cent of base salaries paid to the staff members engaged in the performance of the contract. The foregoing rate, based on an analysis and evaluation by ICA or other appropriate U.S. government agency of relevant data submitted by the Contractor relating to overhead, is provisional and shall be subjected to such audits as may be performed by ICA or other appropriate U.S. government agency to determine whether payments at such rate exceeded Contractor's actual overhead costs allocable to the contract for the period involved, in which event the foregoing rate shall be adjusted accordingly and the Contractor shall promptly refund any such excess to the [Agency]. The rate established by such audits shall become the provisional rate for future billings and shall, likewise, be subject to revision by subsequent similar audit to determine whether actual overhead was exceeded thus necessitating a refund to the [Agency]. (The passage quoted is taken from Amendment 1 to exhibit III of the revised contract covering the operations of Cornell University at Los Baños, dated June 20, 1957.)

22. *Glick Report,* p. 29.

23. For a detailed discussion of these problems by a university business officer, see J. Orville Lindstrom (Business Manager, University of Oregon), "Operational Problems in University Contracting" in Richard Humphrey, ed., *Toward a Foreign Policy for Higher Education: Proceedings of the Fifth Conference on University Contracts Abroad Sponsored by the American Council on Education* (1959).

24. Interview, university campus coordinator.

25. This issue was discussed with a high official in the Agency during this period and a leading representative of the university community. The discovery of differences in benefits tended to occur when university campus coordinators would get together in their annual meetings and compare notes.

26. This opinion was expressed by a ranking university administrator and leading representative of the university community.

27. For a superb general discussion of the underlying issues involved in this type of disagreement, see Guy Hunter, "Education in the New Africa," *African Affairs,* LXVI, No. 263 (April 1967), pp. 127–139.

28. Semi-annual report from participating university files covering the period from October 19, 1955 to April 19, 1956.

29. "Security Clearance": Information submitted for the record by the International Cooperation Administration to the Committee on Foreign Relations, United States Senate, in connection with the testimony of John B. Hollister. *Hearings,* Eighty-Fifth Congress, First Session, pp. 77-78.
30. *Ibid.*
31. *Ibid.*
32. See ICA Staff Memorandum No. 25, "Articles for Publication."
33. For a brief discussion of this and other issues which arose during this period, see E. W. Weidner, *The World Role of Universities* (New York: McGraw Hill, 1962), pp. 177 ff.
34. *Glick Report,* p. 85.
35. *Gelband Report,* p. 6.
36. Officials of these organizations are the first to emphasize that the nature and extent of this "representation" is very hard to define.
37. *Proceedings* of the NASULGC, Sixty-Ninth Annual Convention (1955), Report of the Committee on Foreign Technical Cooperation.
38. *Proceedings* of the NASULGC, Seventieth Annual Convention (1956), Report of the Committee on Foreign Technical Cooperation.
39. Richard A. Humphrey, ed., *University Projects Abroad: Papers Presented at the Conference on University Contracts Abroad* (1955), "Foreword." See also, *Gelband Report,* p. 6.
40. *Gelband Report,* p. 6.
41. *Ibid.*
42. *Gelband Report,* p. 7.
43. Interview, High official in the American Council on Education who participated in the conference.
44. Interviews, High official in the American Council on Education, high official in the NASULGC and participating university president.
45. Interview, High Agency official.
46. American Council on Education, *President's Annual Report,* 1956-57.
47. *Gelband Report,* p. 7.
48. *Ibid.,* p. 6.
49. *Ibid.,* p. 4. See also, American Council on Education, *President's Annual Report,* 1956-57, which discusses the "philosophy" of the Committee during its "first grant period."
50. *Gelband Report,* p. 5. The quotation is from a letter from Arthur S. Adams, President of the American Council on Education, to John B. Hollister, dated June 13, 1956.
51. *Ibid.*
52. Letter, Arthur S. Adams to D. A. Fitzgerald, February 19, 1957. *Gelband Report,* p. 5.
53. Letter, Arthur H. Peterson to Edwin H. Arnold, May 29, 1957. *Gelband Report,* p. 5.
54. Circular letter to the presidents of participating universities, July 17, 1957.
55. *Hearings,* Mutual Security Act of 1957, p. 72.
56. *Ibid.,* pp. 99 *passim.* All of these reports are cited above.
57. *Ibid.,* p. 100.
58. *Ibid.*

CHAPTER V

1. The men who served as Director during this period were:
   James H. Smith Jr.: October 8, 1957—January 31, 1959.
   Leonard J. Saccio: (acting) February 1—May 29, 1959.
   James W. Riddleberger: May 29, 1959—February 28, 1961.
   Henry R. LaBouisse: March 1—November 3, 1961.
2. By contrast, all of the Agency and university personnel who had been associated with the program over a long period of time could remember Stassen and cite detailed characteristics of his policies and programs. Almost all of the Agency personnel and most of the university personnel could do the same for Hollister. These men preceded the Directors of this period in time, yet they are much better remembered.

   We should emphasize that we make no judgment about the personal leadership characteristics of the men involved. Though we will not explore all the reasons for the lack of leadership at the top during this period, it is clear that many factors came into play which were more important than the individual characteristics of the appointees to the office of Director. We are here simply reporting the facts of the situation as they were perceived by the persons who were most closely associated with it.
3. Probably the most important of these initiatives was the establishment of the Development Loan Fund in 1958.
4. Richard A. Humphrey, ed., *Blueprint and Experience: Proceedings of the Third Annual Conference on University Contracts Abroad,* "Address of James A. Smith Jr." Smith announced the change in publication clearance policy in his address. However, while Smith supported university contracts, his address was notable for its failure to deal concretely with the major problems which had plagued Agency-university relations.
5. H. Field Haviland Jr., "Foreign Aid and the Policy Process," *American Political Science Review,* LII (1958), 709 ff. The more general discussion in Richard J. Fenno Jr., "The House Appropriations Committee as a Political System: The Problem of Integration," *American Political Science Review,* LVI (June 1962), 310–324, is also relevant.
6. Congressional Quarterly Service (Thomas N. Schroth, ed.), *Congress and the Nation: A Review of Government and Politics in the Post-War Years* (Washington: Congressional Quarterly Service, 1964), p. 184. For a general discussion of Congressional activity with respect to the foreign assistance program, see pp. 163 ff.
7. See, for example, Aaron Wildavsky, *The Politics of the Budgetary Process* (Boston: Little Brown & Co., 1964). Wildavsky observes: "agency officials are continuously engaged in 'feeling the pulse' of Congress. . . . The likes and dislikes of influential Congressmen are well charted. Hearings on the preceding year's budget are carefully perused for indications of attitudes on specific programs and particularly on items that may get the agency into trouble" (p. 26).
8. The great power of committee and sub-committee chairmen in the House of Representatives has been noted by many observers. See, for example,

Fenno, *op. cit.*, and Holbert N. Carroll, *The House of Representatives and Foreign Affairs* (Pittsburgh: University of Pittsburgh Press, 1958), Chapters 3, 4.
9. Haviland, *op. cit.*, p. 711.
10. In *Witness for AID* (*op. cit.*), Frank M. Coffin refers to this process as "The Annual Minuet" (Chapter 4). He observes: "In terms of the time involved, intensity of preparation, controversy of debate or uncertainty of results, this obstacle course has few, if any parallels in government" (p. 49).
11. For a general discussion of these problems, see Coffin, *op. cit.*, and Chapter X.
12. Interviews, ICA officials. See also, "The University Contract Process," Information submitted for the record by ICA in connection with the testimony of John B. Hollister before the Committee on Foreign Relations, U.S. Senate on the Mutual Security Act of 1957. *Hearings*, p. 97.
13. James A. Smith is said to have remarked in a moment of frustration, "Nothing ever comes up in this damn agency and I can never get anything down."
14. Most university contracts were under the direct operational control of the Office of Food and Agriculture or "O-Food," as it was called by Agency personnel. The director, E. N. Holmgreen, was one of the originators of the university-contract program.
15. *Glick Report*, p. 32.
16. *Ibid.*
17. Interview, ICA official.
18. Interview.
19. *Gelband Report*, p. 7.
20. American Council on Education, "Request to Ford Foundation for Grant Extension," dated April 2, 1957.
21. We have quoted rather extensively from relevant CIPA reports and statements because, despite their clarity and perceptiveness, they seem to be much less well known among university and Agency personnel than more recent documents of a similar nature.
22. Richard Humphrey, Memorandum to C. Tyler Wood, May 5, 1958. *Gelband Report*, p. 9.
23. Richard Humphrey, letter to Leonard Saccio (acting ICA Director), May 29, 1959. *Gelband Report*, p. 10.
24. *Ibid.*, p. 11.
25. Richard Humphrey, letter to E. E. Kunze, August 5, 1960. *Gelband Report*, p. 11.
26. American Council on Education, Commission on Education and International Affairs, Document 60-5, May 10, 1960, pp. 2-3. *Gelband Report*, p. 8.
27. "Bloomington Conference on the Impact of University Contracts Upon the American University," *Education and Foreign Operations*, IX (November 1958), 2.
28. See *The Annapolis Conference on International Education* (Washington, D.C.: Bureau of International Cultural Relations, 1958).

Notes

29. Interview.
30. American Council on Education, *President's Annual Report*, 1958–59.
31. *Gelband Report*, p. 12.
32. Richard Humphrey, Memorandum to Arthur S. Adams, July 8, 1960. *Gelband Report*, p. 27.
33. Of course, there was a high degree of interlocking membership between the NASULGC and CIPA.
34. *Proceedings* of the NASULGC Centennial Convention (November 12–16, 1961), Report of International Study Group I.
35. Many of the originators of the program in the Agency would disagree with this statement.
36. Report of International Study Group I.
37. *Ibid.*
38. Adams and Garraty, *op. cit.*
39. In connection with the *Glick Report*.
40. Bronfenbrenner, *op. cit.*
41. Weidner, *op. cit.*
42. TASG materials were made available by Study Group Coordinator, John Ohly.
43. Twenty persons who had been closely associated with the university-contract program in various positions were asked:

    (a) What studies relating to the program they thought were particularly significant?
    (b) What studies they were familiar with, whether significant or not?
    (c) What studies they had heard of, whether they were familiar with them or not?

    From this questioning it was clear that few Agency personnel had even read, much less been influenced by these works. Surprisingly, the response among university personnel was not much better.
44. Glick, *op. cit.*
45. Mosher, *op. cit.*
46. Interview.
47. Washington: ICA, mimeo., 1961.
48. A typical passage, which illustrates the style of presentation which irritated Agency personnel is the following:

    "... the contract itself is totally unfitted and unsatisfactory as an arrangement to promote maximum use of resources, people, imagination and initiative upon the part of universities as institutions and the people who work in them are concerned. The present contract is a simple purchase order, designed it seems to buy so many packages of pencils or man hours to go through so many motions and bring forth predetermined results which can be recorded by a government auditor or an IBM machine" (pp. 32–33).
49. Interviews and files of Agency officials.
50. Adams and Garraty, *op. cit.*, "Introduction," p. ix.
51. *Ibid.*, p. 156.
52. *Ibid.*, pp. 102–105.

53. *Ibid.*, p. ix.
54. Interview.
55. Two other studies, focusing directly on the university-contract program, appeared during this period. These were Bronfenbrenner's *Academic Encounter (op. cit.)*, a survey of ICA and foundation financed projects in the Far East, and the *Gelband Report,* which reported on the activities of CIPA and has been quoted extensively above. Neither of these studies as far as can be determined, received any particular recognition from the Agency or had any impact on Agency-university relations.
56. Ford Foundation, December 1960.
57. J. L. Morrill, President of the University of Minnesota, was chairman of the Committee.
58. *The University Looks Abroad,* p. xv.
59. Committee on the University and World Affairs, *The University and World Affairs* (New York: The Ford Foundation, 1960), pp. 32–33. (Hereafter cited as the *Morrill Committee Report.*)
60. *Ibid.*, p. 53.
61. *Ibid.*, p. 56.
62. *Ibid.*, p. 80.
63. By establishing Education and World Affairs.
64. See note 43, above.
65. Interviews, Agency and university officials.
66. There seems to be little justification for a university to raise issues relating to "academic freedom" and the "special nature of the university" if its staff members are simply performing direct hire functions along side of, or in place of mission personnel. Regarding this point, see the discussion in Chapter X.

CHAPTER VI

1. *Report to the Congress on the Foreign Assistance Program for Fiscal Year 1962* (Washington: Government Printing Office, 1963), p. 4.
2. One observer has commented that Hamilton was simply not concerned with the operational aspects of the program. He viewed his major function as that of serving as an advocate for foreign assistance before the Congress. See Arthur J. Schlesinger, *A Thousand Days: John F. Kennedy in the White House* (Boston: Houghton Mifflin, 1965), pp. 596–597.
3. Washington, June 30, 1961, mimeo. (Hereafter cited as the *Gant Report.*)
4. Executive Order 10973 and State Department Delegation of Authority 104.
5. This statement reflects the view of the working group, but not necessarily of this study.
6. *Gant Report,* p. 1.
7. *Ibid.*, p. 12.
8. Interview, Agency official.
9. *Gant Report,* p. 49.
10. *Report to the Congress on the Foreign Assistance Program, 1962,* p. 5.
11. Interview, Agency official.

Notes

12. This exact phrase was used to characterize Dr. Fitzgerald's role in the Agency by three Agency officials, a former high Agency official and a high NASULGC official.
13. "Musical Chairs in the Foreign Assistance Program," press release, November 16, 1962; reprinted in David A. Baldwin, ed., *Foreign Aid and American Foreign Policy: A Documentary Analysis* (New York: F. A. Praeger, 1966), p. 134.
14. *Ibid.*, pp. 137, 138.
15. Washington: Government Printing Office, 1963. (Hereafter cited as the *McGee Report*.)
16. *Ibid.*, pp. 1–2.
17. *Ibid.*, p. 7.
18. For a detailed analysis of the 1957 hearings, see Haviland, *op. cit.*
19. *Report to the Congress on the Foreign Assistance Program, 1962*, p. 4.
20. "Musical Chairs in the Foreign Assistance Program," *op. cit.*, p. 135.
21. Coffin, *op. cit.*, pp. 47 ff.
22. Interview, ACE official.
23. Interview.
24. Interview.

CHAPTER VII

1. Much of the information on this period necessarily comes from interviews. In preparing this study, we spoke at some length with Mr. Bell himself and more than fifteen other individuals who had worked with him during his tenure.
2. Interview, university official.
3. Interview, university official.
4. We should make it clear that no assessment regarding the success of this arrangement is implied. In fact, we do not believe it was particularly successful. The point is that it represented a positive response by the Administrator to a long-expressed need of the university community.
5. John W. Gardner, *AID and the Universities: A Report to the Administrator of the Agency for International Development* (New York: Education and World Affairs, 1964). The *Gardner Report* is discussed in greater detail below.
6. An outstanding example is his participation in the International Rural Development Conference. Bell concluded his introductory remarks by stating: "We in AID recognize fully that if we are to achieve these objectives [of closer cooperation in the pursuit of mutual goals], we first of all must change many of our own patterns of work, many of our own attitudes, many of our past practices." One university official who participated in the Conference remarked, "After Bell's introductory speech, there was really no need for the Conference, he had expressed what we were feeling so well." The Conference is discussed in greater detail below.
7. Copies of the report were also brought forth for reference or were in a

readily accessible position in offices of university presidents, campus coordinators and NASULGC officials.
8. It should also be noted that the report was the subject of major articles and editorial comment in both the *New York Times* and the *Washington Post.*
9. *Gardner Report,* EWA Edition, p. ix.
10. Interview.
11. Foreign Assistance Act of 1961, as amended, section 601.
12. *The Scope and Distribution of United States Military and Economic Assistance Programs:* Report to the President of the United States from the Committee to Strengthen the Security of the Free World (March 20, 1963), p. 4.
13. *Foreign Assistance Act of 1961,* section 620.
14. *Ibid.,* section 604.
15. In the 1966 *Hearings* (Part II, p. 41), Passman made the following observation during Bell's testimony: "I predict that you will eventually wind up as president of some great institution, possibly even Vice President or President of the United States, as I think you are one of the finest men I have ever known. You have a quick, alert mind. I just do not agree with you."
16. Interviews, Agency officials (L.A. Bureau).
17. Incorporated in section 622b of the *Foreign Assistance Act,* as amended.
18. A particularly interesting observation was made by an official who had joined the Agency after the reorganization, served for about two years in a regional bureau and then been transferred to a central office reporting directly to the Administrator. "When I was in the [regional] bureau," he stated, "I opposed centralized control. However now that I have served in the [central office] for a while, I can see that there is a need for more centralization. We could still achieve the same results and have a lot more uniformity within the Agency if we could establish a little more flexible, centralized control."
19. To some degree, Dr. Long had already been performing this function informally.
20. "Memorandum for record regarding conference on March 11, 1963 at 9:30 A.M. in the office of the Administrator of the A.I.D. programs, in the Department of State" (prepared by I. L. Baldwin), pp. 1, 2.
21. *Gant Report,* p. 50.
22. *Gardner Report,* p. 40.
23. *Ibid.,* p. 44. An interesting sidelight on this section of the *Gardner Report* is that Gardner was encouraged to include it by high TCR officials. It was hoped that this would bring what we have called the "status problem" of TCR more forcefully to the attention of the Administrator.
24. According to officials in other bureaus, the similarities between the period of proliferation and the developments in the Latin American Bureau went beyond the expansion and diversification of university contracting. In fact, it is possible to interchange some interview descriptions of the two periods with little change in meaning.

25. A good example of the earlier type is the FOA contract with the University of Minnesota to assist Seoul National University (1954).
26. *The University Looks Abroad,* pp. 206, 207.
27. AID Contract (AID–la 49), "Between the United States of America and the Iowa State University of Science and Technology," Appendix B (Operational Plan).
28. See *The University Looks Abroad,* p. 271. We are referring in particular to the Wisconsin contracts in Brazil and Nigeria.
29. Some Agency officials (especially in the regional bureaus) felt that by administering these projects, TCR was assuming operational responsibilities which exceeded the spirit, if not the letter, of its assigned responsibilities as a staff office in the Agency.
30. However, the approach was not entirely without precedent. In the early days of TCA, Stanley Andrews had supported research on the technical assistance process at the University of Chicago.
31. *Ibid.,* p. 153.
32. *Proceedings of the Meeting of the Alliance Steering Committee on Rural Development* (September 6–8, 1962, mimeo.), p. 26.
33. *The University Looks Abroad,* p. 207. The Vicos project in Peru has been a major element of this program.
34. *Ibid.*
35. See Preface above. The major portion of this study was initially prepared as a minor sub-project of the CIC–AID group.
36. Members of the Consortium for the Study of Nigerian Rural Development included (as of 1965): University of Wisconsin, Michigan State University, Colorado State University, Kansas State University, U.S. Department of Agriculture, U.S. Department of the Interior and the Research Triangle Institute. For an overview of the project, see the *Final Report* of the Phase I Planning Team (East Lansing: Michigan State University, mimeo., September 10, 1965).
37. The reader will recall that during the period of genesis, all of the contracts were in the rural development area.
38. It is true, however, that a somewhat higher level of experience in working with universities existed in the Office of Food and Agriculture than in other bureaus of FOA and ICA. This office handled most of the agricultural and rural development contracts.
39. One Agency official told us that he did not think there would be any point in focusing specifically on the rural development area in examining the history of Agency-university relations.
40. *Proceedings of the Meeting of the Alliance Steering Committee on Rural Development,* p. 1.
41. *Ibid.*
42. *Ibid.*
43. *Ibid.,* p. 2.
44. The Steering Committee meeting preceded Hamilton's resignation by a few days. The policy decisions leading up to the meeting were made during the early months of his term in office. However, as far as we can

determine, except for the brief address before the Committee, he was not an active participant.

45. *Proceedings,* p. 7.
46. "Activities in which A.I.D. Should Take Responsibility," a section of the concluding statement of the Steering Committee meeting. *Proceedings,* pp. 7, 8.
47. "Check list of Resources Available to A.I.D. Programs," *Proceedings,* p. 10.
48. "Establishment of Committee of the Association of State Universities and Land-Grant Colleges on A.I.D. Relationships," *Proceedings,* pp. 11, 12. The proposed "instrumentality" was described as follows:

"Within the committee structure of the Association of State Universities and Land-Grant Colleges a standing committee should be established to concern itself with maintaining orderly and effective relationships between AID and the member universities of the Association. Without excluding other activities, this standing committee would be responsible principally for receiving from AID, requests for participation of one or more Land-Grant universities or colleges in programs of agricultural education, research or extension. In response to such requests, this standing committee —on the basis of information previously obtained by the committee— would make specific recommendations to AID concerning the Land-Grant university resources available for meeting specific needs. . . . To provide continuity and to provide a single point of contact for AID, there should be assigned to this standing committee a full time executive secretary or coordinator with offices in Washington."

49. *Proceedings,* p. 13.
50. Interviews, AID officials. Most officials in other bureaus and in the central administration with whom we talked about this issue, felt that the L.A. Bureau went "too fast" and that its programs were unintegrated and poorly administered. (For a list of attendees at the Steering Committee Meeting, see the *Proceedings,* Appendix A, pp. 16–17.)
51. Minutes, Meeting of the International Affairs Committee, NASULGC, Sunday, November 11, 1962.
52. The Rockefeller, Ford and Kellogg Foundations each contributed sixty thousand dollars to cover the operating expenses of the office.
53. *Memorandum for the Record Regarding Conference on March 11, 1963.*
54. AIDTO CIRCULAR LA 190, May 24, 1963. The circular read:

"The association of State Universities and Land-Grant Colleges has established in Washington, D.C., a Rural Development Office, with a Director, to work under the guidance of a special Land-Grant college committee with AID and other interested government agencies and private foundations on rural development problems. Contracts will be negotiated directly between AID and individual universities.

. . . however the Rural Development Office will exercise liaison functions, improving the process of communication between AID and the universities and of coordination with USDA and other suppliers of technical assistance resources. It will obtain and make available information on personnel, interests, resources, and experience available at the different member universities, to serve as a guide to AID in selecting universities for specific assignments. It will foster fuller mutual understanding by AID and the universities of their respective needs, problems and responsibilities. It will work with AID to develop improved contracts and other arrangements between AID and the universities to minimize unnecessary friction and maximize quality of performance.

AID, on its part, is taking such action as is necessary to improve, simplify and coordinate channels of communication from AID to the USDA and to the Land-Grant universities. The Administrator has designated the Director of Agriculture Service, Office of Human Resources and Social Development, to formulate coordination arrangements governing regional contracts and to serve as the Agency's central channel of communication with the USDA and Land-Grant Rural Development Office.

Each Regional Assistant Administrator will similarly designate a single point of contact. . . . Each of these contacts will be responsible for obtaining and channeling decisions at his respective level. Within the broad Agency policy and coordination framework, regional contact with the USDA and with the Land-Grant colleges and their Rural Development Office will be kept as direct as possible.

55. We have focused on the early period of the Office's existence because it was during this period that its basic patterns of operation were established and because detailed information on this period was available.
56. This summary of the activities of the Rural Development Office is taken from the "Report of I. L. Baldwin, Director, International Rural Development Office, Association of State Universities and Land-Grant Colleges," February 5, 1963—June 30, 1964. We are grateful to Dr. Baldwin for the information on the activities of the Office which he made available to us from his personal files.
57. Interviews, NASULGC and AID officials.
58. Interview, NASULGC official.
59. *Proceedings of the Conference on International Rural Development,* p. 16.
60. *Ibid.,* p. 78.
61. Interviews. See also, "Follow-up on International Rural Development Conference," a list of conference recommendations prepared by AID.
62. This point will be elaborated in Chapters IX and X.
63. The basis of this somewhat tentative assertion is our own interviews and interviews of other members of the CIC–AID project.
64. This seemed to be the opinion of many Agency and university officials. In fact, the terms quoted were often used.

CHAPTER VIII

1. Interview, university official.
2. *Proceedings,* pp. 24, 25.

3. See Herbert Simon, *Administrative Behavior: A Study of Decision-Making Processes in Administrative Organization* (New York: Free Press, 1957, second edition), Chapter 3. Some authors use the term, "means-ends calculus" in discussing the same kinds of issues.
4. *Proceedings,* Sixty-Seventh Annual Convention (1953).
5. "Follow-up on International Rural Development Conference," p. 27.
6. Semi-annual report from participating university files covering the period October 19, 1955 to April 19, 1956.
7. *Gardner Report,* EWA Edition, p. 8.
8. *Ibid.,* p. 9.
9. See, for example, the *Memorandum of Agreement between the Technical Cooperation Administration and Oklahoma Agricultural and Mechanical College,* May 16, 1952.
10. See, for example, *Mutual Security Agency Letter of Commitment No. 92-2,* July 23, 1952; and *Contract Between the Agricultural Colleges of the University of the Philippines at Los Baños and Cornell University under Technical Assistance Authorization No. 92-250-380-2611.*
11. In the case of the Indian agricultural development project, essentially the same contract was written for each of the five universities involved.
12. Arthur H. Peterson, letter to Edwin H. Arnold, May 29, 1957.
13. *University Contracts,* pp. 32-33.
14. *Ibid.*
15. *Glick Report,* pp. 102-103.
16. *Ibid.,* p. 87.
17. *McGee Report,* p. 7.
18. *Gardner Report,* EWA Edition, p. 24.
19. See *Proceedings,* pp. 61-72, 143-159.
20. We are referring to grants to conduct overseas technical assistance projects and not grants to universities to create "centers of strength" in teaching and research in areas related to AID operations. The latter were authorized by Congress in 1966, but no funds were appropriated.
21. During the period of retrenchment, for example, two universities established prerequisite conditions for contract extension which the Agency was unable or unwilling to meet. Following extended negotiations, the universities simply refused to renew their contracts and the projects were discontinued. Subsequently, the Agency recruited other universities to continue essentially the same work.
22. Occasionally, the Agency has issued "statements of intent" to renew a contract for periods of up to five years or even longer. However, such statements have no binding legal status.
23. Participating university files. The report covers the period from April through October of 1961.
24. *Ibid.*
25. Participating university files.
26. *Gardner Report,* EWA Edition, pp. 26, 27.
27. Data collected by the University of Illinois Research Group of the CIC-AID Project under the direction of Professor William Thomson.

CHAPTER IX

1. On this important issue in social science research, we ascribe to the "methodological individualist" position. In other words, we believe that these linkages must be established in terms of individual predispositions. For further discussion, see J. W. N. Watkins, "Ideal Types and Historical Explanation," *The British Journal for the Philosophy of Science*, III (1952), reprinted in Herbert Feigl and May Brodbeck, *Readings in the Philosophy of Science* (New York: Appleton Century Crofts, 1953), pp. 723-743; May Brodbeck, "Methodological Individualisms, Definition and Reduction," *Philosophy of Science*, XXV (1958), pp. 1-22, reprinted in May Brodbeck, ed., *Readings in the Philosophy of the Social Sciences* (New York: Macmillan, 1968), pp. 280-304; and James A. Buchannan, "An Individualistic Theory of the Political Process" in David Easton, ed., *Varieties of Political Theory* (Englewood Cliffs: Prentice Hall, 1966), pp. 15-38.
2. For an excellent discussion of this point as well as some of the general issues which underlie the concept of an indicator and its use, see P. J. D. Wiles, *The Political Economy of Communism* (Cambridge: Harvard University Press, 1962), especially Chapter 4.
3. As we use it, the term importance is synonymous with the concept, *centrality*, used by Phillip M. Converse. For a detailed discussion, see his "The Nature of Belief Systems in Mass Publics" in David Apter, ed., *Ideologies and Discontents* (Glencoe: Free Press, 1964), pp. 206-262.
4. Formally, these rules have the status of axioms in a theoretical explanation.
5. Watkins, *op. cit.*, pp. 741-742.
6. The principal references are Simon, *Administrative Behavior (op. cit.)*; Simon, *Models of Man, Social and Rational: Mathematical Essays on Rational Human Behavior in a Social Setting* (New York: John Wiley & Sons, 1957), Part IV; and James March and Simon, *Organizations* (New York: John Wiley and Sons, 1958), Chapters 5-7.
7. See the discussion in Simon, *Administrative Behavior*, Chapters 4, 5.
8. *Ibid.*, pp. xiii-xiv.
9. *Ibid.*, p. xvii.
10. For an analytic study emphasizing organizational maintenance values, see William J. Gore, *Administrative Decision-Making: A Heuristic Model* (New York: John Wiley and Sons, 1964).

CHAPTER X

1. Early TCA contract, dated June 16, 1952.
2. Contract ICAc-1395, February 26, 1960.
3. A most interesting discussion of this phenomenon from a social-psychological perspective is found in Carolyn M. Sherif, Muzafer Sherif and Roger E. Nebergall, *Attitude and Attitude Change: The Social Judge-*

ment–Involvement Approach (Philadelphia and London: W. B. Saunders Co., 1961).
4. For the membership of the working group, see *Proceedings,* p. 103.
5. *Proceedings,* p. 109.
6. *Ibid.*
7. *Lincoln Report,* p. 11.
8. *Ibid.,* p. 32.
9. *Report to the President on Government Contracting for Development* (Washington, 1962, mimeo.), p. 16.
10. *University Contracts,* pp. 28–29.
11. *Research Supplement* of the Task Force on AID–University Relations (New York: Education and World Affairs, 1964, mimeo.), p. 83. See also, *Legislation on Foreign Relations, With Explanatory Notes* (Washington: Government Printing Office, 1965).
12. *Research Supplement,* p. 83.
13. *Legislation on Foreign Relations.*
14. *Ibid.* The *Research Supplement,* pp. 83–85 examines essentially the same issues in much the same way and was an extremely valuable guide in preparing this section.
15. This phrase is used in the *Glick Report,* p. 32.
16. One high AID official spoke of contract officers who had instigated a "reign of terror" in the Agency during the early 1960's.
17. Another agency instrumental in determining "parameters" is, of course, the General Accounting Office. Clearly, there is even less identification with individual project goals among GAO officials than among contract officers.
18. *Gardner Report,* EWA Edition, p. 21.
19. See, for example, the *Bibliography on Planned Social Change* (With Special Reference to Rural Development and Educational Development), prepared by the Center for Comparative Political Analysis, Department of Political Science, University of Minnesota (mimeo., 1967).
20. *Proceedings,* p. 11.
21. A convenient summary of these studies is presented in "Excerpts from Previous Studies of the Foreign Aid Program Relating to Technical Assistance and University Contracting" (An unpublished staff study prepared by EWA for the Gardner Task Force). See also, Haviland, *op. cit.*
22. For example, in 1967 and 1968, the Senate Committee on Foreign Relations refused to act on the foreign aid bill until the Secretary of State testified regarding Administration policy in Viet Nam.
23. Senate Foreign Relations, House Foreign Affairs, House Appropriations and Senate Appropriations, usually in that order.
24. Coffin, *op. cit.,* p. 47.
25. *Ibid.,* p. 48.
26. For an extensive discussion of this point, see Coffin, *op. cit.*
27. *Ibid.,* p. 40.
28. *Gardner Report,* EWA Edition, pp. 31–32.
29. Two recent works which emphasize these variables are K. W. Deutsch,

The Nerves of Government: Models of Communication and Control (Glencoe: Free Press, 1963) and Harold Welinsky, *Organizational Intelligence: Knowledge and Policy in Government and Industry* (New York: Basic Books, 1967).

30. See the very interesting discussion of this issue in Welinsky, *op. cit.*, pp. 54 ff. Welinsky argues that a regionally based organization (specialization according to geography) is the only one with clear disadvantages over other possible types.
31. Based on our own interviews, more than thirty interviews conducted by the Illinois research group of the CIC–AID project and previous studies of the university-contract program.
32. A similar point regarding foreign assistance in general is made in John D. Montgomery, *The Politics of Foreign Aid: American Experience in Southeast Asia* (New York: F. A. Praeger, 1962), p. 197.
33. Glen Taggart of Michigan State, one of the originators of the university-contract program, would be an example of this type of individual.
34. Most of this material is based on interviews conducted by the University of Illinois research group of the CIC–AID project. An unpublished paper by J. A. Rigney, "The Optimum Role for U.S. Advisors," was also helpful.
35. The University of Illinois research group.
36. *Proceedings*, p. 75. At the time she made her address, Mrs. Jacobson was the Assistant Secretary of Agriculture for International Affairs.
37. *Proceedings*, p. 75.
38. *Gardner Report*, EWA Edition, pp. 45–48.
39. *Ibid.*

APPENDIX I

Documents Relating to the University-Contract Program

Introduction

THIS APPENDIX INCLUDES additional documentary material, mostly from participating university files, which provides detailed examples of some of the points made in the text. First are some excerpts from reports written during the period of proliferation which illustrate problems of bureaucratic red tape (see Chapter III). Second are some excerpts from reports written during the period of retrenchment which illustrate problems related to autonomy versus control, procedures, delays and security clearance (see Chapter IV). A brief discussion of each issue is included to provide continuity and relate the material to the analysis in Chapters III and IV. Material which would identify the participating university, the country involved or cognizant Agency officials has, of course, been deleted.

Finally, excerpts from David Bell's introductory address to the International Rural Development Conference are included as they provide a succinct statement of his philosophy regarding the use of universities in international technical assistance programs.

I. The Period of Proliferation

BUREAUCRATIC "RED TAPE" PROBLEMS

Problems of red tape arise when Agency and university personnel on the operating level seem unable to work out a satisfactory

Documents Relating to the University-Contract Program 233

solution, within a given organizational environment, to problems associated with the achievement of a goal to which *both* are committed. A series of incidents involving equipment procurement illustrates the types of bureaucratic red tape problems which arose during this period. These excerpts were taken from the files of one of the larger university-contract projects in operation during this period.

> On October 3, 1955, the Coordinator finally received from ICA/Washington a duly signed copy of Amendment No. 5 which provided the necessary funds and authority to initiate procurement and supplies in the amount of $—— for [host university]. Thus ended almost a year and a half of negotiations and delays in the essential rehabilitation of the laboratories, libraries and classrooms for the [host university] colleges of Agriculture, Engineering and Medicine. . . . The Coordinator was informed on August 30, 1954, that FOA had agreed to make an initial allocation of $—— for the procurement and supplies for [host university]. Since the requested screening by [U.S. university] had presumably been acceptable and the last list had been returned on September 3, 1954, it was believed procurement would go forward immediately.
>
> The first indication that difficulties were being encountered with respect to procurement came in a letter from the chief advisor in [host country] dated November 29, 1954.
>
>> "FOA's normal internal funding procedure requires that, to formally obligate the [funds] earmarked for equipment and physical plant rehabilitation for the three colleges, a 'Project Proposal' must be developed with the [host country] government and sent to Washington for approval. This instrument, when formalized by a Project Agreement with the [host country] government, obligates both dollars and [host country] currency required for the project. It will be evident that the lists of equipment alone fall far short of supplying data needed in preparing this presentation.
>>
>> . . . it may be possible to follow the so-called 'firm request' procedure. . . . This procedure reduces processing time.
>
> After this project proposal or firm request action has been completed it becomes the covering authority for so-called 'implementation orders', which are procurement authorization documents. These instruments require specific bills of material, specifications, cost estimates, suggested procurement agency, etc. . . .
>
> [USOM] expects the advice we are by contract obligated to give [host institution] on the selection and use of necessary books,

equipment, and supplies in the fields concerned, and the coordination required of us with respect to basic operating facilities, to result in specifically defined needs bearing the [U.S. university's] stamp of approval. No procurement will be initiated until such approval has been received.

I'm again in the process of reviewing equipment lists for each of the three colleges, since [U.S. university] questions, comments, and suggestions had to be taken up with [host country's] personnel concerned in an attempt to resolve differences . . . [USOM] since it has no procurement department will transmit approved lists to FOA/Washington for purchase action. At FOA/Washington, the lists will be screened to insure that standard items are specified whenever possible, that items are bought at the lowest price available, and that extra items which add nothing to utility are not ordered. The lists would then be sent to the General Services Agency for procurement.

. . . Even under the most optimistic schedule no actual procurement can be initiated in less than three to four months. . . .

After procurement has been initiated, the experience of [USOM] program personnel is that delivery of the smaller, standard items should not be expected in less than six months, with other items taking up to a year or even longer to appear on the scene."

Further time elapsed during which lists went back and forth between [host institution], [U.S. university], and Washington and were gone over by faculty members of both institutions and by FOA personnel. The first completed list (Part I for Engineering) was sent to Washington on March 1, 1955. Other lists followed. Yet not until March 17, 1955 was the essential 'firm request' completed in [host institution]. And it was not until word of its signing reached [U.S. university] that the actual sum available for procurement was known or, for that matter that procurement could be undertaken. However, this word seemed to assure [U.S. university] that all formalities had been completed and the procurement would go forward without delay.

Within two months the procurement situation had changed completely. On May 16, 1955, [Vice President, U.S. university] received a telephone call from [officials] of FOA/Washington stating that the delay in starting procurement was due to the fact that the government purchasing offices were overloaded with work and that FOA had difficulty in obtaining priorities. They also stated that while [U.S. university] had screened the lists, it had not prepared specifications which would permit purchasing. Finally, they agreed that

[U.S. university] had not been asked to prepare specifications but only to screen the lists. They then urged the university to undertake the procurement so as to avoid the delays which would inevitably follow and the serious effect this would have on [host institution] if the government did the purchasing. Upon being informed that [U.S. university] had rejected this idea earlier when it had been proposed, they requested and were given an appointment to come to [site of U.S. university] on May 24, to enter into discussions over procurement.

... Later, on June 14, 1955, the Coordinator and [U.S. university business manager] were invited to meet with FOA officials in Washington to complete negotiations and spell out a contract amendment. At the Washington meeting it developed that not all FOA staff members had yet agreed to all stipulated conditions. By the time the [U.S. university] representatives left to return to [U.S. university], however, agreement seemed to have been reached and, in accordance with [FOA Contract Coordinator's] request, the amendment to authorize the [U.S. university] to undertake the procurement was further revised in accordance with the June 15, 1955 agreement and mailed to [FOA Contract Coordinator]. At this point it appeared that the procurement amendment could now be signed before FOA ended on June 30, so that 55 funds earmarked for procurement could be utilized.

Six weeks passed with no word from Washington. Then, in a letter dated July 26, 1955, a new draft of a procurement amendment was transmitted by [FOA Contract Coordinator]. In spite of previous assurances to the contrary, this draft still failed to meet the conditions stipulated on May 24 and agreed to on June 14 and was consequently rejected. After correspondence and telephone calls between [U.S. university] and Washington, a satisfactory procurement amendment was mailed to the Coordinator by [ICA official] on August 17, 1955. This was signed on behalf of the [U.S. university] and returned to Washington on August 30, 1955.

Further delays ensued while attempts were being made to secure money from 56 funds to replace the 55 funds which had reverted on June 30, 1955, and while the necessary clearances as to the language of the contract were being secured from ICA officials. The signature of ICA's officer for contract relations affixed to Amendment No. 5 on September 29, 1955, at long last made it possible for procurement operations to begin.

... The delays thus far encountered (in procurement) are bound to have an appreciable adverse effect in carrying out contractual responsibilities in all fields. The technical assistance program can proceed effectively only with substantial, timely support of this nature.

II. *The Period of Retrenchment*

A SERIES OF INCIDENTS INVOLVING DIFFERENCES BETWEEN ICA AND A PARTICIPATING UNIVERSITY REGARDING THE MOST APPROPRIATE MEANS FOR ACHIEVING PROJECT GOALS

Negative incidents frequently arose when the Agency refused to authorize a modification of original project plans to meet the needs which subsequently arose in the field. In the case presented below, the increased costs arising from the proposed modification were a significant factor in determining the Agency's position.

> The most serious problem which has been faced since the previous report was issued was the refusal of ICA/Washington to approve our request to employ a college level adviser in each of the three fields under the contract should any further program arranged for the [host country university faculty members studying at the U.S. university] necessitate such service. The question arose in October 1955, when our engineering adviser in [host country] prepared a tentative plan involving six months observation tours for eight senior engineering faculty members, mostly department heads who constitute the core of the present engineering faculty at [host country institution].
>
> This plan, which proposed observation and consultation at the [U.S. institution] and elsewhere, rather than a registration for courses, was designed to provide a more sympathetic atmosphere for the younger faculty members when they resumed their faculty posts after graduate study in the United States. It was obvious that its implementation would require the services of a senior faculty member in engineering.
>
> The proposal was further amplified and refined in later communications from [host country]. It was then approved by [Dean of the College of Engineering, U.S. university] and his associates, by the Coordinator and then by the project advisory committee [which included two university vice-presidents and had direct access to the president of the university]. The committee directed the coordinator to request authority from ICA/Washington for the employment of a college level advisor, together with the services of a secretary at not

Documents Relating to the University-Contract Program 237

to exceed half time, for each of the three fields under the contract. Although in all probability such services would not be required in either agriculture or medicine, and in the case of engineering would only be used for such special programs involving the eight senior engineering faculty members, the application was made so as to apply equally to all three colleges.

The request for approval, dated January 19, 1956, outlined the problem in great detail and set forth the reasons why such service was being requested and its importance to the successful operation of the contract.

The reply from [ICA official], dated February 1, 1956, was not focused on the real issues involved. Instead, the request was denied with the assertion that 'the handling of participants at [U.S. university] is already being paid for at rates far in excess of any of our other university contracts.' The request for approval was renewed in a letter to [ICA official], dated February 7, 1956. In this letter it was pointed out that the [U.S. university] had no desire to recover in indirect costs more than the actual expenses involved in carrying out its responsibilities under the contract. It was also stressed that no one had anticipated, at the time the contract was negotiated that the [host institution] faculty members would need more individual services than were provided for other foreign graduate students. Finally, attention was called to the fact that the work of the proposed College Level Advisor would consist in caring for [host country institution] faculty members not as students, but as observers of administrative, laboratory and teaching techniques and procedures.

Two weeks later, when no further reply had been forthcoming from [ICA official], the matter was brought to the attention of [ICA official], then Deputy Director for Technical Services. His reply, dated March 6, 1956, used the same argument about overhead rates as did [ICA official] in denying the request.

A follow-up letter (March 23, 1956) closed with this statement: 'I find it hard to add anything to what I have written previously or to what [Dean of College of Engineering] has said. The [U.S. university] wishes to do a creditable job and no one would deny that it has the resources in administration and staff to plan and carry out its responsibilities. How can it do so, however, unless it is given the freedom to so operate as to achieve optimum results.'

In a letter dated April 5, 1956 [Deputy Director for Technical Services] reported that he had discussed our request with [Director, ICA] and that the latter had seen no necessity for making a personal review since authority rested by his delegation with the Deputy Director for Technical Services. But [Deputy Director] did point out that ICA was not opposed to reasonable discussions and suggested that further pursuit of the matter be addressed to [ICA official], head of the Contract Office.

In line with the above suggestion, a letter was addressed to [Deputy Director], with a copy to [head, Contract Office] in which the five major points were made and amplified:

(1) This proposal will not increase overhead.
(2) The 'contingencies' item in our budget was intended to cover just such unanticipated costs.
(3) Similar services performed in [host country] cost far more than in the United States.
(4) Other special programs cannot be undertaken if the present request is not granted.
(5) Overhead reimburses for indirect costs, not for actual operations.

. . . unless ICA reverses its ruling, the [U.S. institution] will be unable to plan any special programs, regardless of the need for them.

This issue was ultimately resolved in favor of the participating university. However, the unfavorable attitudes which had been generated on both sides during the course of the dispute persisted.

A SERIES OF INCIDENTS INVOLVING DIFFERENCES BETWEEN ICA AND A PARTICIPATING UNIVERSITY REGARDING PROCEDURAL MATTERS RELATED TO THE PARTICIPANT TRAINING PROGRAM

The modification of "standard procedures" within the Agency was (and is) a complicated process undertaken reluctantly by Agency representatives. However, as the case below illustrates, rigid adherence to such procedures sometimes affected programs adversely.

The immediately preceding report indicated our dissatisfaction with the arrangement insisted on by ICA under which health service fees were not collected either from the [host institution] faculty members or from ICA funds provided under the contract. Instead, each [host institution faculty member] is required to pay $3.09 per month for health and accident insurance carried by ICA with a commercial insurance company.

During the present period, the very crisis has arisen about which ICA was warned even before the first [host country participant trainee] arrived. Several bills for medical and/or hospital services provided for [host country] faculty members were refused payment by the insurance company. The contention was that the condition for which treatment was provided had been in existence before the faculty member left [host country] and under the insurance contract, there was no liability on the part of the insurance company. One of these bills was a rather substantial one, $431.20.

ICA/Washington was asked at that time to approve payment under the contract of this bill and all others for hospital and medical care which the insurance company refused to pay. The initial request received the following reply:

'Following our usual practice, the participant should be requested to pay for his medical expenses, even if it is necessary for him to appeal to his home university or government. It is our understanding that he was given a physical examination before being accepted for training and that he came over with the knowledge that medical expenses would be covered for only those illnesses incurred in the United States. As you are aware, we have to guard against persons who might wish to come to the United States primarily in order to obtain free medical treatment.'

ICA was asked to reconsider in a communication, dated March 8, 1956, which pointed out, among other things,

'It seems to me to be completely unrealistic, at this late date, to suggest that Professor Y—— or any other [participant] be made to pay a bill as large as this was. It is our feeling that to ask him to appeal to his home university which is so inadequately financed so as to make it impossible as it is to pay adequate faculty salaries would create bad feelings toward the United States government rather than the good will we all attempt to get.

Early in our contract we had many discussions concerning the matter of providing the usual services of the University Health Service for these [host country] faculty members but, against our protests, FOA insisted that there be no health service fee charged for the [participant] faculty members but that they be covered under the blanket insurance policy with the [Insurance Company]. We pointed out at the time the likelihood that a situation such as the one facing Professor Y—— would certainly arise. Had our plan been accepted we would not now be contesting your ruling.'

It is to be hoped that even at this late date, ICA/Washington will allow the [U.S. institution] to substitute the services of its Health Service for the present commercial insurance coverage. Is there any good reason for denying this request when the benefits of the proposed arrangement are carefully weighted.

The exasperation of the university representatives over this series of incidents was increased by the fact that the Health Service coverage which they proposed would have cost no more than the commercial policy.

SOME INCIDENTS INVOLVING DELAYS

Delays in decision-making by the Agency often had long-term consequences for project effectiveness. This was particularly true in cases where delays in contract actions retarded program planning and prevented timely recruitment of university field personnel.

> The overwhelming current problem is the lack of action on the part of ICA with respect to contract matters. Though a contract extension to September 1958 has been received, this helps very little with respect to the proposed program for 1957–59. So much time has elapsed in contract considerations that it will be very difficult, if not impossible, to recruit more than a fraction of the personnel that are necessary to continue an effective program. Further definitive consultation with [host country] counterparts is impossible until contract matters are settled.

Delays in taking action on relatively routine matters also interfered with the achievement of program objectives as the case below illustrates.

> Considerable confusion developed at the last moment when the scheduled departure date for participants arrived and passed and most participants did not have ICA/Washington clearance for their study tours. The bulk of the bio-data forms for these participants were sent to the mission on May 1, 1957, which we in the field thought was early enough to have the necessary approvals before September.

Delays in the Agency were frequently not deliberate. Nor could they, as university personnel quickly found out, be traced to any specific person. However, these facts did not lessen the dissatisfaction of home campus and field personnel with situations in which projects with which they were involved were adversely affected.

SOME INCIDENTS INVOLVING SECURITY CLEARANCE

The area of security does not lend itself to flexible interpretation by subordinate personnel. However, in some instances uni-

Documents Relating to the University-Contract Program 241

versity representatives felt that the enforcement of security regulations was carried to unreasonable and illogical extremes.

> For some time, even library assistants who did nothing but help order and process books which we sent to [host institution] under our contract had to have a security clearance and this process often took weeks.
>
> These assistants were working on a part-time basis and we could not afford to wait for weeks before they could be paid out of contract funds.
>
> At one time I was informed by ICA that we would have to obtain security clearances for students who took packages of books from the library to the post office for shipment to [host institution]. Since we used different students for this none too dangerous work, this was impossible as well as absurd.

This issue was resolved within a month after it was brought to the attention of the Agency. However, the president of the participating university was so aroused that he brought it to the attention of members of the Senate Committee on Foreign Relations.

III. *The Period of Harmony*

EXCERPTS FROM DAVID BELL'S ADDRESS TO THE CONFERENCE ON INTERNATIONAL RURAL DEVELOPMENT

> Its a great pleasure for those of us in the Agency for International Development to join with the Land-Grant universities and the Department of Agriculture in this Conference on International Rural Development. We are convinced of the very great importance of improving the effectiveness of United States assistance to rural development in the less-developed countries. And we are convinced that the sponsors of this Conference jointly command the strong resources of competence and experience to achieve that end. Together we can do far more than has been done thus far to enlarge the horizons and enrich the lives of rural people in Asia, Africa and Latin America.
>
> Everyone knows of the enormous impact upon life in the United States of the work of the Land-Grant universities and the Department of Agriculture over the last century. The results of this mutual effort by the universities and the Department are visible not only

in our country's highly productive agriculture and our prosperous rural communities, but also in the productivity and strength of our entire national economy. Moreover, the results of this century of mutual effort are also found in the structure and workings of our nation's free institutions—urban as well as rural—political and social as well as economic.

... all of us in the United States would like to see in the developing countries a growth in agricultural productivity and in rural living standards, coupled with a strengthening of local public and private institutions, just as we have seen these things happen in the United States over the last century. If we can bring this about, it will benefit the United States as well as the people of the developing countries....

We have been taught correctly by the anthropologists that village life in different countries is tremendously varied in cultural and historical background, in languages and leadership, in the methods with which change is accomplished. . . . Nevertheless there are common threads of poverty, of exposure to disease, and brief life spans, of narrow horizons of knowledge and opportunity, which run through village life in all the Continents.

It is therefore permissible to generalize about the rural development problem, so long as we do not forget that every generalization has to be adapted to the particular circumstances of each cultural setting.

... I would suggest to this Conference that a good deal has been learned in the last two decades about how to deal with the problem of rural development.

First, I suggest that we have learned that rural development requires much more than an improvement in agricultural technology. Along with better agricultural techniques, rural development requires improvements in marketing and transportation, in education and health facilities, in better institutions of local government and of private cooperation. Without such broad changes in the local scene, improvements in agricultural technology will neither take root nor be effective.

A second suggestion which may be derived from the experience of the last two decades is that rural development is not a single factor problem. The experience under the Marshall Plan in Europe was misread by some to indicate that there was something very close to "instant development"—just add capital and stand back. We have long since recognized, however, that restoring effective economies in Europe, and creating effective economies in Africa, or Asia or Latin America, are problems of very different kinds.

There was a time, also, when some were dazzled by the apparent magic of transferring know-how. Just take hybrid corn, and contour plowing and artificial insemination and teach them to the farmers of the world and the millennium would follow. Hard experience has demonstrated the contrary. All of us know today that what works in Bozeman may not work at all in Bolivia. . . .

A third and final suggestion which may be derived from the experience of the past two decades is that rural development must be achieved from within.

. . . We, in the United States, can help create educational institutions of high quality in the developing countries. . . . All of us know how difficult, how sensitive, how slow these tasks can be. But all of us know also the very great "multiplier effect" that can follow from the success of a well-planned, well-educated project of this kind— a project like that of Michigan State at Nsukka in Eastern Nigeria or that of Cornell in the Philippines.

It is quite clear . . . to anyone who examines [our] experience that most projects have been rather narrow in concept, and in most cases the United States institutions involved . . . have been used rather narrowly. . . . This has begun to change and it is a fundamental assumption underlying this conference that it should change further and faster.

It is our firm conviction that we must seek to engage the resources of the Department of Agriculture and the universities more broadly than they have been engaged thus far in international rural development work. We would like to involve the Department and the universities more than we have in the past in country planning processes —both in helping our overseas missions to decide which activities the United States can most usefully conduct in different countries, but more importantly, to assist less developed countries with the development of their own plans and policies. We would like to involve the Department and the universities more than has often been the case in project planning and evaluation, as well as project execution. We would like to conduct more of our projects in the future through contract relations and fewer through direct hire staff. We would like to assist in the substantial strengthening of the competence and capacity of the Department and the universities in research and training, both here and abroad, in the broad spectrum of fields which are relevant to rural development.

We in AID recognize fully that if we are to achieve these objectives, we first of all must change many of our own patterns of work, many of our own attitudes, many of our past practices.

Source: Conference *Proceedings,* pp. 9–17.

APPENDIX II

An Alternative to the Rationalistic Paradigm

CHAPTER IX contains a brief outline of a a theoretical framework which represents an essentially new posture with regard to the development of a paradigm[1] for political science. While it seemed inappropriate to include a lengthy discussion of the theoretical and methodological commitments which underlie this approach in the analysis of AID-university relations, omitting reference to them entirely also seemed inappropriate. Hence this appendix.

The examination of a relatively delimited set of social phenomena, such as AID-university relations from 1950 to 1966, would not seem to pose insurmountable problems for the analyst. Yet if he is honest in his commitment to the goal of scientific explanation,[2] he must come to grips with almost all the problems which plague the social sciences in general, within the microcosmic context of his own substantive concerns. To be sure, there are observable patterns and relationships which almost seem to "cry out" for inclusion in any analysis. In this study, for example, the relationship between the priority of the university-contract program and delays in Agency decision-making would seem to fall within this category. But what are the theoretically relevant aspects of such phenomena; more important, how are significant relationships to be explained by valid scientific laws? In the absence of a generally accepted paradigm, these problems can not be easily resolved. To ignore these problems entirely, however, is not a satisfactory solution for the investigator whether his concerns are primarily substantive or theoretical.

In this appendix, particular attention will be directed to the theoretical element of a paradigm. This element provides the general laws which are linked to empirical phenomena by rules of interpretation.[3] Of course there are other important elements of a paradigm as well, especially the *conceptual element*,[4] which constrains the practitioner to focus on certain aspects of reality in preference to others, and the *criteria of admissibility*,[5] which provide a basis for determining whether a given explanation is valid in terms of the paradigm. The core element of any paradigm, however, is its theoretical element.

To begin the discussion, it is necessary to specify rather explicitly what is meant by a *theoretical element* or *formal theory*. Following Brodbeck,[6] we define a theory as a deductively interrelated set of laws which are, depending on their logical position with respect to one another, either axioms or theorems.[7] The axioms of a theory are a limited number of independent and consistent[8] laws which are logically prior to a much larger set of laws, the theorems. In a sense, the axioms are laws assumed to be true in order to see what other laws, the theorems, they imply. The seven postulates of Euclidian geometry are an example of a set of axioms. So are Newton's three laws of motion. In economic theory, the behavioral characteristics of rational man have axiomatic status.[9]

Any theory, whether it relates to empirical phenomena or not, can be represented abstractly as a set of descriptive and connective symbols, where the descriptive symbols are interrelated by the connectives in a set of logically consistent, if-then statements or propositions. For a theory to be useful in explaining related sets of empirical phenomena, however, it must be the case that (a) some (but not necessarily all)[10] of the descriptive symbols refer to instances of observable empirical phenomena and (b) wherever instances of such phenomena are observed, they are interrelated in the ways which the propositions of the theory specify.

Although the axioms are *logically prior* to the theorems in the formal structure of a theory, in the development of empirical theory, the theorems are usually chronologically prior to the axioms.[11] The development of Newtonian mechanics provides an often cited case in point. In a pre-paradigmatic discipline or area of investigation, there are usually a fairly large number of verified empirical laws which are accepted as true by most practitioners. However, they are not related to one another in any systematic way. Indeed, a set of axioms gains paradigmatic status among practitioners in a particular discipline because of its capacity to logically imply a hitherto unintegrated set of empirical laws. It should be emphasized, furthermore, that the validity of a set of axioms is often untested and sometimes not even susceptible to direct test. Rather, as additional theorems are validated, the usefulness of the axiomatic base tends to be confirmed.

The problem of theory development just described is essentially the one which was faced in a small way in the research for this study. From the investigations for this project and the investigations of others, it was possible to devise a large number of propositions regarding the occurrence of negative incidents, the persistence of behavioral patterns in the Agency and the universities and so forth. But relationships between these propositions were unclear. There was no set of axioms which tied the propositions together in an integrated, coherent theoretical structure. Thus it could not be claimed that this analysis really explained anything.

In order to devise a set of axioms which will systematize empirical laws regarding social behavior, the practitioner must resolve two basic issues which are related, but distinct. First, he must determine what will be the basic behavioral unit in his formulation. The basic behavioral unit is the entity whose behavior will be specified axiomatically. There has been little consensus in the social sciences with regard to this issue. In different theories (or alleged theories), *individuals, groups, political systems, societies* and many other entities have been specified, either implicitly or explicitly as the basic behavioral unit. Having decided upon a basic behavioral unit, the practitioner must then determine the set of axioms which will characterize its behavior. Again, little consensus exists on this question. For most behavioral units which have been incorporated into general use in the social sciences, several sets of behavioral axioms have been postulated.

The way the first issue is resolved in this formulation has been generally labeled methodological individualism. Given the individual as the basic behavioral unit, we say that the observable manifestations of his behavior result from a process of conscious choice among alternatives in a series of decision situations. In making his choices, it is assumed that the individual follows four basic decision rules, which are based on Herbert Simon's notion

An Alternative to the Rationalistic Paradigm

of intendedly rational or *satisficing* behavior.[12] These rules expressed in propositional (if-then) form are the axioms of our theory. Because of their fundamental importance to the analytical style used in this study, it will be useful to elaborate on these points.

One of the best discussions of methodological individualism is in an article by the British philosopher of science, J. W. N. Watkins.[13] "An understanding of a complex social situation," Watkins emphasizes, "is always derived from a knowledge of the dispositions, beliefs and relationships of individuals. Its overt characteristics may be established empirically, but they are only explained by being shown to be the results of individual activities."[14] He elaborates as follows:

> An explanation requires a general statement as its major premise and when we postulate a typical disposition, we assert that all men (with trivial exceptions and minor deviations, perhaps within a limited historico-geographical area) are prone to behave in a certain kind of way and this gives us the generality we require. . . . The ultimate premises of social science are human dispositions, i.e. something familiar and understandable, though not introspectable since they are not mental events. They are so much the stuff of our everyday experience that they have only to be stated to be recognized as obvious. And while psychology may try to explain these dispositions, they do provide social science with a natural stopping place in the search for explanations of overt social phenomena.[15]

It should be made quite clear that the methodological individualistic posture does not require a theory which focuses exclusively on the behavior of individuals *qua* individuals. Macro-economic theory, for example, is derivable from a set of individualistic axioms. In the formulation used here, moreover, many of the theorems refer to the behavior of large numbers of individuals in organizational settings and could properly be termed laws (or theorems) of *organizational* behavior. We would maintain, however, that to the degree that laws regarding aggregate behavior are verified empirically, it should be possible to formulate a set of individualistic axioms from which they could be derived. In other words, such laws would have the status of theorems in an empirical theory whose axioms were individualistic. Indeed, it is difficult to see how relationships between aggregate phenomena can be convincingly explained in the absence of such axioms since it is clear that the variables defining such phenomena are related through a surrogate of individual dispositions and actions which, unless specified, have unknown properties.

Now we turn to the question of a specific set of axiomatic decision rules for our individualistic behavioral units. The discussion to this point might be interpreted as a defense of the growing body of social science theory based on the rationalistic postulates of economic theory.[16] However, as noted above, we do not ascribe to this position, but to the alternative formulation suggested by Herbert Simon. Although the relevant issues have been thoroughly discussed by Simon,[17] a brief comment may be in order.[18]

The rationalistic paradigm has, of course, gained wide acceptance in economics. However, despite the important contributions of Downs, Olson, Tullock and Buchannan and others, it has not been similarly accepted in the non-economic social sciences. One reason may perhaps be found in the history and sociology of knowledge of different social science disciplines. However, there is a more crucial and more fundamental explanation. Despite the formal elegance of rationalistic behavioral theory, the range of phenomena to which it has been fruitfully applied is quite limited. Even theorists such as Downs and Tullock have been forced to deviate from the axioms of rationality in order to examine phenomena which they found intrinsically interesting.[19] Moreover, it should be noted that this observation does not only apply to the non-economic social sciences. In the areas of developmental economics and the study of non-market economies such as the Soviet Union, the rationalistic paradigm has been found to have limited application.[20] In view of this situation, it seems likely that a set of axioms which conform more closely to intuitive notions about human behavior may provide a more appropriate foundation for a general theory of social behavior. Simon's critique of more than twenty years ago still seems valid:

> Real behavior, even that which is ordinarily thought of as "rational" possesses many elements of disconnectedness not present in this idealized picture [of the rationalistic paradigm]. If behavior is viewed over a stretch of time, it exhibits a mosaic character. Each piece of the pattern is integrated with others by their orientation to a common purpose, but these purposes shift from time to time with shifts in knowledge and attention and are held together in only slight

An Alternative to the Rationalistic Paradigm 249

measure by any conception of an overall criterion of choice. It might be said that behavior reveals "segments" of rationality—that behavior shows rational organization within each segment, but the segments themselves have no very strong interconnections. . . .

Actual behavior falls short in at least three ways, of objective rationality:

(1) Rationality requires a complete knowledge and anticipation of the consequences that will follow on each choice. In fact, knowledge of the consequences is always fragmentary.

(2) Since these consequences lie in the future, imagination must supply the lack of experienced feeling in attaching value to them. But values can be only imperfectly anticipated.

(3) Rationality requires a choice among all possible alternative behaviors. In actual behavior, only a very few of all these possible alternatives ever come to mind.[21]

A theory based on the idea of satisficing would seem to provide a desirable alternative to the rationalistic paradigm for three reasons. First, it is consistent not only with intuitive notions about behavior, but also with recent theoretical formulations in anthropology[22] and social psychology[23] which are based upon empirical research. Second, since rationalistic or optimizing behavior constitutes a limiting case of satisficing behavior, where a specific cost-benefit function can be attached to every alternative considered, the axioms of satisficing are also consistent with the theorems of the rationalistic paradigm. In fact, it can be demonstrated that the axioms of the rationalistic paradigm become theorems in a theory of satisficing behavior which are applicable in a limited set of decision-making situations. Finally, the theory is specifically applicable to settings where goals and alternatives are noncomparable in terms of a rational calculus, and (regrettably perhaps) this type of setting seems to predominate in the reality.

The purpose of this appendix is not to provide a detailed elaboration of the rather complex set of definitions and derivations which provide the logical basis for the conclusions presented in Chapters IX and X. However, some of the more significant elements of the formulation and some instances where it has been fruitfully applied should be noted.

The basic idea of satisficing is that a decision unit chooses alternatives which are satisfactory or good enough, and that choices are made sequentially from among finite sets of alternatives in an environment of multiple and not necessarily comparable goals.[24] An additional important point made by Simon is that only operational goals affect the choice process significantly. General, vaguely defined goals are unimportant in actual decision processes regardless of the importance which may be attached to them in some normative sense by a decision-maker.[25] All of these ideas are incorporated into our model in essentially the way that Simon has presented them.

We postulate that decision-making activity (or behavior) takes place in a "setting" which is environmental to the decision unit. Specific decision situations are initiated when the decision unit receives a disequilibrating environmental stimulus.[26] Given a particular stimulus, behavior is uniquely determined by the setting and other specified environmental characteristics.[27] The parameters of the setting are (a) a set of operative goals and (b) a set of alternatives. Each operative goal partitions the set of alternatives into subsets of *functional, dysfunctional* and *neutral* alternatives.[28] Functional alternatives are "satisfactory" in the sense that Simon uses the term. Dysfunctional alternatives are unsatisfactory in the sense that if chosen, they will lead to adverse consequences with respect to the particular goal in question. Neutral alternatives have no effect, either positive or negative. Alternatives may also be "costly" in the sense that other ongoing activities which are functional for some goal will have to be foregone if they are chosen. This factor is taken into account by treating costly alternatives as elements of the set of dysfunctional alternatives for such goals.

Other alternatives, or bits of information about goals and/or alternatives which would change the partitioning of alternatives in the setting may also be present in the environment. However, neither of these are regarded as part of the setting. In order to incorporate an alternative or bit of information into the setting, the decision unit must be willing to pay the *search costs*[29] which the "discovery" of these elements requires. The total cost of an alternative not in the setting, then, is the sum of search costs and any intrinsic costs.

Thus, in any decision situation, the decision unit may select an evoked alternative or search for a new alternative. In addition, it may decide to do nothing at all, that is, to continue its present activity in essentially the same way. It is assumed that at any point in time, the decision unit is engaged in activities which are the result of previous decisions and are judged to be satisfactory for that particular point in time. "Continue present activity" (or "no change") then, is simply treated as another evoked alternative which is evaluated in every decision situation.[30]

A decision unit is unable to make optimal judgments with regard to most of the alternatives in his environment. Instead, as Simon suggests, the choice process is much simpler. We have already postulated that every goal defines a partitioning of the set of alternatives in the setting. This, in a sense, changes the decision process from a choice among alternatives to a choice among goals. However, most of the goals in the setting are not comparable in terms of any rational calculus. The way in which a decision unit copes with this problem is suggested by what Simon calls the *mechanism of identification*,[31] i.e., preponderant influence of operational goals on the decision process. Thus we postulate that the *degree of operationality* is the principal attribute in terms of which one goal is ordered with respect to another in a decision process. Only if two goals are equally operational (and therefore comparable) does their relative importance or saliency become a relevant consideration. Essentially this introduces two notions of preferredness into the decision process, although the decision unit is, in a sense, only aware of the second. Given a decision situation where a decision unit must choose among a set of alternatives or where present activities are unsatisfactory for some other reason, the first thing evaluated is the relative operationality of any goals which seem relevant. Often, this is sufficient and a choice is made at that point by selecting a functional alternative in the set defined by the most operational goal. If goals are equally operational, then the more salient (or important) will govern the choice of an alternative.

To digress for a moment, the university-contract program provides an interesting example of a set of situations where this mechanism is frequently operative. Because many of its goals are relatively non-operational, they simply do not enter into Agency decision processes at all. Only where goals are equally operational (and thus comparable) is their relative saliency or importance a consideration. Here the mechanisms of choice which apply in economic theory come into play, except that choices are made with respect to a partitioning of a limited set of alternatives rather than an ordering of the set of all possible alternatives.

To simplify the statement of our basic choice axioms, we use the term *determinacy* to refer to the preferredness of one goal to another in a decision process. However, this is nothing more than a parsimonious way of characterizing the choice mechanism described above. Thus, given a set of two operative goals in a decision situation, if A is more operational than B, then A is more determinate than B. If A and B are equally operational and A is more important than B, we also say that A is more determinate than B. It should be emphasized, perhaps, that in our formulation, the term, determinacy of a goal, has meaning only in the very restricted way specified by this definition. Though it will not be fully apparent here, this convention becomes very useful when the concepts defined above are represented symbolically and additional theorems are derived through algebraic manipulation.

With this preliminary background, our basic behavioral axioms may now be presented. First, they will be stated explicitly, then their implications will be considered briefly.

(1) In a setting where A and B are operative goals and A is more determinate than B, then if a_1 is a functional alternative with respect to A and a dysfunctional alternative with respect to B and a_2 is a functional alternative with respect to B alone, the alternative chosen by the decision unit will be a_1.

(2) In a setting where A and B are the operative goals and A is more determinate than B, then if a_1 is a dysfunctional alternative with respect to A and a functional alternative with respect to B, the alternative chosen by the decision unit will be "continue present activity."

(3) In a setting where A and B are the operative goals and A is more determinate than B, then if a_1 is a functional alternative with respect to both A and B and a_2 is a functional alternative with respect to A alone, the alternative chosen by the decision unit will be a_1.

(4) In a setting, where A and B are the operative goals and A is more determinate than B, then if a_1 is a functional alternative with respect to A and a_2 is a functional alternative with respect to A and a dysfunctional alternative with respect to B, the alternative chosen by the decision unit will be a_1.[32]

The way in which decision processes are dominated by more determinate goals (which are usually more operational goals) is made explicit by these axioms. Less determinate goals will only affect the choice of alternatives where the type of congruence be-

An Alternative to the Rationalistic Paradigm

tween partitionings denoted by (3) and (4) exists. Moreover (1) indicates that the choice of alternatives which are actually dysfunctional for less determinate goals will occur under certain conditions.

From these axioms, the basic relationships of complementarity, negative complementarity, parametric constraint and conflict among goals may be derived. These relationships can be most simply expressed in the following 2x2 table. In the table, it is again assumed that A and B are the operative goals in a setting and A is more determinate than B.[33]

	Functional alternatives defined by B	Dysfunctional alternatives defined by B
Functional alternatives defined by A	Alternatives which are functional for A and B	Alternatives which are functional for A but dysfunctional for B
Dysfunctional alternatives defined by A	Alternatives which are functional for B but dysfunctional for A	Alternatives which are dysfunctional for A and B

Thus, we say that A and B are *complementary goals* if and only if a set of alternatives exists where the elements of the set are functional for both A and B. We say that A and B are *negative-complementary* goals if and only if a set of alternatives exists where the elements of the set are dysfunctional for both A and B. We say that A is a *parameter* (or is parametric) with respect to B if and only if a set of alternatives exists where the elements of the set are dysfunctional for A, but functional for B. Finally, we say that A *conflicts* with B if and only if a set of alternatives exists where the elements of the set are functional for A but dysfunctional for B.

The basic theorems of our formulation, then, are propositions about the likelihood of goal attainment or the selection of a particular subset of alternatives in a setting under different conditions. In general, it should be clear that the likelihood that a particular goal will be attained will depend on the patterns of congruence between the sets of functional and dysfunctional alternatives which it defines *and* those defined by other goals. Moreover, these patterns of congruence may be more important than the operationality or importance of the particular goal itself. For instance, alternatives which are functional with respect to a relatively non-determinate goal may often be chosen if a high degree of complementarity exists between that goal and goals which are more determinate. Also, a decision unit may choose alternatives which are dysfunctional for a relatively determinate goal if a more determinate one conflicts with it.[34] In fact, some of the more puzzling characteristics of behavioral phenomena involving a complex organization become quite clear when the possibility of conflicting and parametric relationships among operative hierarchies of goals is taken into consideration.

In the study of empirical cases, we have found it helpful to introduce several additional assumptions even though we can not represent them with the same degree of precision as the framework presented above. These assumptions have been presented in a general way in the latter part of Chapter IX (pp. 162–165 ff); however, it will be helpful to review them here. First, it is assumed that any individual actor in a setting will be influenced by three distinct sets of goals which are normative with respect to that setting. *Personal goals* refer to the objectives of advancement, remuneration, prestige and security of the individual *qua* individual. *Organizational maintenance goals*[35] are those objectives which are directly related to the stability and prestige of the organizational unit with which he identifies. *Substantive goals* are those tasks or objectives which are, in a sense, the reason for being of an organizational unit. For organizational units in complex organizations they are usually specified as normative by some recognized higher authority. Furthermore, it is assumed that in general, there is some subset of the set of operative personal goals in a setting whose elements will be more operational and important than all other goals. Any other assumption seems implausible since it would mean that individual members of an organizational unit would consistently be involved in decision situations involving the choice of neutral or even dysfunctional alternatives with respect to their personal goals. Similarly, if the demise of an organizational unit is not our concern, we assume that there is some subset of the set of operative organizational maintenance goals in a setting whose elements will be more operational and important than the substantive goals of the organizational unit. Again, this seems a reasonable assumption since an organizational

An Alternative to the Rationalistic Paradigm

unit could not survive if alternatives which were neutral or dysfunctional with respect to its maintenance goals were consistently chosen. This implies that the substantive goals of an organizational unit will be attained only if complementary relationships exist between personal, organizational maintenance and substantive goals and if there are relatively few conflicting or parametric relationships. We would argue that the overriding concern of "management science" is the design of organizational structures which achieve this desirable pattern of congruence. Unfortunately, in political life other patterns frequently predominate.[36]

The reader will note that up to this point the discussion has been confined to the behavior of decision units and to organizational units presumed to have many goals in common, thus avoiding the very substantial problems of aggregation which arise when empirical cases involving the "organizational behavior" of very large complex organizations are considered. Problems of aggregation have been a major concern in economic theory,[37] and they pose even graver difficulties for the theorist who attempts to model the behavior of complex organizations *qua* organizations. However, in most instances, we take a very different approach to the analysis of "organizational behavior." The underlying philosophy of this approach is outlined by Simon:

> It is clear that the actual physical task of carrying out an organization's objective falls to the persons at the lowest level of the administrative hierarchy. . . . The nonoperative staff of an administrative organization participate in the accomplishment of the objectives of that organization to the extent that they influence the decisions of the operatives—the persons at the lowest level of the administrative hierarchy. . . .
>
> In the study of organization, the operative employee must be at the focus of attention, for the success of the structure will be judged by his performance within it. Insight into the structure and function of an organization can best be gained by analyzing the manner in which the decisions and behavior of such employees are influenced within and by the organization.[38]

Simon's philosophy is reflected in the concern with positive and negative incidents in this analysis of AID-university relations. Moreover, we believe that in general, organizational behavior must be resolved into sets of behaviors of the decision units within the organization if it is to be studied meaningfully. The structure of the organization of a whole, then, is only relevant to the degree that it influences the settings of those decision units.

It will be useful to conclude this appendix with a somewhat more specific discussion of the way in which the framework presented above guided the examination of the university-contract program.

As noted above, any analysis of a social phenomenon must begin with the identification of those sets of patterned behavior which comprise it. These sets should be delimited as explicitly as possible with respect to (a) the period of time in which they occur and (b) the decision units (or individuals) involved. This analysis was principally concerned with the persistence of negative incidents involving Agency and university personnel and with a set of issues which seemed to be associated with that persistence. Where changes in AID-university relations had occurred, we were interested in concomitant policy and organizational changes which seemed to be associated with those phenomena. The problem of analysis was compounded by the fact that although a single (albeit vaguely defined) set of substantive goals was associated with the university-contract program, the individuals involved in negative incidents were associated with not one, but two organizations. Thus we faced the opportunity (and problem) of applying our framework to a situation involving symbiotic and conflicting relationships between two very different kinds of organizational structures. The analysis focused on typical types of decision situations related to the university-contract program which involved members of both organizations and on the goals which seemed to be operative for each of them. Since this approach had not been used in previous studies of the university-contract program, a major portion of the interviewing was directed to this concern.[39]

As the operation of the university-contract program involved constant interaction between Agency and participating university decision units, it was clear that negative incidents would be likely to arise wherever there was little or no complementarity between the operative hierarchies of goals of the two decision units. A symbiotic relationship would only be attained where complementarity existed between the organizational maintenance goals of the two decision units. This symbiotic relationship would also contribute to successful operations overseas if complementarity existed between substantive project goals and the organizational maintenance goals of the two decision units.[40] In most projects it has been extremely difficult to identify large numbers of alternatives which satisfied these conditions. Indeed, most disagreements have not been concerned with the substance of project operations at all, but with the organizational maintenance goals of the respective decision units.

The usefulness of this style of analysis can be further illustrated by the specific issue of the priority of the university-contract program. We have argued that substantive project goals have had a low priority within both the Agency and the universities and that this has contributed to the occurrence of negative incidents. The framework provides a clearer indication of why this would be the case. We would argue that the priority of a substantive goal for an organizational unit is nothing more than the degree of complementarity between that goal and the organizational maintenance goals which are operative in a given setting. If the assumptions upon which the framework is based are correct, this is the only reason why it is ever possible for an organizational unit to make progress toward the attainment of non-operational substantive goals. If the maintenance goals of an organizational unit are defined by a higher authority, as is frequently the case, and if that authority specifies that an alternative will be functional for maintenance goals only if it is functional for the non-operational substantive goal, then the organizational unit will incur whatever search costs are required to make the substantive goal more operational and/or to discover alternatives which are functional for that goal in its environment.

The reader will recall that Harold Stassen used this approach to expand the university-contract program, but unfortunately not to ensure that project operations were conducted effectively. This issue also underlies the argument that an agency structured along regional lines (such as AID) was, all other things being equal, likely to have more difficulty operating a university-contract program than an agency structured along functional lines. The organizational units of a regionally structured agency must inevitably be responsible for the attainment of a variety of objectives within their geographic area of competence. Assuming that no program is singled out for very special attention, the non-operational goals will inevitably receive least attention. An agency structured along functional lines reduces this problem by establishing complementarity between particular substantive goals and the organizational maintenance goals of relatively powerful organizational units. Here the activity of the organization as a whole is a result of bargaining activity between its components, and non-operational goals may fare reasonably well. However, as the tasks of the organization *qua* organization become more complex, the problems of coordination and integration between organizational units multiply and the whole operation is likely to bog down in a mass of "red tape." This is especially likely to occur in the absence of strong leadership at the top. What happened in ICA during the period of inertia was that it became necessary for its component units to devote an increasing amount of time to the search for alternatives which would not impinge on the maintenance goals of other units. At the same time Congress was reducing the resources of the Agency and consequently increasing the costs of each alternative chosen. It is not surprising under these conditions that intra-organizational bargaining became such a time-consuming activity in ICA during its twilight years.[41]

The decision-making structure of the universities has been no more conducive to a high priority university-contract program. Here the problem has been that university administrators are not authoritative decision units with respect to academic departments. The personal goals of university faculty members and the departmental organizational maintenance goals are determined by considerations which lie outside of the university organizational structure. The mark of a successful university administration is the degree to which it facilitates the choice of functional alternatives with respect to the personal and maintenance goals of its constituent components. But the Agency, for the most part, has been unable to structure a program which would meet these criteria.

Many additional examples from the history of the university-contract program could be included to illustrate other aspects of the framework, but the thrust of the argument should now be clear. We believe that formal theory founded on a set of individualistic axioms is an essential requirement for the systematic study of organizational behavior (or for that matter any social phenomenon). But we also believe that there are viable alternatives to the rationalistic paradigm. Our objective in writing this appendix has been to illustrate the potential usefulness of one such alternative.

Notes

1. See the rather special meaning of this term discussed in Thomas S. Kuhn, *The Structure of Scientific Revolutions* (Chicago: University of Chicago Press, Phoenix edition, 1964). More detailed explication is presented in Robert T. Holt and John M. Richardson Jr., "Competing Paradigms in Comparative Politics" in Robert T. Holt and John E. Turner, eds., *The Methodology of Comparative Research* (New York: Free Press, forthcoming). In the simplest terms, a paradigm is a pattern or framework that gives organization and direction to a given area of scientific investigation. In a discipline where a paradigm has been accepted, many of its aspects are taken for granted by scientific practitioners. In a pre-paradigmatic discipline, however, there is considerable debate about both theory and methodology. A paradigm includes six basic elements: (1) concepts, (2) a theory (i.e. a deductively interrelated set of empirical laws), (3) rules of interpretation for relating concepts to real world phenomena, (4) a set of relevant problems or puzzles (The term "puzzle" is used because the problems are known to have a solution, within the context of the paradigm), (5) criteria of admissibility for puzzle solutions, and (6) an "ontologic predictive" element which suggests what the paradigm will look like when it is fully articulated.
2. A useful explication of this rather slippery term is found in John Kemeny, *A Philosopher Looks at Science* (Princeton: D. Van Nostrand, 1959), p. 135. Kemeny's "four properties of a good explanation" are defined as follows: "(1) We must have general theories; (2) These theories must be well established; (3) We must be in possession of facts which are known independently of the facts to be explained; (4) The facts to be explained must be a logical consequence of the general theories and the known facts." For a general discussion of science *qua* science, see Herbert Feigl, "The Scientific Outlook: Naturalism and Humanism" in Herbert Feigl and May Brodbeck, eds., *Readings in the Philosophy of Science* (New York: Appleton Century Crofts, 1953), pp. 8–18.
3. See note 1, above; also, Kemeny, *op. cit.*, p. 133. According to Kemeny, rules of interpretation "tell us which of the statements in our language describe observable phenomena and just what observations will establish whether the predictions of a given theory are right or wrong."

4. See note 1, above. According to Holt and Richardson, "The conceptual element [of a paradigm] contains the concepts that are used in the theoretical propositions and which, directly or indirectly provide a focus for empirical investigation. In other words the conceptual element of a paradigm provides an answer to the question 'of what is reality composed?' "
5. See note 1, above. According to Holt and Richardson, "these criteria emerge from the deductive elaboration of the theoretical element and from the rules of interpretation. The question which must be posed to the scholar who has formulated a particular 'solution' is not simply, can this formulation be derived from *some* set of general premises and rules of interpretation, but rather, can it be derived from that set of general premises and rules of interpretation which is defined by the paradigm."
6. For a general discussion of Brodbeck's orientation to the philosophy of the social sciences, see May Brodbeck, ed., *Readings in the Philosophy of the Social Sciences* (New York: The Macmillan Co., 1968), pp. 1–12.
7. See Brodbeck, "Models, Meaning and Theories" in *Readings in the Philosophy of the Social Sciences,* pp. 582–583.
8. Morris R. Cohen and Ernest Nagel, "The Nature of a Logical or Mathematical System" in Feigl and Brodbeck, eds., *op. cit.,* pp. 140–144.
9. See Milton Friedman, "The Methodology of Positive Economics" in Brodbeck, ed., *Readings in the Philosophy of the Social Sciences,* especially pp. 518–528.
10. *Ibid.;* also Holt and Richardson, *op. cit.*
11. Cohen and Nagel, *op. cit.,* pp. 131–132.
12. See Chapter IX, note 6, above.
13. "Ideal Types and Historical Explanation." See also Chapter IX, note 1, above.
14. *Ibid.,* p. 732.
15. *Ibid.,* pp. 738–741.
16. See especially, Anthony Downs, *An Economic Theory of Democracy* (New York: Harper and Row, 1957); Gordon Tullock and James M. Buchannan, *The Calculus of Consent: Logical Foundations of Constitutional Democracy* (Ann Arbor: University of Michigan Press, 1965); Mancur Olson Jr., *The Logic of Collective Action: Public Goods and the Theory of Groups* (Cambridge: Harvard University Press, 1965) and William D. Riker, *The Theory of Political Coalitions* (New Haven: Yale University Press, 1962).
17. See especially, "Rationality and Administrative Decision Making," "A Behavioral Model of Rational Choice," and "Rational Choice and the Structure of the Environment" in *Models of Man, Social and Rational.*
18. Essentially the same arguments are present in the section on "Formal Models" in Holt and Richardson, *op. cit.*
19. While the authors might disagree, I believe that this is the conclusion which must be drawn from Downs, *Inside Bureaucracy* (Boston: Little, Brown, 1967) and Tullock, *The Politics of Bureaucracy* (Washington: Public Affairs Press, 1965).

Notes

20. See especially, Edward Ames, *The Soviet Economic Processes* (Homewood, Ill.: R. D. Irwin, 1965) and P. J. D. Wiles, *The Political Economy of Communism* (Cambridge: Harvard University Press, 1962).
21. *Administrative Behavior*, pp. 80–81.
22. See especially, Charles J. Erasmus, *Man Takes Control: Cultural Development and American Aid* (Minneapolis: University of Minnesota Press, 1961), Chapters 2–5; F. G. Bailey, *Tribe, Caste and Nation: A Study of Political Activity and Political Change in Highland Orissa* (Manchester: Manchester University Press, 1960), Chapters 1, 9; and John H. Kunkel, "Value and Behavior in Economic Development," *Economic Development and Cultural Change*, XIII, No. 3 (April 1963), 257–277.
23. See particularly, Carolyn W. Sherif, Muzafer Sherif and Roger E. Nebergal, *Attitude and Attitude Change: The Social Judgement-Involvement Approach* (Philadelphia and London: W. B. Saunders Co., 1965).
24. *Administrative Behavior*, pp. xiii–xiv.
25. *Administrative Behavior*, pp. xvii. Simon refers to this as the "mechanism of identification."
26. Simon and March, *Organizations*, pp. 10–11.
27. Especially the availability and cost of information and alternatives. See Simon and March, *Organizations*, pp. 120–123, 176.
28. In developing our theory, we have found it helpful to represent many of these concepts symbolically and define them using a relatively few primitive terms. For interested readers we will present illustrative examples in notes at appropriate points. For example, functional alternatives are represented as $a \in H(G)$, dysfunctional alternatives as $a \in \overline{H(G)}$ and neutral alternatives as $a \in H(G) \cap \overline{H(G)}$ where a is any alternative, $H(G)$ refers to the "hierarchy of goals" defined by the goal G. $\overline{H(G)}$ refers to the complement of that hierarchy. To elaborate a bit further, a hierarchy of goals comprises a *normative goal* and its factors. A normative goal is one which (for purposes of analysis at least) is not a sub-goal, i.e. a normative goal is desired "for its own sake" not because it contributes to the attainment of another goal. The factors of a goal are the sub-goals and premises of activity (sub-goals at low levels of generalization) which conduce to its attainment. The complement of a hierarchy is the set of negative factors associated with its goal. A negative factor is any alternative which, if chosen, is followed by a change in the criterion of its associated goal in a negative direction. For further discussion of these concepts, see Simon, *Administrative Behavior* and Simon and March, *Organizations*.
29. See Simon and March, *Organizations*, pp. 105 ff.
30. An evoked alternative is any alternative for which the search costs are the empty set. Thus for an evoked alternative $C_T(a) - C(a) = C_S(a) = \emptyset$ where $C_T(a)$ refers to the total cost of the alternative, $C(a)$ refers to its intrinsic cost and $C_S(a)$ refers to its search cost.
31. See note 25, above.
32. Symbolically, these axioms are represented as follows:
    (1) $A \triangleright B \longrightarrow \triangle [a_1 \in H(A) \cap \overline{H(B)} \wedge a_2 \in H(B) \xrightarrow{D} a_1]$
    (2) $A \triangleright B \longrightarrow \triangle [a_1 \in \overline{H(A)} \cap H(B) \xrightarrow{D} a_0]$

(3) $A \mathrel{\dot{\triangleright}} B \longrightarrow \triangle [a_1 \in H(A) \cap H(B) \wedge a_2 \in H(A) \xrightarrow{D} a_1]$
(4) $A \mathrel{\dot{\triangleright}} B \longrightarrow \triangle [a_1 \in H(A) \wedge a_2 \in H(A) \cap \overline{H(B)} \xrightarrow{D} a_1]$
Where $\xrightarrow{D}$ means "choose," $\mathrel{\dot{\triangleright}}$ means "is more determinate than," $\triangle$ is a decision unit and the brackets denote a decision process. To simplify the symbolic representation of decision situations, we adopt the convention that alternatives are neutral with respect to all hierarchies of goals except where inclusion is explicitly stated.

33. Using symbols, this table is represented as follows:

	$\{a \in H(B)\}$	$\{a \in \overline{H(B)}\}$
$\{a \in H(A)\}$	$\{a \in H(A) \cap H(B)\}$	$\{a \in H(A) \cap \overline{H(B)}\}$
$\{a \in \overline{H(A)}\}$	$\{a \in \overline{H(A)} \cap H(B)\}$	$\{a \in \overline{H(A)} \cap \overline{H(B)}\}$

34. The form which the theorems take requires further elaboration however. We define the concept of an *alternative space*, $S\{a\}$ as the number of alternatives in a set of alternatives. The likelihood that a particular goal will be attained is a function of four coefficients. The *coefficient of complementarity* of a goal $\theta_C(A)$ is equivalent to the ratio of $S\{a|a \in H(A) \cap H(G|G \mathrel{\dot{\triangleright}} A)\}$ to $S\{a|a \in H(A) \cup H(G|G \mathrel{\dot{\triangleright}} A)\}$. The *coefficient of negative complementarity*, $\theta_C(\overline{A})$ is equivalent to the ratio of $S\{a|a \in \overline{H(A)} \cap \overline{H(G|G \mathrel{\dot{\triangleright}} A)}\}$ to $S\{a|a \in \overline{H(A)} \cup \overline{H(G|G \mathrel{\dot{\triangleright}} A)}\}$. The *coefficient of exclusion* (for parametric goals) $\overline{\theta_C}(A)$ is equivalent to the ratio of $S\{a|a \in H(A) \cap \overline{H(G|G \mathrel{\dot{\triangleright}} A)}\}$ to $S\{a|a \in H(A) \cup \overline{H(G|G \mathrel{\dot{\triangleright}} A)}\}$. The *coefficient of conflict* $\overline{\theta_C}(\overline{A})$ is equivalent to the ratio of $S\{a|a \in \overline{H(A)} \cap H(G|G \mathrel{\dot{\triangleright}} A)\}$ to $S\{a|a \in \overline{H(A)} \cup H(G|G \mathrel{\dot{\triangleright}} A)\}$. $\theta_C(G)$ and $\theta_C(\overline{G})$ vary between zero and plus one and $\overline{\theta_C}(G)$ and $\overline{\theta_C}(\overline{G})$ vary between zero and minus one respectively. Given these coefficients it is then possible to talk about a coefficient of attainment for a goal, $\theta_T(G)$, which is equivalent to $f[\theta_C(G) + \theta_C(\overline{G}) + \overline{\theta_C}(G) + \overline{\theta_C}(\overline{G})]$ as we have noted.

35. A study which places particular emphasis on this concept is William J. Gore, *Administrative Decision-Making: A Heuristic Model* (New York: John Wiley & Sons, 1964). See especially, Chapters 1, 5.

36. The most frequent conflict is between organizational maintenance and substantive goals. This leads to "obstructionism" and "bureaucratic red tape."

37. For a brief but useful discussion of this problem, see R. G. D. Allen, *Mathematical Economics* (London: Macmillan and Co., 1963, second edition), Chapter 20.

38. *Administrative Behavior*, pp. 2–3.

39. Some of the officials interviewed were puzzled and even irritated by a style of questioning which seemed to be focused on the minutiae of specific types of decisions rather than the broader overriding issues which they believed to be more relevant.

40. The reader will recall that in the conclusion, we observed that harmonious Agency-university relations by no means assure successful projects.

41. See the discussion of "organizational slack" in March and Simon, *Organizations,* pp. 126–127. The authors observe that "when resources are relatively unlimited, organizations need not resolve the relative merits of subgroup claims. . . . When resources are restricted and this slack is taken up, the relations among individual members and subgroups in the organization become more nearly a strictly competitive game. From this we predict that as resources are reduced . . . intergroup conflict tends to increase."

Selected Bibliography

I. BOOKS AND ARTICLES

Adams, Walter and John A. Garraty. *Is the World Our Campus?* East Lansing: Michigan State University Press, 1960.

Albert, Michael. *The Role of International Technical Cooperation in the Inter-Regional Development of Peru.* Unpublished Doctoral Dissertation, Ohio State University, 1962.

Allen, R. G. D. *Mathematical Economics.* London: Macmillan and Co., 1963, second edition.

Ames, Edward. *The Soviet Economic Processes.* Homewood, Ill.: R. D. Irwing, 1965.

Apter, David, ed. *Ideologies and Discontents.* Glencoe: Free Press, 1964.

Badeau, John S. and Georgiana G. Stephens. *Bread From Stones: Fifty Years of Technical Assistance.* Englewood Cliffs: Prentice Hall, 1966.

Bailey, F. G. *Tribe, Caste and Nation: A Study of Political Activity and Political Change in Highland Orissa.* Manchester: Manchester University Press, 1960.

Baldwin, David A. *Foreign Aid and American Foreign Policy: A Documentary Analysis.* New York: F. A. Praeger, 1966.

Boulding, Kenneth E. *Conflict and Defense: A General Theory.* New York: Harper and Row, 1962. Torchbook Edition, 1963.

Brodbeck, May, ed. *Readings in the Philosophy of the Social Sciences.* New York: The Macmillan Co., 1968.

Bronfenbrenner, Martin. *Academic Encounter: The American University in Japan and Korea.* Glencoe: Free Press, 1961.

Carroll, Holbert N. *The House of Representatives and Foreign Affairs.* Pittsburgh: University of Pittsburgh Press, 1958.

Clawson, Marion, ed. *Natural Resources and International Development.* Baltimore: John Hopkins Press, 1964.

Coffin, Frank M. *Witness for AID.* Boston: Houghton Mifflin, 1964.

Cohen, Morris R. and Ernest Nagel. "The Nature of a Logical or Mathematical System" in Feigl and Brodbeck, eds., *Readings in the Philosophy of Science,* pp. 129–147.

Congressional Quarterly Service (Thomas N. Schroth, ed.). *Congress and the*

Nation: A Review of Government and Politics in the Postwar Years. Washington: Congressional Quarterly Service, 1964.

Converse, Phillip M. "The Nature of Belief Systems in Mass Publics" in Apter, ed., *Ideologies and Discontents*, pp. 206–262.

Curle, Adam. *Educational Strategy for Developing Societies: A Study of Educational and Social Factors in Relation to Economic Growth.* London: Tavistock Publications, 1963.

Dahl, Robert A. and Charles E. Lindblom. *Politics, Economics and Welfare: Planning and Politico-Economic Systems Resolved into Basic Social Processes.* New York: Harper and Row, 1953.

Downs, Anthony. *An Economic Theory of Democracy.* New York: Harper and Row, 1957.

Downs, Anthony. *Inside Bureaucracy.* Boston: Little, Brown and Co., 1967.

Durish, Lawrence L. and Robert E. Lowry. "The Scope and Content of Administrative Decision—The TVA Illustration," *Public Administration Review*, XIII, No. 4 (Autumn 1953).

Education and World Affairs. *The University Looks Abroad: Approaches to World Affairs of Six American Universities.* New York: Walker and Co., 1965.

Elder, Robert Ellsworth. *The Policy Machine: The Department of State and American Foreign Policy.* Syracuse: Syracuse University Press, 1960.

Enke, Stephen. *Economics for Development.* Englewood Cliffs: Prentice Hall, 1963.

Erasmus, Charles J. *Man Takes Control: Cultural Development and American Aid.* Minneapolis: University of Minnesota Press, 1961.

Feis, Herbert. *Foreign Aid and Foreign Policy.* New York: St. Martins Press, 1964.

Fenno, Richard F. Jr. "The House Appropriations Committee as a Political System: The Problem of Integration," *American Political Science Review*, LVI (June 1962).

Feigl, Herbert. "The Scientific Outlook: Naturalism and Humanism" in Herbert Feigl and May Brodbeck, eds., *Readings in the Philosophy of Science.* New York: Appleton Century Crofts, 1953, pp. 8–18.

Forster, George M. *Traditional Cultures and the Impact of Technological Change.* New York: Harper and Row, 1962.

Fort, Raymond. *Development of U.S. Technical Assistance Programs in Iran.* Unpublished Doctoral Dissertation, Cornell University, 1961.

Friedman, Milton, "The Methodology of Positive Economics" in Brodbeck, ed., *Readings in the Philosophy of the Social Sciences*, pp. 518–528.

Glick, Phillip M. *The Administration of Technical Assistance: Growth in the Americas.* Chicago: University of Chicago Press, 1957.

Gore, William J. *Administrative Decision-Making: A Heuristic Model.* New York: John Wiley and Sons, 1964.

Hambridge, Gove, ed. *Dynamics of Development: An International Development Reader.* New York: F. A. Praeger, 1964.

Harwood, Ruth. *An Experiment in Community Development in El Salvador.* Unpublished Doctoral Dissertation, Columbia University, 1963.

Haviland, H. Field, Jr. "Foreign Aid and the Policy Process," *American Political Science Review*, LII (1958).

Holt, Robert T. and John M. Richardson Jr. "Competing Paradigms in Comparative Politics" in Robert T. Holt and John E. Turner, eds., *The Methodology of Comparative Research*. New York: Free Press, forthcoming.

Huntington, Samuel P. *The Common Defense: Strategic Programs in National Politics*. New York and London: Columbia University Press, 1961.

Institute of Research on Overseas Programs, Michigan State University. *The International Programs of American Universities: An Inventory and Analysis*. East Lansing: State Board of Agriculture, 1958.

Jones, Garth N. *Planned Organizational Change: A Set of Working Documents*. Center for Research in Public Organization, School of Public Administration, University of Southern California, 1964.

Kardner, Abram, M. D. *The Individual and His Society: The Psychodynamics of Primitive Social Organization*. With a foreword and two ethnological reports by Ralph Linton. New York and London: Columbia University Press, 1939.

Kemeny, John. *A Philosopher Looks at Science*. Princeton: D. Van Nostrand, 1959.

Kim, Young Hum. *Technical Assistance Programs of the United Nations and the United States: A Comparative Study*. Unpublished Doctoral Dissertation, USC, 1960.

Kuhn, Thomas S. *The Structure of Scientific Revolutions*. Chicago: University of Chicago Press, Phoenix edition, 1964.

Kunkel, John H. "Value and Behavior in Economic Development," *Economic Development and Cultural Change*, XIII, No. 3 (April 1963), 257–277.

LaPalombara, Joseph. *Bureaucracy and Political Development*. Princeton: Princeton University Press, 1963.

Leibenstein, Harvey. *Economic Backwardness and Economic Growth: Studies in the Theory of Economic Development*. New York: John Wiley and Sons, 1957.

Leonard, Glen E. and Charles P. Loomis. *Readings in Latin American Social Organization and Institutions*. East Lansing: Michigan State College Press, 1953.

Lindblom, Charles E. *The Intelligence of Democracy: Decision Making Through Mutual Adjustment*. New York: Free Press, 1965.

Luce, R. Duncan and Howard Raiffa. *Games and Decisions: Introduction and Critical Survey*. New York: John Wiley and Sons, 1958.

McCamy, James L. *The Conduct of the New Diplomacy*. New York: Harper and Row, 1964.

March, James G. and Herbert Simon. *Organizations*. New York: John Wiley and Sons, 1958.

Matthews, Donald R. *U.S. Senators and Their World*. New York: Random House, Vintage Edition, 1960.

Montgomery, John D. *The Politics of Foreign Aid: American Experience in Southeast Asia*. New York: F. A. Praeger, 1962.

Mosher, Arthur T. *Technical Cooperation in Latin American Agriculture.* Chicago: University of Chicago Press, 1957.
Neustadt, Richard E. *Presidential Power: The Politics of Leadership.* New York: John Wiley and Sons, 1960.
Olson, Mancur, Jr. *The Logic of Collective Action: Public Goods and the Theory of Groups.* Cambridge: Harvard University Press, 1965.
Pye, Lucien W., ed. *Communications and Political Development.* Princeton: Princeton University Press, 1963.
Riggs, Fred W. *Administration in Developing Areas: The Theory of Prismatic Society.* Boston: Houghton Mifflin Co., 1964.
Riker, William D. *The Theory of Political Coalitions.* New Haven: Yale University Press, 1962.
Robinson, James A. *Congress and Foreign Policy-Making: A Study in Legislative Influence and Initiative.* Homewood, Illinois: The Dorsey Press, 1962.
Rosenau, James N. *Public Opinion and Foreign Policy: An Operational Formulation.* New York: Random House, 1961.
Rosenau, James N. *International Politics and Foreign Policy: A Reader in Research and Theory.* Glencoe: Free Press, 1961.
Sapin, Burton M. *The Making of United States Foreign Policy.* Published for the Brookings Institution, New York: F. A. Praeger, 1966.
Scott, Andrew M. and Raymond H. Dawson. *Readings in the Making of American Foreign Policy.* New York: The Macmillan Co., 1965.
Selznick, Phillip. *TVA and the Grass Roots: A Study in the Sociology of Formal Organization.* Berkeley and Los Angeles: University of California Press, 1949.
Shearer, John. *Manpower Resources in Overseas Operations, Brazil and Mexico.* Unpublished Doctoral Dissertation, Princeton University, 1959.
Sherif, Carolyn W., Muzafer Sherif and Roger E. Nebergall. *Attitude and Attitude Change: The Social Judgement-Involvement Approach.* Philadelphia and London: W. B. Saunders Co., 1965.
Simon, Herbert A. *Administrative Behavior: A Study of Decision-Making Processes in Administrative Organization.* New York: Free Press, 1957, second edition.
Simon, Herbert A. "Birth of an Organization, The Economic Cooperation Administration," *Public Administration Review,* XIII, No. 4 (1953).
Simon, Herbert A. *Models of Man, Social and Rational.* New York: John Wiley and Sons, 1957.
Snyder, Richard C., H. W. Bruk and Burton Sapin, eds. *Foreign Policy Decision Making: An Approach to the Study of International Politics.* Glencoe: Free Press, 1962.
Tullock, Gordon. *The Politics of Bureaucracy.* Washington: Public Affairs Press, 1965.
Tullock, Gordon and James M. Buchannan. *The Calculus of Consent: Logical Foundations of Constitutional Democracy.* Ann Arbor: University of Michigan Press, 1965.

Watkins, J. W. N. "Ideal Types and Historical Explanation" in Feigl and Brodbeck, eds., *Readings in the Philosophy of Science*, pp. 723-743.
Weidner, Edward W. *The World Role of Universities*. New York: McGraw Hill, 1962.
Wharton, Clifton Jr. *The Economic Impact of Technical Assistance, Capital and Technology in the Agricultural Development of Minas Gerais*. Unpublished Doctoral Dissertation, University of Chicago, 1959.
Wildavsky, Aaron, *The Politics of the Budgetary Process*. Boston: Little, Brown and Co., 1964.
Wilensky, Harold. *Organizational Intelligence: Knowledge and Policy in Government and Industry*. New York: Basic Books, 1967.
Wiles, P. J. D. *The Political Economy of Communism*. Cambridge: Harvard University Press, 1962.

II. GOVERNMENT DOCUMENTS, CONFERENCE PROCEEDINGS AND MISCELLANEOUS

Act for International Development: A Program for the Decade of Development. Summary Presentation to Congress, 1964.
Administration of National Security. Staff Reports and Hearings Submitted to the Committee on Government Operations, United States Senate, by its Subcommittee on National Security Staffing and Operations. Washington: Government Printing Office, 1965.
AID in Summary. Washington: Government Printing Office, 1966.
AID Contract Operations. Report and Hearings Conducted by the Committee on Government Operations, U.S. Senate. Washington: Government Printing Office, 1963.
Alliance for Progress. Report Prepared by the Government of the United States of America for the Second Annual Meeting of the Inter-American Economic and Social Council at the Expert and Ministerial Levels, Sao Paulo, Brazil. October-November. Washington, D.C.: Agency for International Development, 1963.
The Ambassador and the Problem of Coordination. A Study Submitted by the Subcommittee on National Security Staffing and Operations to the Committee on Government Operations, United States Senate. Washington: Government Printing Office, September 13, 1963.
American Institute for Research. *A Study of Some Key USAID Jobs: The Program Officer*. 1963.
Andrews, Stanley. *Technical Assistance Case Reports: Selected Projects in Nine Countries*. A report prepared for the Office of International Programs, Michigan State University. East Lansing, 1961.
Andrews, Stanley. *University Contracts*. A report prepared for the Technical Assistance Study Group (TASG), ICA. Washington: AID, 1962.
The Annapolis Conference on International Education. Summary prepared by the Bureau of International Cultural Relations, Department of State. Washington, 1959.

Changes in Administration, January, 1961—January, 1963. Report prepared by the Bureau of Administration, U.S. Department of State. Washington, 1963.

Commission on Foreign Economic Policy: Report to the President and the Congress. The "Randall Commission Report." Washington, 1954.

Conclusions and Recommendations of the International Development Advisory Board. Report to Harold E. Stassen regarding U.S. participation in technical cooperation programs for underdeveloped countries. Washington, 1953.

Duncan, Richard L. *Technical Assistance and Institution Building.* Unpublished paper prepared for the Annual Conference of the Society for International Development. 1964.

The Ford Foundation. *Personnel for Overseas Development.* December 1962.

Gelband, Carla S. *University Contract Programs: Educational Support to Developing Nations.* A paper prepared for the American Council on Education. Washington, 1961.

Humphrey, Richard A., ed. *University Projects Abroad.* Papers presented at the Conference on University Contracts Abroad, November 17–18, 1955. Washington, 1956.

Humphrey, Richard A., ed. *Blueprint and Experience.* Addresses and Summary of Proceedings of the Conference on University Contracts Abroad, November 14–15, 1957. Washington, 1958.

Humphrey, Richard A., ed. *Education Without Boundaries.* Addresses and Summary of Proceedings of the Conference on University Contracts Abroad, November 13–14, 1958. Washington, 1959.

Information Brochure, University Contract Presentation. Prepared by the Office of Contract Relations, ICA for the World Wide Education Conference, November 15, 1960.

Lincoln, George A., Special Advisor to the Administrator, AID. *Improving AID Program Evaluation.* The "Lincoln Report." Washington: AID, 1965.

Notes on the World Wide Conference of ICA Chief Education Advisors. November 1960 (unpublished).

Ohly, John H. *A Proposed Outline for the Study of Technical Assistance to Less Developed Nations.* Washington: ICA, 1960.

Ohly, John H. *The Mobilization of Federal Resources in Support of the Foreign Aid Program.* Washington: AID, 1962.

Overseas Economic Operations. A Report to the Congress by the Commission on Organization of the Executive Branch of the Government, Herbert Hoover, Chairman. Washington, 1955.

Partners in Progress. A Report to President Truman by the International Development Advisory Board, Nelson A. Rockefeller, Chairman. New York, 1951.

"Partnership for Progress: International Technical Cooperation," *Annals of the American Academy of Political and Social Science.* May 1959.

Personnel Administration and Operations of the Agency for International Development. Report of Senator Gale W. McGee to the Commission on

Selected Bibliography

Appropriations, U.S. Senate. The "McGee Report." Washington: Government Printing Office, November 29, 1963.

Personnel for the New Diplomacy. Report of the Committee on Foreign Affairs Personnel. The "Herter Report." Washington: Published by and under the auspices of the Carnegie Endowment for International Peace, 1962.

Positive Contracting for AID: Marshalling and Strengthening the Nation's Resources for International Development. Report of the President's Task Force on Foreign Assistance, Working Group on Contracting. The "Glick Report." Washington, 1961.

Proceedings of the Conference on International Rural Development. Washington, 1964.

Report to the President by the President's Citizen Advisers on the Mutual Security Program. Benjamin F. Fairless, Coordinator. Washington, 1957.

Sanders, Irwin T. *The U.S. Academic Professional Abroad: Role Perception by Professional Fields.* Paper prepared for the Sociology Colloquium, University of Wisconsin, October 22, 1965. Madison, 1965.

Sanders, Irwin T. *Satisfaction and Problems of Overseas Work as Reported by United States Academic Professionals.* Address presented at a public meeting of the Seminar on Institutional Structures and Cultural Values as Related to Agricultural Development, Sponsored by the Agricultural Development Council. Pullman, Washington, 1965.

Sanders, Irwin T. *Differences in the American's Professional Role at Home and on a Foreign Assignment.* Paper prepared for a Conference on the Role of the Younger Professional Person in Overseas Development Programs. Princeton, 1965.

The Scope and Distribution of United States Military and Economic Assistance Programs. Report to the President of the United States from the Committee to Strengthen the Security of the Free World. The "Clay Report." Washington, 1963.

The Special Role of Land-Grant Colleges and State Universities in Meeting the Needs of Developing Nations. Report of International Study Group I to the NASULGC Centennial Convention, November 12–16, 1961.

Statistics and Reports Division, AID. *AID Management Report: Program Implementation During Fiscal Year 1962.* Washington, 1963.

Task Force on AID-University Relations. *Rationale for University Contracts and Changing Objectives of Foreign, Economic, Technical Assistance Programs.* Unpublished staff study, 1963.

Task Force on AID-University Relations. *Summary of Study Commentary on Procedural Problem Areas in the University-AID Contract Relationship.* Unpublished staff study, 1963.

Task Force on AID-University Relations. *Research Supplement.* New York: Education and World Affairs, mimeo., 1963.

Technical Assistance Study Group, ICA. *Forms of Donor-Host Government Operational Relationships: U.S. Contractors.* Summary of Files. Washington, 1961.

Technical Assistance Study Group, ICA. *Forms of Donor-Host Government Operational Relationships: Third Party Contracts.* Summary of Files. Washington, 1961.

Technical Assistance Study Group, ICA. John B. Stabler, ed. *University Contracts.* Summary of Files. Washington, 1962.

The University and World Affairs. Report of the Committee on the University and World Affairs. New York: Ford Foundation, 1961.

Weidner, E. W. *Another Look at University Technical Assistance Projects Abroad.* A Report Prepared for the Ford Foundation. New York: Ford Foundation, 1962.